Beyond the Dark Depths

Beyond the
Dark Depths

A Memoir of
Depression and Recovery

Hannah Nash

Beyond the Dark Depths
Hannah Nash

Published by Aspect Design 2021
Malvern, Worcestershire, United Kingdom

Printed by Aspect Design
89 Newtown Road, Malvern, Worcs. WR14 1PD
United Kingdom
Tel: 01684 561567
E-mail: allan@aspect-design.net
Website: www.aspect-design.net

A copy of this book has been deposited
with the British Library Board

ISBN 978-1-912078-14-1

To my dear friends Ann and Margaret
and my faithful dog Llewelyn

PREFACE

It was not until my seventieth year that depression first hit me. I had no history of mental illness and never before during my life had I suffered anything like this. So when, at the age of sixty-nine, depression hit me full force it was a great shock and I found it very difficult to understand and, indeed, to *believe* what was happening to me.

I had been married to my husband, Don, for over forty years. We had weathered various ups and downs in our marriage and with our children over the years but had overcome difficulties and enjoyed many pleasurable times together. Of course there had been sadness and times when I was unhappy or miserable but mainly I had been fortunate with a happy and secure childhood, a good education, successful career and a stable marriage. I found it a mystery and very difficult to believe that here I was in a completely new world.

Retired for over ten years, I had previously had a varied and successful career where I was used to solving problems and helping others, rather than being the problem myself or depending on others for help. My life changed so suddenly and completely that I literally didn't know who I was any longer. I felt that my being was shattered into a thousand pieces and scattered in places that I couldn't reach.

One of the things that helped me most through this difficult time was reading books by other people who had experienced this mind-blowingly dreadful illness. I still don't really understand why this helped so much; perhaps it helped me feel less isolated, not completely alone in what I was suffering; maybe less ashamed and guilty, or maybe it gave me hope to know that people, some of whom suffered more severely than I, do recover. Maybe it was a little of all of these.

It was reading the memoirs of others that helped me to know that people, often high achievers in various fields and with successful lives, could be struck down as low as I had been but they found ways through the dark depths and eventually came out the other side. Most of them were ill for much longer than I, even though at the time it seemed like eternity to me.

We were very different people – different ages, different backgrounds, different lives, different personalities, different symptoms and with different events causing our depressions – but I was struck by how similar our darkest feelings were. It was a shocking and humbling experience to read these accounts but they reached me in a way that words from my GP, counsellor or psychiatrist could not. This is my main reason for attempting to record my own experiences, in the hope that this may help someone, somewhere, somehow.

This book is simply a memoir; it describes what happened, how I felt, how I coped and eventually came through it, along with some of the things I discovered during this treacherous journey. It was my journey and I make no claims that what helped me would work for everyone. I know this is not true and that everyone must find their own way on this lonely and difficult path.

Although I do not have the literary skills and experience of other authors, and in some ways my depression does not seem as serious as that experienced by them, one dreadful night I plunged low enough to come very close to suicide, an experience that shocked me profoundly. So I think I can truthfully say mine *was* a serious depression and if, by sharing my experiences, this book can reach out to just one person and give them hope during their dark times then it will have been worthwhile.

Chapter One
WRECKED

My depression arrived suddenly and, it seemed, unaccountably, engulfing my very being – that special, indefinable inner part that is 'me' – my personality, my mind, my soul, my spirit. It numbed my senses, clouded my thinking, skewed my perception and reduced me to a desolate shell.

Sunday 8 September 2013

The first sign indicating that something strange was happening to me came without warning one Sunday morning in September. An ordinary Sunday morning, I was cooking lunch as I do most Sundays when, the roast meat and potatoes in the oven and the vegetables prepared, I was quite suddenly overcome with emotion and began to cry. Not a sobbing or wailing type of crying, but silent tears were streaming down my face and wouldn't stop.

This was so unusual, as I am not generally given to dramatic displays of emotion, and certainly not to weeping in mid-morning when there was nothing obvious wrong. Not wanting to face questions or to distress my husband who, fortunately, was absorbed in some Sunday morning television programme, I hastened quietly to my bedroom where I could do nothing but allow the tears to flow for a while, then lay on my bed distraught until I stemmed the flow. I felt totally drained of life, so exhausted and numb, with heavy limbs that did not want to move. Shocked by this outpouring, I rationalised that I must be tired, having not slept well the previous night. After half an hour or so lying there, I managed to regain control of my recalcitrant body, made myself get up and return to the kitchen to finish cooking the lunch, though between tasks I would cat nap on my bed again.

Whilst my brain and my body still functioned fairly normally, they seemed to do so automatically, robotically; they felt separated and detached from 'me', just linked by an indistinct thread.

That afternoon, I had planned to go for a walk and call on a friend but once lunch was eaten I was overcome again by terrible tiredness and total lethargy. I lay on my bed again and slept lightly for nearly three hours. On waking, I tried to read but found that I couldn't concentrate or engage with the book, *Les Misérables,* in which, over the past two weeks, I had previously been living along with the characters. *What's happening to me?* I thought as I lay there, worried about my feelings of total despair. I just wanted to lie down and die so that I wouldn't have to worry about or do anything ever again. All I could do was dream about dying; I had no energy to do anything more drastic, either positive or negative, and was conscious of withdrawing into myself, not wanting to see anyone, talk to anyone or do anything. I recognised that I was completely emotionless, with no feelings for anyone else, real people, including those closest to me, or the fictional characters in the book I had tried to read.

In the evening, I tried to watch TV but, flicking through the channels, all the programmes seemed trite rubbish and completely pointless. I couldn't find anything that would remotely interest me. That again was unusual as, although I don't watch a great deal of television, the programmes that I did watch were normally greatly enjoyed.

Now the essential being, 'me', felt as if it had disintegrated, like a smashed car windscreen where the fragments of crushed glass are just held together precariously but of no use; or a digital television picture during a storm when the pixels separate, creating a weird, distorted picture which is continually changing but with no meaning. I no longer recognised myself or knew who I was any more. By now I was beginning to be horrified and frightened by my feelings but I also felt powerless to do anything about them except cry quietly into my bed. Still tearful after several hours, I finally went to bed and slept for a few hours.

Monday 9 September

Two o'clock in the morning. I woke to find tears streaming down my face once more. I wasn't thinking of anything and I wasn't dreaming but utter despair came flooding into my consciousness, along with feelings of panic and anxiety as to why I was reacting like this. Tossing and turning for three hours, I relived Sunday in my mind, everything turning over and over but I could find no explanation there. Then a strange incident from Saturday, that I'd tried to bury, pushed its way into my consciousness and I knew that this was related in some way to a car accident in which Don and I had been involved two weeks previously. On Saturday afternoon, my recorder group had been playing some pieces in a concert in our local park. Our group was one of several performers in a mixed programme and just played for a couple of ten minute slots. As we were playing one piece, an arrangement of the Volga Boat Song, we went wrong. The music seemed to shriek and scream discordantly in my ears. It sounded like the brakes of a car screeching and it was hard to bear. Our conductor stopped us and we played the piece again without further mishap but I had been devastated by this experience, hardly able to move or speak and filled with a sense of shame and guilt that perhaps it had been my fault. I forced myself to move and take a seat back in the audience where I sat silently, trembling, choked and breathless. Looking round I could see that no-one else appeared to be upset by what had happened and they didn't notice the state I was in. I couldn't get the shrill, screeching sound out of my head and as soon as there was an opportunity, I left and went home. The music continued to go round and round in my head, haunting me all evening This was the reason why I hadn't slept well on Saturday night, and now here I was reliving it once more. Eventually I must have dropped off into an exhausted sleep.

At 8.00 am I awoke again and made an effort to act normally by dressing, eating breakfast, washing-up and so on. That Monday was the second Monday of the month, which meant there was a U3A Meeting. I had belonged to U3A (University of the Third Age) for several years since I retired and I always looked forward to these meetings every month. So I busied myself with getting ready but, to my surprise and horror, I was again overwhelmed by a suffocating feeling which came over me as I tried to decide what to wear – not that it would have mattered what I chose – and everything was all too much. I was completely unable to make this simple and unimportant decision. I felt so pathetic and useless. The tears started again and this time wouldn't stop.

By this time, I knew that something was seriously amiss – it was so much more than just being tired or upset. I felt as if my world was collapsing around me and my whole being was disintegrating within the chaos. This time, there was no quiet escape to my bedroom. My husband, Don, could see my distress and began concerned questioning about what was wrong.

'Nothing,' I kept saying because I couldn't identify any particular thing that was wrong, and then, 'Everything' – the whole world seemed dark, desolate and pointless.

Don was nonplussed – whatever had brought this about? We sat and talked for a while, all thoughts of going to the U3A meeting abandoned, but still I couldn't move and the tears wouldn't stop. Eventually, in desperation and choked with tears, we telephoned the doctor's surgery but there were no appointments available until the following week. I was told that if it was an urgent matter, I could attend the assessment clinic that morning or to ring again at 8.00 am the following day in case there were any cancellations.

Don persuaded me that I was in no fit state to drive to the assessment clinic and he tried patiently to talk me through what had happened, recent events and possible worries or causes. We talked for over an hour and, whilst this helped a little, nothing I could say made sense to him – or to me – and I became more and more distressed at my own incoherence and despair. Don made me a cup of tea and I took some paracetamol tablets and went back to my bed again until after lunch.

That afternoon, I needed to go to Tesco to buy some bread. Somehow I dragged myself there, feeling completely wrung out after all the crying and emotion of the morning but, on encountering a friend there, the emotions overcame me again. She could see that something was wrong and asked me if I was okay. The tears welling up in my eyes, I stammered, 'Yes, just don't talk to me,' and hurried away from her concern and sympathy. With difficulty I controlled the crying sufficiently to drive home and then gave in, having reached the sanctuary of my bed once more where I cried and cried and worried and worried about what was going on. What was all this crying about?

I had scarcely eaten all day – most unlike me and yet another cause for concern and worry – and all I could manage that evening was a bowl of soup and some toast, with no appetite for anything more substantial. Many thoughts kept whirling in my head as I struggled to make sense of why I was in such distress, why the floodgates had opened and let the tears rush out.

I had to accept that suddenly I wasn't fit enough to live my normal life, to engage in my usual activities. I hadn't gone to U3A that morning or to swimming that afternoon, and it was clear that

I wouldn't be able to go to my recorder group the following day. Having to accept all this, I was stunned and shocked to realise that I was no longer the strong person that I thought I was. I was used to being able to cope and sort out problems both for myself and for other people, so when this hit me it was devastating. This new perception of myself was one I didn't like at all and it made me feel totally distraught.

Tuesday 10 September

I woke at about 4.00 am feeling anxious and nauseous but, after an hour or so, drifted off into a fitful sleep until 7.30 am. I watched the minutes and the seconds count down on my digital alarm clock by the bedside and at exactly 8.00 am, phoned the doctors' surgery to see if there were any cancellations. To my amazement, there was a cancellation and I was given an appointment to see one of the doctors at 11.30. This was a huge relief to both me and my husband, Don, who accompanied me. Our surgery is a group practice and although patients are assigned to a particular GP they are also able to see any doctor of their choice or who may be available sooner. Over the past ten or more years, I had only ever needed to consult a doctor sporadically so I had no particular relationship with or preference of which GP I would see. I was just relieved to be able to see someone, and on this occasion the vacant appointment was with Dr Alice. I think I had seen her once before, about fifteen or twenty years ago but had no real recollection of this and she clearly did not remember me.

Haltingly and with much help from Don, between us we told the doctor about the car accident in which we'd been involved two weeks ago on the bank holiday Monday at the end of August whilst travelling to visit my daughter and our grandchildren. It was a warm, sunny day and we were looking forward to seeing our grandchildren, including the latest arrival, a baby boy of just six weeks old, whom Don had not yet seen. I was driving as Don, now eighty-four, had given up his licence some years ago due to ill health. The traffic in the mid-Wales countryside wasn't heavy, despite it being a bank holiday, but, as we drove through a village, a car had driven out of a side road, crashing into our car and damaging it severely on the passenger side. Whilst neither of us had been physically injured or lost consciousness, immediately the accident occurred I had completely lost my memory. I scrambled out of the car and collapsed on the ground, unable to walk or move from the kerbside. Don must have been in shock, not only from the crash itself, but also by the state of my obvious confusion. Some people walking their dog had witnessed the accident and could see that there was something very wrong with me so they had called an ambulance and the police. Completely disorientated and unable to process anything that was happening to me, I was taken to hospital some miles away by ambulance, accompanied by Don, whilst the police interviewed the other driver and witnesses and also arranged for the damaged car to be taken to a local garage. The hospital staff telephoned my daughter and she arrived at the hospital shortly afterwards with her husband and young baby.

Various tests eliminated the cause as a stroke, heart attack or an epileptic seizure but I was admitted to an assessment ward for observation. I knew who I was and could recognise my husband and my daughter but not my son-in-law or my daughter's baby. I kept asking her whose baby it was, having no awareness that I had been present at his birth six weeks previously. I had no recollection of the accident and kept asking the same questions, 'What's happened? Where are we? Can we go home now?' completely unable even to process the replies to the questions. My daughter told me afterwards that she had been devastated at the state of my mind and thought something very serious had happened to me. After several hours she and her husband took Don home with them for the night, promising to return the next day. Over the next few hours my memory gradually started to return and to function again. I became aware that I was in a hospital ward and I remember wrapping myself up tightly in a sheet, feeling safe at last and sleeping for a while.

After an agitated and disturbed night my memory had begun to work properly again in that I knew where I was and, although I still remembered nothing of the accident, I could process information again and could remember what I had been told. Apart from one incident of panic I was thinking clearly once more, able to eat breakfast and was given permission to have a shower. I felt greatly refreshed after my trip to the bathroom, but on returning to my bed – still wearing my hospital gown – I realised that I had no clothes to put on which caused me to panic. I looked around the ward, noticing that all the other patients were old, obviously ill and confined to their beds. Memories of a book I'd been reading recently flashed into my mind, *The Secret Scripture*, the story of a woman who was incarcerated in a mental hospital for most of her long life, and I was suddenly apprehensive that I had been left in that ward with no clothes, no phone, no money. It was a dreadful feeling of being abandoned and trapped in this place with no means of escape, and for a few minutes I was overwhelmed by panic. Fortunately, it did not last long as, when I looked under the bed, I found my clothes neatly folded in a plastic bag! This, at least, was reassuring and I no longer had to picture myself wandering outside in a hospital gown. It gave me the confidence, once dressed, to ask the nursing staff if I could use a phone to call my daughter to find out what was happening, and later that morning they arrived to take me home once I was discharged.

Now, at the doctors' surgery, Don and I together explained these circumstances to Dr Alice and then talked through with her what had happened since – the fact that my memory was working again (although I still could not remember the accident at all), how I had appeared to be making a recovery, getting back to normal but then, at the weekend, had collapsed into this state of distress and tearfulness.

Dr Alice was brilliant. When I reached the part about not knowing who I was any more, my distress overcame me and she could see how distraught I was. Not only was she very professional, patient and thoughtful, but also very caring. She reached out and touched my hand in sympathy. This gesture was so important to me, that she cared enough to do this. I came to realise much later that the smallest word, gesture or smile, when sincere and genuine, can have an enormously powerful effect on people, particularly when they are in such an emotional state.

After carrying out a few physical tests – blood pressure, heart, lungs, reflexes – Dr Alice diagnosed the loss of memory as 'transient global amnesia' or TGA and gave us a brief explanation of this condition.

TGA is an episode involving a sudden onset of memory loss and confusion during which a person is unable to make new memories. The person will know who they are and can recognise people close to them but they are disoriented in time and place and will often ask the same questions over and over again as they are unable to process or memorise the answers. Events stored in their long term memory will not be affected but they may be unable to recall recent events and, as no memories are made during a TGA episode, the person will never remember what happened during this period. TGA typically lasts for several hours, but can last up to ten hours. The cause is not known, though one of the likely triggers is thought to be emotional or psychological stress. There is no specific treatment but it usually resolves on its own and most people have only one episode during their lifetime.

Now, at least I could make some sense of this part of the problem.

No-one at the hospital had mentioned the term TGA (at least I don't remember anything said along these lines) but when I looked it up on the Internet later at home, the symptoms fitted exactly with my experience. It was a relief to know that it can happen to anyone and that recovery is almost always rapid and complete.

Dr Alice's tests showed that everything in my body seemed to be working normally, so there was no indication of any physical brain injury but she said she would ring the radiologist at the hospital later, to see if I should have an MRI scan. She then explained that I now seemed to be suffering from depression and talked through the benefits of taking some anti-depressant pills for a short time, prescribing Citalopram. Knowing very little about depression or anti-depressants, I naively thought she meant just for a few days and, as I was so desperate to feel better, I agreed to this. I also experienced huge relief when she said that, although it wouldn't be illegal, I should avoid driving, except just locally around the town if necessary, but no more than this. Her other advice was to take everything very easy, to engage in activities if I felt like them but not to undertake anything strenuous. She suggested just taking a walk if I felt up to it, rather than attempting pilates or other structured exercise. I had no idea at the time how important this suggestion would prove to be in my recovery or how walking would become one of the most important parts of my life. She asked me to ring her if I had any questions over the next few days and to see her again in a week's time.

On leaving the surgery, my relief was overwhelming. I felt as if I had been rescued from the very bottom of a deep, dark abyss and dragged up to rest on a ledge a little way up the side of the pit. This was the first of my 'thinking in pictures', not normally something I would do but something that became quite common during my illness. As I walked out, I was conscious of the feeling when Dr Alice reached out and touched my hand. It was so unexpected but so comforting and, although I was not at all religious at this time, I felt it was like Jesus reaching out as he did so often to heal through touch. Although I had a long and treacherous pathway ahead, I think this was an important first step for me on my road to recovery.

Don and I went straight from the surgery to the chemist to collect the prescribed anti-depressants and I took half of the first one, as instructed, at lunchtime, then slept all the afternoon. When I woke I felt nauseous so couldn't face anything to eat or drink but had been warned that this was a common side effect and any nausea would probably wear off in two or three days. When I went to bed that night, although a bit restless at first, I slept well, only waking once in the night. I felt calmer and more relaxed but vivid picture images kept invading my mind. The image of the doctor pulling me up from the bottom of an abyss to a ledge where I could rest and feel safe was still there before going to sleep. I welcomed this respite which I thought would enable me to recover enough gradually to climb to the top where I could see patches of sunshine and blue sky. I knew it was a massive challenge still but I felt I had ropes to help me climb up a few steps at a time.

Looking back now, I believe that I began to think in pictures as I had no words to express the powerful feelings of disintegration and desolation and had to think metaphorically to verbalise them. I can see now that the picture images were a way of helping to sort out my thoughts and feelings but, at the time, it struck me as very strange and I was concerned that my mind was working in a different way from usual and worried about the significance of this. The images are still vivid in my mind but even they don't show the strength and depth of emotion that engulfed me, blocking out all rational thought, leaving me with just feelings.

The most powerful image of all was that experienced on waking during that night when I saw myself slumped like a wreck on the hard, rocky seabed, deep under the ocean, stranded and smashed, silent in the dark waters. My main structure was still present but very battered and damaged, with pieces of wreckage falling off, drifting away, becoming lost or entangled in sinister, writhing fronds of seaweed; other pieces hanging by a strand but worn, damaged, fragile and in danger of breaking off and becoming lost; the joints loose and wobbly; other pieces rotting and corroding; loose ends swaying aimlessly; pieces crushed out of all recognition, grating and scraping on the jagged bare rock, looming menacingly; the murky waters blurring my vision; no sounds, just a deep muted silence as if I were deaf. I had no option but to lie there, slumped still and hopeless on the desolate seabed, my broken self submerged in the water, engulfed by its deep dark depths.

Chapter Two
SUBMERGED

Wednesday 11 September 2013

I woke in the morning feeling terrible; very sick and with an awful headache. I seriously questioned whether I would be able to continue taking the anti-depressant tablets if I was going to suffer such bad side effects. But I made and drank a cup of tea in bed, even though I didn't really want it, thinking of it as a 'kill or cure' approach. As I sat in bed drinking the tea, I began to feel better, less sick and the headache easing, but it was very hard to wake up properly even after all those hours of sleep that I'd managed the previous afternoon and all night. Although I felt drowsy and heavy, at least I was calm and not tearful and for this I was grateful.

Later, I got up and pottered around throughout the day, deliberately trying to avoid sleeping in the daytime and, in spite of my dozy state, I managed to achieve a few simple tasks like picking some beans from the garden, renewing my library books online, sending a couple of emails and even, in the afternoon, making a cake. I had to fight off the drowsiness continuously and waves of nausea came and went but carrying out these small, simple tasks seemed like a huge achievement and gave me a sense of doing something useful instead of being a complete waste of space. The shipwreck image was still very pervasive but at least no more bits fell off or were washed away, in spite of strong currents and waves. I felt I was hanging on despite the difficulties.

Over the next week or two, sometimes I felt as if I was floating up towards the surface as I made small achievements but these occasions were usually short-lived and inevitably I would soon sink down again, back to the hard, rocky ocean floor, submerged and held prisoner there by the pressure of the dark waters above and around me.

Thursday 12 September to Friday 13 September

The achievement of the previous day was short-lived. Thursday was my first day of taking a whole 20 mg. Citalopram tablet and this turned me into something resembling a zombie. Not only was I feeling sick, sometimes faint and always heavily sleepy but I also had the feeling I was living in a parallel world where nothing seemed to matter very much. I felt completely numb, totally emotionless and didn't care about anything or anyone. I knew I should feel guilty about not caring but couldn't even feel that emotion.

Thursday and Friday just melted away. I slept a lot and just slumbered and plodded through the days, forcing myself to do what was essential but in a sort of daze, as if I were instructing my body to perform actions from a different plane. Emotionally, I still felt numb but became aware that this was at least a relief from the intense emotions of the past week.

I know that, during these two days, I spoke on the phone to both my children and in person to several neighbours but somehow I was on a kind of automatic pilot and felt no engagement at all in these communications, though apparently I appeared fairly normal, if quieter than usual, to other people.

Saturday 14 September

This was a strange day. I must have slept fairly well until 5.15 am but, on waking at this early time, I had very dark thoughts, wishing that we had been killed in the car accident. This was such a strong feeling of complete hopelessness and a wish for relief in the form of death so that I wouldn't have to cope with everything. I must have fallen asleep again until nearly 8.00 am, when it was not only difficult to wake up properly but I also felt a huge reluctance and resistance to wake and, even more so, to get up and face another day.

However, I did get up and made an effort to appear alright to Don. I sensed strongly that he was, by now, finding my illness extremely difficult and was getting to the limits of what he could take. Fourteen years older than me, Don was in his early eighties and had been in poor physical health for some years, suffering from angina, COPD, and arthritis. Also I knew, even then, that his mental capacity was deteriorating, though he was reluctant to admit this and very resistant to seeking medical help. Gradually, I had taken over most of the tasks and responsibilities that we used to share and so now he was finding it particularly difficult when I was struggling and I did not want to add to his problems or anxieties.

My efforts of trying to seem normal worked and Don was pleased that I was apparently feeling 'better'. Encouraged by this success, I continued to make an effort, to take control of my feelings, to put on a brave face and I decided to go into town to do a few necessary tasks.

But all was not well. As I stood waiting in the library to return some overdue books and to sort out the fine, feelings of panic started to engulf me. I felt hot, sweaty and breathless, as tense as a spring, with my legs feeling wobbly but I just about managed to remain calm on the surface and escaped without major incident. But it happened again, even more severely, when going on to the chemist where I had to stand in a long queue. The panic returned making me feel both hot and sweaty and cold and clammy, my head about to burst with the pressure. Thinking I was about to faint, I had to leave the shop to get away from people and to breathe some fresh air. I went outside and trudged along the street, aware of nothing except trying hard to control my body. As I gradually started to feel normal again, I then managed to return to Boots, relieved to see that the queue had dispersed and I was able to collect some prescriptions without further difficulty.

Yet it was not all over, for going into Tesco was even worse; I started to tremble all over, feeling very strange and, when noticing several people that I knew in the store, I felt a strong urge to hide, skulking behind the shelves in the clothing section until they had moved away. It took me some time to complete my few purchases and get through the checkout. This outing took a tremendous effort and I was very glad to get home again to peace and safety. It made me realise that I was really not functioning well, however much I might try to appear normal.

That day, I was no longer feeling sleepy but agitated, on edge, ready either to spring into action or flee when feeling threatened. Still feeling restless after lunch, I decided to take Dr Alice's advice and go out for a walk, hoping that the exercise and fresh air might calm me down. The first half of the walk was uneventful as I walked a mile or two to a neighbouring village. I remember little about this first walk other than a vague enjoyment of being outside, alone in the peaceful countryside and being mildly pleased that I was doing something positive as recommended by my doctor.

This walk did not end well, however, for on the way back I was overcome by a terrible, crushing tiredness. It was the last stretch uphill that floored me. My legs were leaden, so heavy that it took an enormous effort literally to put one foot in front of the other. I had to stop and rest after every few steps, propping myself up against the wall of the cemetery. Very anxious about the state I was in, I wondered whether I could make it home, as I felt so absolutely weak and exhausted; it required a huge effort to keep walking at all but, step by step, with many rests in between, I finally made it home.

Faint with relief, I collapsed on my bed and fell asleep for an hour or two until Don woke me with a cup of tea. Once again, I didn't tell him about the difficulties I'd had, as I didn't want to worry him but I was very shaken by this experience. I realised that, as well as being mentally unwell, I was also physically fragile. This realisation came as something of a shock.

Physical illness, as well as mental illness, was not something of which I had very much personal experience. Unlike my friends, I had gone through childhood avoiding all the usual illnesses like chicken pox, measles, mumps, and rarely seemed to catch colds or anything more serious. Polio was a big fear during the 1950s; it seemed to arrive every summer and in spite of all municipal precautions, including closing the town swimming pool and prohibiting swimming in the river, it descended on people all around the town. It was a dreaded disease which, even if it did not kill, could cause paralysis, leaving its victims unable to walk or having to wear metal leg supports and heavy boots. Polio hit several families that we knew, seeming to attack children especially, but fortunately my own family remained untouched.

It always seemed to me that, in our family, being ill was something to be ashamed of. We were brought up to be healthy and strong, never going to the doctor, never breaking any bones and shaking off a cold or cough with some aspirin or cough mixture from the chemist. Going to hospital was unheard of, even as an outpatient. Perhaps we were just lucky. The only time I remember the doctor coming to our home was when my mother was ill with quinsy – abscesses on the throat. She was in bed and my father warned my brother and me not to go near her bedroom so we were not allowed to see her for a week or two, which was distressing for all of us. Of course the NHS did not come into being until 1948 when I was four years old, so some of my parents' attitudes towards healthcare had been formed in the days when people had to pay for medical attention and they were slow to adapt to the new free services available.

These attitudes were reinforced by my school, a girls' grammar school, where good attendance was praised and encouraged, both directly and indirectly. In the first three years there was a monthly 'Honours' system whereby pupils whose work across all subjects gained marks of 80–90 per cent were awarded Red Honours and those with 70–80 per cent Black Honours. No allowance was made for pupils who had missed work through illness and the names of the pupils gaining honours were read out during morning assembly in front of the whole school. If my name was missing from the list, even if I had been absent through illness, I felt dreadful, guilty and ashamed.

As for mental illness, I had never really had any experience of this as a child and it wasn't something my family or friends ever talked about. For several years, when I was about eleven or twelve, we lived quite close to a mental hospital, known locally at that time as the 'loony bin'. I just knew that the patients there were 'mad', a frightening thought but I had no real understanding of what that meant. Sometimes when I cycled to school with my friend, we would see male patients working in the fields bordering onto the road at the back of the hospital. Although they always appeared very calm, just getting on with their work, we were quite fearful as we passed by and would cycle as fast as we could to get past.

Later, when in the sixth form of my grammar school, one of the girls in my history group became ill. She was a very clever girl who always had top marks but she gradually stopped eating, became painfully pale and thin and started to faint quite frequently. One day, quite close to our A-levels, we were told by the headmistress in quiet, hushed tones that she had been withdrawn from school and would not be taking her exams. We were all very surprised and shocked, especially as we all thought this girl could have passed her exams without doing any revision, but this was about 1961–62 when no ordinary person had heard of illnesses such as anorexia or bulimia No-one talked about what had happened in any detail and we certainly knew nothing of such an illness. Again, it seemed to be something to be kept quiet as if it were 'shameful'.

After that, I never gave much thought to mental illness; for many years it was just not part of my experience. Gradually, over the years, I gained more awareness of mental illness, particularly when, as a result of the 1959 Mental Health Act, many mental hospitals were closed over the next three decades, with patients discharged into the community. Mental illness started to become something that was talked about more, in the news, no longer kept hidden.

Working as a probation officer in East London during the late 1960s, one of my first clients was a teenage girl on probation for shoplifting. She lived with her family in a block of flats and seemed to have lived an uneventful life with no indication of mental illness. The shoplifting was a first offence and seemed out of character but she kept her job and appeared normal. We started to build a good relationship but, after a few weeks, communication became strange and strained. I visited her at home with her family, who also had noticed a change, and we agreed they should consult her GP as she seemed to be deteriorating rapidly. Shortly after this, I was notified that she had been diagnosed with schizophrenia and admitted to a mental hospital. I visited her once in hospital but she was a changed person, due in part to the medication she was receiving. I was staggered to have witnessed the rapid change in her mental state and to realise that she was suffering with a severe illness, and it then became inappropriate for the Probation order to continue.

In more recent years as a working adult, I became aware of staff going off sick with 'stress'. Later still, I was conscious of my responsibilities as a manager, offering support to staff who had been sick and introducing provision for counselling, return to work interviews and a staggered return to work but even then, I had no real sense of the strength or depth of pain and anguish that can result from anxiety or depression.

Although I had no concerns about using doctors and hospitals myself, I think some of my experiences and my parents' and school's underlying attitudes had shaped me and I still found it shameful to be ill for any length of time, expecting to recover from minor illness in just a few days. It certainly never occurred to me that I might suffer from mental illness. I was always the one who would support others. Now here I was both physically and mentally unwell.

Sunday 15 September

This day started out better. I woke at 4.30 am but didn't experience the same dark thoughts as the previous day and slept again until 7.30 am. After a cup of tea and a Citalopram in bed, I felt quite good and got up at 8.45 am feeling much more 'connected', with even a little energy. Don, though, was very tired; he hadn't slept well and admitted he was worrying about me and our future. We talked things through together and his mood picked up a bit but, disappointingly, my new energy soon expired.

By mid-morning, I was so tired again that I had to lie down on my bed for an hour and really struggled to cook the roast lunch. My legs were trembly all the morning, especially going up and down the stairs. I had to hold on tightly to the bannister and I had frequent bouts of pins and needles in my arms.

It was a wet and windy day with gales forecast so I was glad that I had been out the previous day to do a few things, even though I had found it all so difficult. After lunch I slept again in the afternoon, feeling totally exhausted once more, with no energy, enthusiasm or feelings, just total exhaustion.

Monday 16 to Wednesday 18 September

This pattern of feeling a little better, then sinking back into panic, exhaustion and numbness continued over the next few days. I would wake up feeling less tired and sleepy and more connected to the world, make an effort to undertake a few tasks and return to normal life, only to keep realising that what I could do was very limited before I would collapse in some way.

Friends started to contact me, offering me lifts and encouraging me to go to various activities but just the thought of engaging with people filled me with dread and I declined them all. I only felt 'safe' in my own home and wanted to withdraw from contact with anyone else. It was like pulling a cloak around myself so that people could not see my shattered self and I felt like a wounded animal, hiding away to lick her wounds in private.

On Monday morning, when the solicitor's firm appointed by my insurance company telephoned, I found it impossible to talk coherently about what had happened, becoming completely overwhelmed by emotion and tearfulness. This extreme reaction took me by surprise and I was shocked at my vulnerability. I told them I couldn't cope with the phone interview and they agreed to send printed forms for me to fill in.

I knew that I couldn't continue living like this. So, recognising my limitations and difficulties, I decided to break my life down into manageable 'bite sized chunks' and do one small challenge a day, including going out somewhere. This decision made me feel slightly better, that I was going to start to take control again.

So, on this Monday my challenge was to attend an appointment with the dental hygienist, a lovely person whose kindness and sensitivity helped me get through a 'scale and polish' session. It was obvious that she could see how fragile I was and, again, this shocked me into realising that I couldn't even hide my state when faced with certain situations. I was shaking so much and my legs were so trembly walking back to the car afterwards that I don't know how I made it but I did and with great relief went back home to escape the world again.

My challenge for the following day was to attend a meeting of my Book Group. With this in mind, I made an effort and managed to finish reading the book which we would be discussing, *The Secret Scripture* by Sebastian Barry. It is the powerful story of an old lady nearing her hundredth birthday who, incarcerated in a mental hospital in Ireland since her youth, faces release, or rather displacement, into the much changed world of the twenty-first century, now that the Victorian hospital is about to be demolished. It deals with the themes of love, hatred, betrayal, loss, suffering and trauma as her story unfolds in discussions with her psychiatrist in an attempt to prepare her for life outside the institution. When I started this book several weeks previously, I had found it very moving but now I was quietly amazed and somewhat shocked that, on finally finishing it, I had no feelings at all. I felt no connection with the characters and was not moved by the traumatic events they endured. This state of unresponsiveness and emotional numbness left me feeling that I would have nothing to contribute to the Book Club discussion which in turn made me very anxious. I tossed and turned in bed that night before falling asleep, then woke at 2.30 am, feeling as if huge clouds were descending on to my head ready to burst and swamp me. These clouds were to be frequent visitors of the next few months but somehow that night I eventually managed to hold their downpour at bay and finally slept a restless sleep.

In spite of being very tired and apprehensive, I not only resisted the urge to stay in bed and sleep but took the plunge and went to the Book Group on Tuesday afternoon. The other members were obviously pleased to see me and interested to know about the recent car accident but, when I started to tell them what had happened, I found that I couldn't talk about it, just froze and felt the tears coming and emotions overwhelming me. This was so strange because, straight after the accident, I seemed to want to talk about it all the time and I found this new feeling upsetting. The room felt constricting, with the walls pressing in all around me. Realising that I was feeling somewhat claustrophobic, I took a seat opposite the window so that I could gaze at the view outside, which helped me relax a little as the meeting progressed into discussion about the book.

I know that I avoided eye contact with everyone and I didn't participate in the discussion. Aware of my failure to engage, I felt strangely detached, as if I were there but encased in a big glass prism which enabled me to observe everything, including myself, but with distorted vision, from a safe distance. It was a most peculiar feeling and I became so uncomfortable that, as soon as the opportunity arose, I went out to the kitchen to make the coffee.

Convinced that people must have noticed how strange and uncommunicative I was, I felt very guilty and worthless because I had made no contribution to the discussion about the book. However, at the end of the meeting, my dear friend Catherine, who had chosen the book we discussed, asked me if we could meet the following morning for a coffee. We had planned to meet a couple of weeks earlier but I had to cancel that arrangement as the car accident happened the day before our meeting and I was still in hospital that morning.

Catherine was a wonderfully brave person who, at that time, had been battling with breast cancer for over a year. She had gone through months of gruelling chemotherapy and had herself only just started, two or three months previously, to get out and about again and resume a normal life. I knew that she would understand my fragility and so I felt able to accept this invitation without feeling threatened and was relieved that I would then achieve another of my 'bite-sized chunk' targets.

The following morning we met in the Hotel Metropole, a large hotel in the centre of town and Catherine's favourite place for coffee. She arrived carrying a bunch of lovely yellow roses for me, a gesture which I found very touching. During her illness over several months, I had spent time each week trying to support her, visiting, taking flowers and sending chatty emails when she was feeling too rough to meet after a tough chemo session. Now here we were together and it was Catherine who seemed to be doing well and encouraging me.

Full of her own new-found energy and enthusiasm for life, she tried hard to interest me in the new activities she had just started, knowing that we have many interests in common. Whilst I appreciated her positivity and was glad to see how she was improving, the thought of doing anything like joining an art class with her was the last thing I wanted to do. I was struggling so hard to do one essential thing a day! To take on anything new was an overwhelmingly awful thought. We were able to talk, though, to empathise with each other, and found we shared a lot of common thoughts and feelings. She seemed to understand something of what I was experiencing as this was very similar to her own struggle to get her life back on track but I felt very guilty that I had collapsed over such a relatively minor thing, compared with what she had been undergoing for months.

After a largely pleasant morning, the day once more deteriorated, as Wednesday afternoon was very stressful. The garage that had been repairing my car phoned to say it was ready and they wanted to return it that afternoon. Instead of being pleased at this news, all I felt was anxiety and horror. I wished that someone would drive the car over a cliff and wreck it completely. I had no wish to see the car again, let alone to drive it. That thought was too terrifying.

Then the garage told me that I would have to pay a £200 excess, even though the insurance company had previously told me there would be no charge as the other driver had accepted full responsibility. I found this conflicting information hard to cope with and became very tense and upset. It wasn't only the thought of paying £200 but more about the need to deal with people and try to sort the problem out. I was certainly not up to this.

Added to this, Don was annoyed that we hadn't been to inspect the car before they returned it, as he was convinced it would not be up to a good standard. All this conflict and anxiety was devastating. I was in tears – the first time I'd cried since starting the anti-depressants. My stomach was in knots and my throat choked from trying to hold the tears at bay.

Fortunately, when the car arrived it was fine; two new doors had been fitted and a good repair job carried out. Even Don could find no fault with it! The garage also confirmed that, having been in touch with the insurance company again, there was no excess payment due. So all was sorted out satisfactorily but I felt I had slipped right down the steep sides of the dark pit again. Not quite to the bottom but I was wounded, shocked, exhausted and devastated at having to face the effort of climbing back up again.

That afternoon, I re-lived much of the dreadful feeling of depression – tension; anxiety; anguish; despair; worthlessness and had a very restless night with only fitful sleep, negative thoughts and high anxiety. Until then I had felt that I'd been making progress – even if it was just a small step each day – but today had proved to be a serious setback which had taken a lot out of me and I was faced again with another long, exhausting journey to reclaim the little progress I had made.

Chapter Three
THE SALVAGE OPERATION BEGINS

Thursday 19 September 2013

Things did start to improve though, as I took advantage of the help and support I was offered. I attended my appointment with Dr Alice on Thursday morning and, in spite of getting very tense and stressed whilst waiting in the waiting room, it was worth it. She seemed genuinely pleased that I had made such good progress in a week and thought my setting a target of going out and doing one thing a day was a good strategy. She thought the structured approach would be helpful, and stressed the importance of achieving a balance between doing too much too quickly or not enough. She suggested that I should try to drive a bit further now but advised against undertaking a long journey yet. This was a relief and made me feel less guilty that I had not been and did not want to drive to see my daughter, son or other family. Now that I had my doctor's official advice, this took the burden of guilt and responsibility off my shoulders.

Dr Alice recognised that, in spite of making progress, I was still experiencing significant problems associated with meeting people and that I was not sleeping well, being besieged by negative thoughts and worries during the nights. She asked whether I thought a course of counselling might help. I told her that I had been offered some telephone counselling sessions by my insurance company and, although she seemed a little doubtful about how useful these might be, we agreed that I would try them for the time being as it would take a month or so for face to face sessions to be arranged at the surgery.

I came away feeling so much more positive and even managed a slight smile as I left the doctor's surgery – the first smile for over two weeks or more. Encouragement, praise and approval from Dr Alice helped a great deal to give me some confidence in myself, while the prospect of professional counselling gave me hope that I would receive support in my long climb up from the bottom of the dark depths which seemed to be all around me.

That afternoon, I felt absolutely exhausted and slept for several hours. Later a friend from my Recorder Group brought some music round, thinking that I might like to practice and keep up to date with pieces on which the group was working. Although I had no real wish to do so, I unpacked my recorder which had been left in its case since the start of my breakdown and tentatively played a few pieces. This made me realise how much I had missed playing and it was very good to enjoy this activity again, even just for a short time. I didn't play very much, being careful not to overdo things, but I felt that this was one big step forward. It was an activity that totally absorbed me and with my mind focused on playing the music, it could not worry and cause me anxiety. Most of the music we play in our group is fifteenth or sixteenth century, a time when the recorder was a popular instrument and, when played with a variety of instruments is very pleasant, a far cry from the shrill notes of descant recorders on which children usually learn in primary school. Our group, one of the many interest groups offered by our U3A, has around fifteen members playing treble, tenor and bass recorders as well as the ubiquitous descant. It is a friendly group whose members enjoy making music together from which I gain great pleasure, so I was pleased and relieved that playing with the group again may not be too far away in the distant future.

Friday 20 September
Much to my own amazement, I got up at 8.00 am, went to my

pilates class and did all the exercises quite well. Once more I was very pleased at such progress. I actually felt 'normal' with much more energy, although I didn't know whether I had really made some recovery or whether it was just the anti-depressant tablets taking effect. Whatever the reason, it was good to feel alive again.

In the afternoon, I used my new found energy to mow both lawns, front and back, then made a real effort to start to fill in the insurance claim form. This, however, was much more difficult. Whilst I seemed to be recovering physically, I was still finding it impossible to concentrate for long on anything that required mental energy. I therefore decided to set myself a target of completing one page of this lengthy form each day. With a more manageable goal, it felt less threatening and I managed to complete the first page that afternoon. I was aware that I felt quite 'high' today and recorded in my diary that I hoped that it wouldn't all collapse.

Saturday 21 September

It did collapse, but not too badly. After a restless night I was very tired, slow at everything, with no enthusiasm, and very apprehensive of becoming tearful once more. Fortunately, nothing went wrong so I managed some shopping and cooked lunch, including runner beans which I picked from the garden and which were delicious. It was small things like the lunch going well that were tremendously important in keeping my spirits up and my emotions stable. If it had gone badly, I know that the collapse would have been much worse, the achievements of the day forgotten and the world seeming a bleak place once more, full of problems that I had neither the energy nor the will to solve.

In the afternoon, I slept for several hours, then spent some time pottering in the garden and talking with my neighbours across the road. I also received a nice email from my friend, Ann, who offered to come with me to Recorder Group the following Tuesday if I felt up to it. These interactions with friends and neighbours assumed a huge significance. I was so in need of friendship and kindness that the smallest gesture played an important role in keeping me from disintegrating. For the first time, I fully realised how important people are to each other and what a powerful effect we can have on each other, just in everyday contacts. Most of the time we just take our communication with others for granted but now I was relishing these contacts and treasuring the caring friendship that was offered. They were a great support.

My first telephone counselling session was due the following day and, although I only had a vague idea of what it might involve, I spent some time writing down things in preparation, knowing that my brain was not yet up to speed and my thinking processes were slow. I always find that writing things down helps to move my thinking on and ensures that I do not forget something important. I did not want to waste the precious time that I'd been allocated and I think this activity not only prepared me well to make good use of the counselling time but also helped me start to sort out my very jumbled and confused thoughts and emotions.

My insurance company had offered these sessions after the car accident and I had already spoken for a short while with a counsellor, Brian, who had explained that during the sessions we would concentrate on tackling the problems I was currently experiencing, to help me readjust to a normal life, and that we would not be delving into the past to deal with unresolved issues. I was impressed with Brian's calm and reassuring approach during this initial discussion and he made me think differently about responsibility. I had mentioned how I was besieged with 'What if?' questions that not only made me extremely anxious but also made it very difficult for me to make everyday decisions.

What if my grandchildren had been in the car with me when I was involved in the accident and lost my memory? What if I gave my grandson the money to buy a laptop for his twelfth birthday and he became the victim of online abuse? What if I gave my ten-year-old granddaughter money towards a pony for her birthday and she was injured in a riding accident?

The world seemed a frightening place where potential threats lurked everywhere and consequently I was avoiding making decisions and hiding away from everyone and everything.

As well as encouraging me to think things through rationally and consider the evidence and likelihood of potential hazards and threats, Brian also made me think afresh about 'responsibility', stressing that, instead of assuming total responsibility for everyone and everything, I should ask myself *Am I totally responsible for this decision? Who else should share the responsibility?* With regard to all the questions about the grandchildren, it was clear that their parents would have to be consulted and agree to these gifts, so the parents would also have a responsibility to ensure that they were controlled and used safely. This concept of shared responsibility, although it may seem obvious to others – and it also became clear to me when thinking it through rationally – had a huge effect on me and lightened the burden, not through just abandoning it but by sharing the load and understanding that I do not have to take on total control and responsibility for everything. It is permissible and advantageous to share it with others.

After this initial conversation with Brian I felt very reassured, knowing that someone would be there for me if I needed him and, because it was his job, I need not feel that I was boring or irritating him as I might if I kept on about my difficulties with family or friends, who may become bored or impatient. Brian was a good listener and somehow he succeeded in prodding my brain into starting to work through some issues in a more positive way. After this initial discussion, he offered me a full session in a fortnight's time. It was this session that was now due on the following day.

Sunday 22 September

Knowing that the counselling session was due at eleven o'clock, I was very on edge and apprehensive all morning. Doing mundane, practical tasks like preparing the lunch in advance helped me get through to the appointed time without becoming too stressed.

This first session was an introductory one and it went well. Brian, the counsellor, and I talked for about forty minutes on the phone, which turned out to be easier than I thought, no doubt helped by my preparation the previous day. He stressed that my expectations for a quick recovery were not realistic and that it was going to take much longer than I thought or hoped. I should try to accept this and not put additional pressure on myself by expecting more rapid progress. He encouraged me to accept my feelings; in particular, feelings of guilt about not being strong. These would pass and I should just allow myself to feel them as this is a natural reaction. He told me that I was 'allowed' to be upset; being upset doesn't mean you are not a strong person, just that you are human, not superhuman, and that it is okay to let grief show. Somehow, being given 'permission' to have such feelings was helpful. We agreed that I might benefit from a regular programme of fortnightly sessions, starting on 3 October. He said I must spend some time before then thinking about what I wanted to get out of the counselling and what I expected of him. This would help us both focus on what was important to me and also would prevent unrealistic expectations which, if unmet, would simply add to my distress. After the session, I felt much calmer and it made me start thinking more logically than I had for some time. I was surprised at how well my brain could function in a safe and structured situation where my thoughts and feelings were not allowed to run riot. Although I could not have verbalised this at the time, I think this is when I began to take back control of my life from my unruly, negative mind.

After lunch I went for another walk, following the same route as previously but on this occasion, by chance, I met two friends, Ann and Dorothy, who were also out for an afternoon stroll. They invited me to join them for tea at Dorothy's and I accepted as, remembering my problems on the last walk, I thought it would be a good idea to have a rest before tackling the homeward journey. I was quite proud of this achievement, meeting and talking not just to one but two people at once! But, in spite of them both being friendly, lovely and caring, I knew I wasn't really engaging with them. Over tea, I just sat there and let the conversation go on all around me. I was back in my glass prism, observing our communication from a different plane. They gave no indication that they were aware of anything strange about me but it worried me.

Then, that evening, one of my favourite TV programmes, *Downton Abbey*, started a new series, to which I had looked forward with great anticipation, but I was subsequently very disappointed that I didn't enjoy it at all. I found it disjointed and felt no connection with the characters and, like many other things I had previously enjoyed, I found it all completely pointless. Confusion and despair overwhelmed me again. I felt that, once more, I did not know who I was any longer – bits of me were either missing or were so different from how I knew or perceived myself, this perception having been built up over the many years of my life. Where had my being gone? Why was I still submerged? Would I ever be the same again? These were sobering and frightening thoughts. Clearly the salvage operation was not straightforward. It was going to be a lengthy and difficult process.

Monday 23 September

My grandson's twelfth birthday. I didn't phone him as I usually did, as he had school and then gymnastics club. Also, if I'm honest, it was because I was too apprehensive. Don and I had sent him a card and some money and my daughter phoned to say he was pleased with his presents and had bought a new fishing rod with the money we sent. Once again I was aware of my shortcomings, not even being able to speak to my grandson and even worse, not really caring that I couldn't. Guilt and self-loathing reigned again.

I spent the day keeping busy with jobs in the garden, finding it therapeutic to work outside amongst the flowers, butterflies and bees, which were everywhere on this warm autumn day; also I managed to complete another page of the insurance claim, contributing to my bite-sized target of one page a day and in the afternoon, swimming in the over-fifties session at the local pool. This was quite a lot to achieve in one day but raised some new concerns: when working in the garden I'd felt faint when it turned very warm, and then had felt dizzy when swimming, making me cut down to forty lengths from my usual sixty. I didn't know if these physical symptoms were side effects from the anti-depressant tablets or an indication of my physical limitations.

Tuesday 24 September

An important day. My friend, Ann, picked me up in the afternoon and came with me to Recorder Group as promised. This was the first time I'd been to the group since becoming ill and I wouldn't have had the courage to go if Ann had not been there to support me but, with her help and rather to my surprise, I found no real difficulty relating to the other people there. On that occasion, it was just a small group of three others who were all pleased to see me back. However, I found playing the music very difficult and my brain kept getting the notes mixed up, reading D as B, which threw me into a real panic. The tutor was very patient as always, but I felt dreadful about it, anxious and worried at my inability to play properly. I didn't show that I was upset when there but, later that evening, it all came out in floods of tears and terrible feelings of depression, wanting to die and leave all the stress of life behind, just as bad as before I started taking the anti-depressant tablets.

Wednesday 25 September

Although I slept, exhausted from the emotional outburst the previous evening, I felt very tired and all morning I could visualise and actually *feel* a big, dark cloud over my head just waiting to burst. All I wanted to do was give in to it, go to bed and cry but somehow I found the strength to control it by continually taking very deep breaths and by trying hard to appear normal. I was lucky that another good friend, Margaret, phoned me and somehow seemed aware of my state. She suggested going for a walk that afternoon and I agreed. The chilly, misty morning changed into a sunny, warm afternoon both physically and emotionally. We enjoyed a lovely walk in the countryside, taking her neighbour's dog with us and picking blackberries. Since I was a child, I've always loved blackberrying. It was one of my favourite childhood activities, going with my parents and brother into the country on a sunny afternoon, watching out for promising hedges, then filling containers with these shiny, black fruits that stained your hands and lips purple and blue as you picked and ate. We would take a walking stick to help us reach the higher brambles which always seemed to bear the largest, most luscious fruit and, in spite of being scratched by brambles and stung by nettles, we always enjoyed this family activity. I think there is something very comforting about undertaking activities you enjoyed as a child. It takes you back to a safe and happy time that helped to form the person you later become.

With Margaret that afternoon, it was easy to talk while we worked, and being with a kind and thoughtful friend, out in the fresh air in the sunshine appreciating nature, worked wonders on my emotional state. For a couple of hours I actually enjoyed my life again, even though I was conscious of having to work hard at doing so. I was beginning to understand that being outdoors – whether walking, gardening or now blackberrying- was something that helped to calm and restore me to a healthier state of mind.

The following day, I was due to attend another U3A group, Mythology. This group was a larger one with a lot of members and I felt unable to face this so I decided to phone the leader to give my apologies. I even managed to explain to her how difficult I was finding it to mix with groups of people and was glad that I'd made the effort to give this explanation as she was so understanding and sympathetic. I realised how lucky I was to have such lovely people as friends. Their care and concern made such a difference and it was their small acts of kindness that helped me to struggle on through these difficult and painful times.

But, overshadowing these good feelings, I was still distraught that I was unable to concentrate on or to sustain an interest in anything that required mental effort. I was particularly upset about my inability to enjoy reading as this had always, since very early childhood, been something that gave me tremendous pleasure and a means of escaping into another world. I must have learnt to read at a very young age; I don't remember ever being unable to read and was always puzzled at how difficult other children found it. Being a child in the post-war years meant that books were not easily obtained, due to paper rationing and expense as children's books were produced only as hardbacks at that time. Children were not allowed to join our town library until they were seven years old but, knowing how desperate I was for books to read, my mother was able to join the Junior Library and take out books on my behalf. I also remember when, a little older, I would walk around all the bookshops in the town and stand at the book counter rather surreptitiously reading a chapter in each shop. I always expected the shop assistant to realise what I was doing and put an end to my clandestine reading, though this never happened. I came to know intimately the characters in books by many authors such as E. Nesbit, Noel Streatfield, Angela Brazil, Arthur Ransome and of course Enid Blyton, though at one time her books were banned from our town library as some sort of moral protest when she was divorced, which was much frowned upon. Books take you to many places and allow you to share so many experiences, some real, some fantasies, and I have always loved the ability to share in others' lives and adventures, making my life richer through reading. Now that I could no longer read, it seemed that this pleasure was denied to me, leaving me alone and deprived.

It wasn't just the reading that was causing me concern. I was also unable to watch television, even programmes that I would usually find gripping; even more important, I knew that I was not connecting with people. A phone call from my daughter had exacerbated my concerns when she told me some disturbing news and I became aware that I was horrified in a 'knowing' way but not in a 'feeling' way. This state of emotional numbness was something I had noticed on other occasions when trying to relate to people.

Overall, I began to doubt seriously whether my brain was working properly, as I seemed to be experiencing such difficulty in learning anything new and just not wanting to know about so many things that had previously been important to me.

Thursday 26 September

A very dark, difficult day. I slept badly all night and was so tired that day that I felt ill. I managed to cook a casserole for lunch in between lying on my bed and dozing. I had no appetite and couldn't face going out at all throughout the day. I just felt terribly tired and depressed and spent most of the time in bed.

Friday 27 September

I didn't sleep well again, probably as result of spending so much time in bed the previous day, but forced myself to get up in the morning and go to pilates, feeling very apprehensive. Once there with my friends I managed fairly well, only giving up on the exercises near the end of the hour's session. Afterwards, I went with Margaret and another friend to a Macmillan National Coffee Morning which proved to be not a good idea. The room was very crowded and stuffy and I was aware of feelings of claustrophobia and panic rising up and closing in on me. I knew I had to get out of that room and away from all the people – yet another worrying symptom to cope with!

Saturday 28 September

Saturday was a bit of a 'lull before the storm' which, unknown to me then, was to arrive on Sunday. I actually had a real sleep the previous night, the first time without being awake for the long, early hours of the morning, so I awoke feeling refreshed and good.

This lasted sporadically all day and I managed to achieve a few tasks without too much of a problem, using my new found technique of lots of deep breathing to avert tearfulness when this threatened. I found that if I took and held a deep breath when I felt the cloud descending over my head, that this seemed to push it away so that the rain, or tearfulness, did not engulf me.

I also found that working outside in the garden was calming and gave me a sense of purpose and achievement, so I worked for an hour before lunch and again in the afternoon. I even took a few plants to a friend who seemed pleased to see me, and we spent a pleasant hour together looking around her garden and having a coffee. I was pleased that I was beginning to manage one to one relationships better, without feeling that I was just going through the motions of social chit-chat from inside my bubble but sometimes *beginning* to engage with people again. Unfortunately, I seemed to have strained a muscle in my shoulder and this was causing me quite a bit of physical pain and even more emotional stress. I felt I just couldn't cope with anything else, however minor.

Sunday 29 September

My shoulder was very painful during the night, resulting in a dreadful sleep. Consequently, I was very tired and struggled hard to cope, exacerbated by Don being in an angry mood with everyone. Several things had happened to upset him but I found it very difficult to empathise. Listening to his tirade was too much and made me feel quite ill, trembling all over. I realised that all the stress of the accident and my breakdown seemed to have affected him much more than we had realised and that his memory had deteriorated significantly over the past few weeks. I wished he would go to see the doctor but his refusal was adamant. I had no energy or motivation to go out or do anything but withdrew into my unhappy self once more.

Monday 30 September

The weather was gloomy, dull and damp which matched my miserable, lethargic mood. I had intended to do some cleaning but couldn't find the energy and became frustrated and upset at my failure to get through on the phone to my contact at the solicitors' firm appointed by my insurance company.

My daughter phoned me in the evening but I found it hard to talk and was conscious of it being a very stilted conversation but I hadn't the will or the skill to change that. I knew that our relationship was deteriorating because of my poor communication and felt very guilty and afraid.

Wednesday 2 October

Another drizzly, damp day but Don and I decided to brave it and drive to Talgarth to examine the site of the accident so that we could draw an accurate sketch map of the road layout, as requested by my insurance company. Strangely, it was Don now who was very apprehensive about driving. He developed a headache and complained of not feeling well but I persuaded him to take a couple of paracetamol before we set off, and on the way back he became more relaxed. In contrast, I was fine, even though this was a 'big' journey for me, the furthest I'd driven since the car accident. I was hyper-alert and a little tense, intensely vigilant, especially for cars approaching me from side roads, but I managed the driving well. I was apprehensive about seeing the place where it had happened and wondered what effect that would have on me but the answer was, none at all! It brought back no memories of what had happened and I was able to have a good look at the scene and draw an accurate sketch map which I could then send off to the insurance company and so achieve another dreaded task.

In the afternoon, I spent some time preparing for an appointment with my doctor the following day and also for my next telephone counselling session the following evening.

Counselling was to play a very important role in my life over the next months. It wasn't a straightforward process and there were many highs, lows and emotional moments. It was, though, a very useful experience and helped me struggle through one of the most difficult periods of my life. My counsellors were like an anchor, just there, holding me as I floundered about in some very stormy seas.

Brian, with whom I'd had an introductory session, was my first counsellor and we engaged in several structured sessions on the telephone. Although initially a little doubtful about this method, I think in retrospect it was a good way for me to start and to get used to talking about things that I found very difficult to say. Because it was less personal than face to face and because he was far away in a call centre in some unknown location, I gradually lost some of my inhibitions and started to learn how to express what I was feeling.

The rules were very clear; I knew that I only had fifty precious minutes with him and couldn't waste them, so I had to do a lot of thinking before and after each session, planning what I wanted to say or ask. Brian explained that the type of counselling on offer was short-term, with a focus on solution and it was not about dwelling on the past. I would need to have a clear idea of what I wanted to focus on to enable positive change so that I could move on in my life.

Thursday 3 October

The first of my regular programme of six fortnightly sessions with Brian was due at 7.00 pm until 7.50 pm. The arrangement was that I had to telephone him at the appointed time, which I did with some apprehension but as soon as he came on the phone I felt as if I knew him and trusted him, even though I'd only spoken to him during the initial sessions. It was reassuring to have rules that had been carefully explained so I knew what to expect.

Before the session, I considered what I wanted to gain from the counselling and what I expected from the counsellor and I wrote down my thoughts as a way of clarifying them:

What I want to gain from counselling:

1) **Time to focus on me** and what's happening to me, without feeling guilty about taking up too much of another person's time, e.g. my GP or friends. Because of the structure, the limits and the fact that there is no personal relationship or involvement with the counsellor, he would not be telling me about his own problems or experiences but would *focus solely on me.*

2) **To make me talk** – in general, I'm a listener rather than a talker and find it difficult to talk freely about deeply personal thoughts and feelings, especially if I'm ashamed of them. But I know I ought

The Salvage Operation Begins

to talk because it is only after something has been said out loud – and heard – that I can hope to move on and not just be stuck there thinking the same thoughts over and over again.

3) **Reassurance** – where appropriate, that I'm not completely abnormal or going mad. The reassurance must be **genuine.**

4) **Advice** – even if it's not always what I want to hear. This makes it more credible.

What I expect from the counsellor:

1) **Confidentiality** – so that if necessary I could say things that I couldn't admit to anyone close because it might upset them, or to anyone who lives locally as this is a small town where everyone knows someone who knows you, and people talk. This is usually nice but it can be inhibiting.

2) Use of **professional expertise** to help me reconstruct my life out of chaos – whatever that takes.

3) Help to develop a **different perspective** on things, by challenging some of my thoughts, feelings and perceptions of myself.

4) Just being there to **support and accept** all this stuff that I'm dumping on him **without emotion or judgement**, recognising that things are difficult for me but not letting me give up, without making me feel too pathetic.

I found the first session hard work but my preparation beforehand helped me make good use of the time and I was pleased with how it went. It was very reassuring to be able to express my myriad

41

anxieties and doubts about myself in such a controlled and safe environment. I think knowing that I would not be interrupted and that I had his full attention as a professional counsellor who had no emotional relationship with me was particularly helpful.

We spent a long time discussing emotions and how we cannot control them. We don't *decide* how anything will affect us emotionally. What we *can* do is control how we *respond* to our emotions but first we must give ourselves permission to feel them and just accept them, whatever they are.

Brian echoed what my GP had told me, that the way forward would not be straightforward; there would be ups and downs, lows and highs. I needed to accept that these are *understandable and normal*.

He stressed, as others would in the future, the importance of taking things slowly, allowing myself time to gradually build up my abilities and achievements, not trying to do everything at once. He recommended setting small targets, just to achieve one thing, a day, however small, and gave me reassurance that things would get easier as time went on.

As the session drew to a close, Brian suggested some worksheets available on a website www.stopp.gg that he thought might help me deal with my anxieties and feelings between sessions and we set the date for the next session on 21 October.

In spite of it being quite a painful and emotional experience as we tackled some of my difficult feelings, afterwards I felt a deep sense of calm, a feeling that had been absent for months. As I reflected on this session in the following days, I realised that one of the most helpful things Brian had told me was that all the counsellors at his call centre have monthly 'supervision' sessions to ensure their own good mental health. I felt that, if even professionally trained counsellors need support and help sometimes, then somehow that made it okay for me to need it. It doesn't detract from them being essentially strong, mentally healthy people, but just human. This realisation was like another huge weight taken off me as I realised that there was no need to feel guilty about needing help and support and that this need did not intrinsically alter who I was.

I sat in my room for some time after the session had finished, my mind going over all that we had discussed, and the next day I printed off some of the worksheets and read a lot of information on the STOPP website.

Friday 4 October

Feeling more confident and cheerful, I worked hard at pilates and had a generally good day, carrying out my main task for the day which was to update the U3A website.

So far, so good, but what I didn't realise was the effect that my total self-absorption would have on my husband who told me on Saturday how hurt he'd been. I realised then that I had to consider the effect of my behaviour on others and that people close to me might feel threatened by the counselling. Interestingly, one of the first questions both my husband and my daughter asked about the counselling was ,'What did you say about me?' I was quite taken aback by this, as I had seen the session as the one occasion when it was all about me, no-one else.

I did manage to explain to Don how I was feeling after the session, and to apologise for being thoughtless. It was good that we were both able to be open about how we felt, a big step forward. Nevertheless, I was taken aback at my reaction to his accusations with tears, trembling and jumping every time he spoke in a raised voice. After my explanation and apology he was reassured and we became very friendly. We went for a drive to the Elan Valley which Don enjoyed, especially as it was a nice day, mild with sunny spells. Normally this excursion would have filled me with pleasure but on that occasion I would gladly have come home long before we did, and was still close to tears for the rest of the day, even though things between us were good.

On the following day, Sunday, I was still very close to tears all day but managed to cope with cooking the lunch and, despite feeling tired and lethargic, forced myself to go for a walk round the lake in the afternoon, still feeling tearful. By the end of two circuits (about 2 km) I felt better – not brilliant but better than previously. It occurred to me that I might be feeling worse at weekends as there were no structured activities, so I attempted a couple of tasks on the worksheets and found this helped me become more motivated and have the confidence to email (but not to phone) my daughter to ask her for the photos of the car that she had taken on her phone after the accident, so that I could send them off to the legal representative involved in my case. I even drafted an email to this representative expressing my concerns about how the case was being handled, and this action made me feel that I had done something constructive instead of just worrying and taking *all* the responsibility myself. As a result of the counselling sessions, I had learnt to recognise that I could and should *share* responsibility and not take everything upon myself.

Monday started off well as my daughter sent the photos, and I sent them off to the legal firm, accomplishing my main task for the day first thing in the morning. I even did the washing then, which I hadn't been able to face the previous day. This success motivated me to talk to Don more about the counselling and I found that he was very curious and quite scared of what I talked to the counsellor about. I spent some time explaining what the counselling involved and also about the effects of the accident on him, especially his memory which seemed to have deteriorated in recent weeks. This led on to his fear of going to the doctor in case he should be diagnosed with Alzheimer's Disease which would really depress him. His mother had suffered from this illness during her final years and he was afraid of going the same way. He was adamant that he would not like to engage in counselling himself but he could see that it helped me and became quite encouraging about me continuing with it. This was a very useful conversation for both of us and helped us to understand each other's feelings, fears and anxieties.

The day continued well. I went swimming and enjoyed that, then called at the library to collect a book I'd requested to read for Book Group, *Flight Behaviour* by Barbara Kingsolver. To my surprise, I soon became immersed in this book, reading four chapters and actually getting inside the main character, Dellarobia's head, as she attempts to escape her empty marriage and the drudgery of life on a rundown Appalachian farm. I found that I could empathise with her, understanding how she thought and could feel that I was living her life with her. This was such a breakthrough, the first time I had engaged with characters in a book for weeks. After this I even wrote down some of my thoughts about the book to take to Book Group so that I could contribute something to the discussion.

Engaging with this book made me feel as if I had put another piece of the jigsaw of my shattered 'personality' back in place and that I might not be broken for ever. It gave me a glimmer of hope for the future.

Chapter Four
UPS AND DOWNS

This positive behaviour and optimism was sadly short-lived. What a let-down! Each time I seemed to be making progress I would soon go backwards again and be devastated. My GP had warned me that it would not be an easy climb but a staggered one with lots of falls on the way. I was glad she had warned me but it was still so hard to cope with when it happened, bringing more disappointment each time, and resurrecting all my feelings of uselessness and self-disgust. I knew that I wasn't being realistic but this did little to assuage the guilty plunge back into those dark depths.

It all started when I attended the book group meeting the following day. I started off normally, chatting to the other members, and I even felt brave and confident enough to offer to drive several of us to a lecture at Brecon later in the week. I thought this would be a good opportunity to practise driving a longer distance as it was about twenty-six miles each way, but a straightforward, easy drive and I would have the company of other people in the car. But only minutes later, when the formal discussion about the chosen book began, I withdrew into myself, not knowing why but feeling myself becoming distant, sinking down underwater, submerged once more with the pressure of water above and all around me, making me breathless and helpless. The discussion just went on around me. I could hear people speaking but their words had no meaning and I was unable to bring myself to contribute at all. Conscious of the waves buffeting and threatening to overpower me, I concentrated hard on looking calm and composed, whilst underneath becoming restless and agitated. I think I managed to keep my inner turmoil well hidden and, as soon as there was a suitable opportunity, I volunteered to make the coffee and escaped to the kitchen, finding relief in doing something practical that didn't require much thought. The overwhelming panic subsided sufficiently for me to make my exit but I was exhausted, choked and close to tears as I left.

That evening, as I thought about my reaction, I became very apprehensive about the lecture day at Brecon, the thought of both the journey and the event filling me with terror. It was not so much the thought of the driving itself but a fear of being 'trapped' in the confined space of a car with three other people and not being able to escape from being involved in their conversations. Then the thought of attending the lecture itself, being present in a large theatre packed with people and having to converse with them over lunch or in coffee breaks, felt very threatening. Knowing how I would feel in that situation, I worried and worried overnight, tossing and turning, not being able to sleep until finally I decided that I would not go – it was all just too much pressure. Having made that decision, I then started to worry about how I would tell people and extricate myself. I knew that I would have to admit my failure and dreaded the task, thinking everyone would despise my weakness and view me as pathetic, as I did myself.

The next morning, it took me several hours to summon up the courage to ring my friend, Margaret, to explain how I was feeling. I trusted Margaret; she had supported me before and, once again, she didn't let me down. She was very calm and relaxed about it, accepting my explanation easily and said she would drive and let the other members know of the change of plan. She was so matter of fact, not dismissive but understanding, and made it so easy. All those hours of worrying were dealt with in a matter of minutes.

She must have recognised that I was struggling, for she then asked me whether I would like to go for a walk that afternoon to which I agreed with alacrity, feeling that it was just what I needed. I felt such enormous relief about making the decision not to attend the lecture and about the fact that I had summoned up the courage to tell Margaret the truth about how I was feeling and not to make up some excuse. I was slowly learning to be a little more open about myself and how I felt. Our walk was a short one; when it started to rain we decided to go back to Margaret's house for coffee and shared a lot of thoughts about depression and its effects. She actually made me laugh several times, not least when demonstrating how to hula-hoop (her latest fitness activity) in the kitchen and knocking over first the broom and then the washing basket. Laughing – not something I'd done much of lately – was such a pleasure, a medicine in itself, and I felt so much more cheerful when I left. The importance of Margaret's reaction was crucial to my learning that I do not have to aim for perfection in everything I do. When I think about this situation now, it is clear that it was no big deal to her who drove the car and, now that I am better and recovered, I can see this but at the time, it made such a difference to me. It has struck me time and time again how the little things that other people do and the way in which they do them can make a critical difference to someone experiencing difficulty with their mental health.

Throughout the day of the conference, I felt so relieved that I hadn't gone, knowing it was the right decision for me at this point in time. I knew that I would have felt under a great strain all day and would not have been able to concentrate on the lecture. Then I would have had a sense of failure to cope with as well.

The day, however, was not without another 'down' caused by a very minor incident. I went to town, wanting to buy a new glass roasting dish to replace one that had recently been broken. I usually enjoy shopping at the local supermarket, especially if I'm not in a hurry, so it seemed quite a pleasurable task to undertake. But as I walked from the car park to the entrance I was suddenly overwhelmed by strong feelings of panic and depression, thinking, *They won't have what I want . . .* To my horror, tears flooded my eyes, even though I knew this was a completely exaggerated response. I asked myself, 'What would it matter anyway? I could always go to another shop,' but this reasoning didn't seem to help my emotions. I felt such an emotional wreck. In fact, I did find something suitable, even though it wasn't what I had in mind, but the tearfulness remained not far away all morning, partly from being upset by my initial reaction. It was yet another experience of being someone different from the person I always thought I was. I felt so weak and stupid and unable to control my thoughts and feelings which just seemed to run away with themselves out of control.

In the afternoon, seeking some practical task to stop me brooding over the morning's events, I decided to work in the garden, picking the last of the runner beans, taking the canes down, then planting the space with wallflowers ready for next spring. It was very therapeutic to be in the fresh air and to do something practical, rewarding and forward looking. There is something very calming about gardening and about the continuing natural cycle of sowing, planting, flowering, harvesting, then dying down for winter but well prepared with fruits and seeds ready for life again in the spring. Having achieved the tasks that I set out to accomplish that afternoon, I felt much more relaxed and stronger, so much so that I felt able to phone my daughter. On this occasion, our conversation came easily; we had a good chat and caught up with all her news. I was pleased and relieved to know that she was managing well with her baby, now three months old, and finished the day on an 'up' rather than a 'down'.

Once again, this did not last long. The morning started well but then the postman brought a letter from the Police saying the incident (car accident) was 'currently under investigation'. This aroused all sorts of feelings again – panic, fear, anxiety, worry, anger, frustration – will it ever be over? In spite of trying to be rational, the feelings just kept rising up and taking over my whole being. I felt physically unwell, nauseous, trembly and tearful and blundered through the rest of the day until, in the late afternoon, I thought I'd try a bit more gardening. So I went outside and planted a lot of bulbs which had arrived back in August or September but had been ignored ever since. This activity did work, and I felt much better. That evening I amazed myself by enjoying *Strictly Come Dancing* which I'd always enjoyed in the past but hadn't watched at all this series. I especially enjoyed watching the Hairy Biker, Dave Myers, who was hilarious doing the Paso Doble. It made me laugh out loud and I felt really good for a time. Laughter is such a good medicine!

During these days of swinging up and down, it was the small achievements and occasional glimmers of progress that kept me going. Each day brought new challenges but I only had the strength and energy to tackle them just one at a time, being careful not to attempt too much and risk failure. It was hard going but it was these small goals and achievements that gave me enough hope to struggle through each day. Most of the time I felt as if I was stumbling through a fog which now and then lifted for a brief time and then closed in on me once more.

The nights were a different matter altogether. Although feeling constantly tired, my sleep, when it came, was broken and restless and I would almost always wake in the early hours of the morning, sweating and anxious about something. In the dark of the night, the problems seemed overwhelming and it was easy to forget the small steps of progress that I'd made. Eventually, after an hour or two of tossing, turning and worrying, I would fall into an uneasy sleep. My brain would not shut down and I never felt refreshed when I woke in the morning, finding it difficult to get up and face each day. I'm sure that this continual tiredness contributed hugely to my lethargy and lack of enjoyment in everything. Life had become something to be endured rather than lived, something that required ceaseless effort and toil to get through each day. I found that I could no longer bear to watch the news on television; it seemed that the whole world was in such chaos and misery which exacerbated my view that everything was dire and that life was pointless.

It was around this time, realising that I knew very little about depression, that I started to investigate the subject to learn more about its symptoms, its causes and its cures. I had no real idea what I was looking for and just read whatever came to light as I searched the internet. Sitting at my computer just browsing had become something I could do easily with little effort or commitment. It absorbed me for an hour here and there and helped get through the day. At first I had no particular goal in mind and just read everything I came across but, as I gained a little more strength and energy, the browsing became focused on searching for a way out of my miserable existence, and inevitably led me on to look into suicide.

Surprised at how difficult it can be actually to be successful in committing suicide, my browsing became more focused and intense. I became obsessed with finding a successful way that I might use. At this stage, I had no immediate intention of committing suicide and still did not have the energy to carry out such an action but the possibility lodged in my mind that this was a means of escape at some future date if I needed it. I started to research and plan in detail how I could do it effectively and this goal gave me a new sense of purpose.

From day to day the ups and downs continued, with brief periods of ease but with tearfulness very near the surface, likely to erupt at the slightest provocation. As the date for the first of my face to face counselling sessions drew close, I became extremely tense and on edge. The appointment letter had informed me that this would be an 'assessment session' and I felt very apprehensive at the thought of this, while those *What ifs*? were taunting me again. *What if* the counsellor thinks I'm wasting his time? *What if* he thinks my problems are not bad enough to warrant counselling? *What if* he thinks I'm in too bad a state to benefit from counselling? *What if* he thinks I should be certified with mental health problems and locked away? I wrote in my diary the night before, 'I am so afraid.' Although I did not recognise this at the time, looking back on it now I think that a large part of my fear was based on anxiety that it wouldn't work. I was pinning so much hope on this process being my salvation and returning me to my previous stronger self. On that Sunday night, I cried a lot before finally falling asleep exhausted.

Monday 14 October

Monday morning finally arrived – the first day of face-to-face counselling. Still very nervous and apprehensive I went to the local doctor's surgery. I sat in the car until two minutes to ten as I couldn't face the thought of waiting with all the other patients in the waiting room, especially as I would invariably meet someone there I knew. Much to my relief I was called in promptly at ten o'clock to see Caden, the counsellor, who stood in the doorway of the counselling room ready to greet me.

Once I was seated, my whole body shaking and trembling, Caden took a few minutes to explain that he wanted me to feel that the room was a safe place and that everything said there was confidential. He also raised the issue that he had met me once before, some years previously, at a social gathering and in view of this he asked if I was happy to continue seeing him as a counsellor. I was pleased he was so up-front about this contact and that we did not have to pretend that we hadn't met before in different circumstances.

This helped me to feel confident in his honesty and integrity and I agreed that I was happy to continue. However, I had some questions about 'confidentiality', as I knew from the telephone sessions with Brian that there were exceptions to this. Caden also explained that if I was threatening to cause harm to anyone – including myself – he would be duty bound to pass this information on. With Brian this had not been an issue, as I had no such intentions at that stage, but now I was not willing to accept this proviso and argued strongly against it, as much as a matter of principle as any immediate desire to harm myself, although the possibility of my suicidal thoughts becoming reality at some point must have been at the back of my mind for me to be so resolute in my objections. I argued strongly for the right to end my own life, if I so chose, without interference. However, Caden was equally resolute in his stance and would not move away from his 'duty of care'. We spent rather a lot of time on this thorny issue and it probably wasn't the best way to start our relationship. We could both see that we weren't getting anywhere, so decided to park the issue temporarily and to move on to consider why I was there, what had happened to cause my depression. All he knew was that I had recently been involved in a car accident and lost my memory, since which time I had become increasingly depressed. I explained about Dr Alice's diagnosis of transient global amnesia, of which he had not heard before.

In spite of the difficult start to the interview, I found it easy to talk to Caden and we covered a lot of ground. I felt he was very skilled and he established a warm but professional relationship where I was able to be open (except about my suicidal thoughts) and I found I could express my thoughts and worries relatively easily. My telephone sessions with Brian had proved to be a good preparation.

Nevertheless, I found it a very gruelling hour during which I was extremely shaky, trembly, often tearful, none of which seemed to worry Caden at all. He just passed a box of tissues and continued, as if this was perfectly normal and acceptable behaviour. When I apologised for the tears he said he was glad I could cry as this is the natural way humans deal with things. He would be more worried if I couldn't cry, which some people can't. It was wonderful to have this 'permission' to cry and not to have to try to control my tearfulness. This was one of the best things about the counselling and I'm sure it had a very healing effect over the weeks and months.

Shortly before the end of the hour, he asked me to complete a questionnaire and I was surprised to find from the results that I scored higher on *anxiety* than on depression. Caden thought that I was showing some of the symptoms of Post Traumatic Stress Disorder, which he would like to explore further with me in a future session.

Finally, at the end of the interview, we returned to the safety issue. I was still reluctant to agree to him sharing the fact that I was having serious thoughts about suicide but I made a promise to him that I would not do anything to harm myself, in return for him not recording his concerns on my computer record. He did somewhat reluctantly agree to this, saying he would trust me, but as part of this negotiation he made me agree that he could tell my GP verbally about his concerns. Greatly to my relief, we concluded the interview by Caden telling me that he thought he could help me, and arranged another session for a fortnight's time.

After the session, I sat in the car in the surgery car park and cried some more, needing a quarter of an hour or so to compose myself and to feel able to drive safely. I couldn't understand why I was crying like this as I had not really been upset by the session. I concluded that it was about relief, the relief of expressing thoughts that I had never dared to put into words before and sharing them with Caden, without him showing any emotion, anger or distress. Yet at the same time, I was impressed with his caring and empathetic approach and his skills in identifying what I was feeling.

After a while I calmed down, went home and talked to Don for another hour. He wanted to know how I'd found the session and how it compared with the telephone sessions. I explained that I'd found it more intense, warmer and much wider ranging in everything we discussed but, of course, I omitted the discussion about suicide. Although Don was unable to see why I found these sessions so useful, he was supportive and pleased that I seemed to have found something that helped.

As I continued to think about the session, I thought that the other main difference was that I felt that Caden was proactive and in control during the session – it was he who set the agenda rather than me but, as this had been an 'assessment' session, that was to be expected.

For the rest of the day, my head felt as if it was bursting, my brain was in turmoil with so many thoughts and feelings coming and going so quickly that they were all jumbled up. I couldn't catch hold of any of them; they were so fleeting that it was difficult to make sense of anything and they continued to whirl around in my head. When I went swimming later that afternoon, I was filled with a huge amount of energy and went racing up and down the pool, the thoughts and feelings still a maelstrom in my head. This vigorous exercise made me feel a little better, though my brain was still over-active all evening and most of the night, too, with disturbed sleep and vivid dreams.

One positive thing that helped me through all this was Caden's statement that he would trust me when I promised not to harm myself. That statement of trust had a huge impact because it meant that he not only believed me but he believed *in me*. He had given me some respect, something which I had completely lost for myself. In spite of all that I told him, all he knew about me, far more than anyone else, how I was thinking and feeling, he must have believed that I had some integrity. This made me feel that he had given me one missing piece of the smashed up 'me' and put it back in place, not very securely perhaps but this small piece was slotted into place and gave me a small measure of hope. It gave me some faith in myself, a view that I was not completely weak, useless and pathetic but could still be strong – perhaps? I felt very strongly the need to keep my word to him, at least until the next session.

Overnight, my thoughts were still in turmoil, with many emotions raging around and plaguing me. I felt so many contradictory things: feelings of relief, reassurance, a glimmer of hope; feeling safe, secure and calm, along with negative feelings about being invaded, anger, frustration, regret, resentment, and some fear. I could hardly believe that Caden had been able to get inside my head so quickly and deeply and was anxious about what else he might uncover about me when he had managed to stir up all these feelings in just one interview. In spite of being relieved and confident that if anyone could help me it would be him, this was not a comfortable feeling.

Tuesday 15 October

Strangely, when I woke I didn't feel tired, in spite of little sleep the previous night. My mind was still very active with thoughts coming and rushing around in my head, making it very hard to keep or take hold of any one thought. Although I had found talking to Caden helpful and felt relief at sharing things with him, I was still experiencing feelings of indignation, if not anger, about his refusal to accept that any thoughts I might express about committing suicide could not be confidential if I so wished. I could understand the 'duty of care' argument but did not agree with it, not least because I felt it prevented me from talking about this issue at a time when I would have found it so helpful to be able to express openly my overriding wish to die and to share my thoughts and concerns but, because of the clear limits of the confidentiality, I was too afraid to do this, fearing that I might end up sectioned.

I was too mentally aroused and alert to want to commit suicide at that time but nevertheless felt an overwhelming need to have a plan which I could implement if I became desperate. So now I started to spend time on the internet, researching in detail various methods of committing suicide. It was easy to find a great deal of down to earth, factual information but I was surprised and despondent at finding that there is no easy way out. Each method is fraught with potential difficulties and a danger of the action being unsuccessful in ending life but instead causing physical or mental damage. I was looking for something reliable and found my research quite depressing but it did not lessen my urgent need to know that I could have a way out of everything if I needed it. This became my over-riding priority and, over the next week or two, I became obsessed with my search until I eventually came up with a well-researched plan that had every chance of success.

Not only did I find a method that seemed acceptable to me but I also found a suitable place where I could carry out my plan. The place was important; it had to be somewhere that I would not be disturbed or discovered too early, yet within easy walking distance of my home so that I could leave my car and keys behind. This was crucial as I wanted to leave everything in order to make it as easy as possible for my family after I had gone. I spent hours trudging about in the countryside, looking for a suitable place until I found the perfect spot, close to home, sheltered and hidden in between two yew trees that made a 'cave', practically invisible from the path. I could walk here easily, carrying a sleeping bag in which to keep warm whilst the alcohol and tablets took effect. I started to collect together everything that I would need and hide them away secretly where they would not be discovered at home. I compiled a list of all my finances and where details of these could be found. The next task was to write some letters for my husband and children, telling them how much I loved them and explaining everything. This was the most difficult task of all when I started to attempt it.

In spite of reading heart-rending accounts from people whose partners, parents and children had committed suicide successfully, I was absolutely convinced that my family members would be better off without me, being so full of self-disgust and worthlessness, but I found it impossible to put my thoughts into words that they could understand. I put this task to one side temporarily and concentrated on the practical parts of preparation that I could achieve. I must have spent hours researching and compiling my plan, acting it out interminably in my mind to check on all the details of method, time, place and how I would organise all this. I had considerable experience of planning and organising as this had been an important part of my jobs in various senior management positions, and undertaking this planning process gave me a sense of purpose and achievement. I found great satisfaction in working it all out and overcoming potential problems. I was sure it would work and felt much more safe and secure knowing I had this plan in place to be implemented if and when things became unbearable.

Chapter Five
COUNSELLING BEGINS ITS WORK

Monday 21 October

A dark, gloomy day with rain all morning reflecting my mood. I was tired and depressed again but had a telephone counselling session booked for 2.00 pm. I had booked this before going to the initial face-to-face appointment with Caden and had left it in place until I was confident that the face-to-face counselling was going to take place. I knew that I would have to tell my telephone counsellor, Brian, about these arrangements and wondered how he would react.

First, though, I had identified several issues that I wanted to talk through with Brian. These included the way I had opted out of the Lecture Day at Brecon; how difficult I still found the thought of engaging with a large group of people; how apprehensive I was about attending a Recorder Workshop planned for early November, and most difficult but most important of all, my relationship with my daughter and baby grandson.

So we started by talking about my good progress. Brian again stressed the need to give myself time and not to push myself too fast before I was ready, assuring me that my confidence in such situations would come back in time. There was no point in just adding to the pressure by expecting it to happen too quickly. It seemed as if I needed this constant reassurance.

We then talked through what would happen if I did attend the Recorder Workshop and this was helpful. He asked what would happen if I went and led me to see that I might actually be alright and, if I wasn't, I might be able to leave unobtrusively during a break. By questioning me gently, Brian got me to understand that this is what I would do if I was physically unwell and that I should treat being mentally unwell in the same way. There was no need to make a decision yet as the workshop was still two weeks away but it might be a good idea to plan in advance that I would travel in my own car so that I could leave early if I wished. He suggested also that I talk to the group leader or to a reliable friend in advance and explain to them that I might cancel at the last minute or leave before the end. In this way, they would be warned and it would not become a big issue on the day.

When I expressed my concern over the huge swings in mood that I was experiencing, Brian explained that my highs and lows were a natural reaction to the circumstances and that people all react in different ways to trauma. He advised me not to fight against the feelings but to accept that 'this is how I'm feeling today; it's not pleasant but it won't last.' He suggested that I should not dwell too much on the negative but try to do things that I knew I would find pleasant. This fitted in with something my friend Margaret had suggested of identifying some 'treats' that I could give myself at bad times – just simple things like re-reading a favourite book or watching a favourite film or, in my case, having a bath by candlelight, all things that are especially enjoyable to me. She recommended that I should have all these things to hand, so that I could access them easily when needed. If I was feeling low it would add to my distress to have to search for a book or DVD, or to find that I had run out of candles or a relaxing bath gel. I know now what good advice this was and that, however much I might be tempted to wallow in miserable, negative thoughts, it does help to do something nice, especially something that manages to make me smile or laugh. The resulting benefits can be mood lifting. I struggled to choose a favourite book as there are so many books I love and many of those are powerful stories of love, loss, betrayal – probably not the right

thing to read when you are trying to feel good. A film was easier
– *The Devil Wears Prada* had never failed to make me laugh, and
I made sure that I had a good supply of candles in the bathroom.
At that time, eating was still something to be endured rather than
enjoyed, so there was no point in buying special food and I was
avoiding alcohol as instructed by my GP as not being compatible
with taking anti-depressants.

With only a little time left in the session with Brian, I finally
managed to raise the issue that was really worrying me and about
which I was full of guilt. I didn't think I would actually be able to
put into words and say out loud what I had been feeling, so had
written the words down in the hope that I might be able to bring
myself to read them. Even then it was physically hard to do so; my
throat felt constricted and dry, my voice was weak and cracked,
with tears of shame loading in my eyes. I had been so ashamed of
and guilty about my feelings for some weeks, not even wanting to
admit them to myself and certainly not to anyone else, so I was
surprised and shocked at myself when I did manage to force the
words out.

The problem was that I didn't want to see my baby grandson. I
blamed him for being the cause of my breakdown and the resulting
chaos in which I felt my life to have been plunged. Of course, I
knew rationally that it was not the baby's fault but I couldn't get
rid of my feelings of anger and resentment towards him. This was
a complete turnaround from the day of his birth six weeks earlier,
at which I was present. Then I hadn't realised what a rough, tough
process a birth by Caesarean Section was and what physical hard
work was required by the doctors to extract the baby. My daughter,
though conscious, was drowsy and spaced out from the epidural
and pain killers so I was the first person to hold him once he was
born. When he was placed in my arms I was overwhelmed with
love and also fiercely protective towards him, determined that I

would care for him myself if no-one else was able to give him the care and love he deserved. In spite of the July day on which he was born being the hottest day in the year, the baby had difficulty in maintaining body temperature. After a short time, he started to turn blue and had to spend the rest of the day in an incubator. I stayed with him all day, feeling very concerned and protective until my daughter recovered enough to care for him herself. Over the next few weeks, I spent the weekdays staying at my daughter's house to look after her, the baby and the other two grandchildren. At weekends, when her husband was at home, I would return to my home to carry out a frantic round of looking after Don, washing, shopping, cooking, cleaning, keeping the lawns cut and preparing for another week away.

Holding my breath, I waited anxiously for Brian's response to my confession. When it came, so calm and matter of fact, that he thought it was a normal thing to feel, I almost shouted at him, 'You think this is *normal*?' He was unperturbed, still remaining totally calm and rational. He went on to compare coping with trauma with how people cope with bereavement. Often they blame the person who has died and feel angry at them, even though they know rationally that it is not the deceased person's fault. These feelings of anger and resentment are a normal part of grief and a normal part of trauma. He assured me that there was no need to continue with self-criticism, to be ashamed or guilty about feelings over which I had no control and that they would pass in time. I needed to understand the feelings and accept them for what they were, not see them as something with which to criticise myself.

We then agreed that the next step in overcoming these feelings would be actually to see my daughter and her baby and to talk to them. This should be my next challenge! I felt so relieved and grateful for this discussion and, although I knew that taking the next step would be a huge challenge, I also felt that heavy burden of guilt had been lifted from me and was so grateful to Brian for his patient listening and understanding. He suggested that I speak to my daughter before meeting her and explain that I may seem a bit different from normal.

Before we finished, I told Brian that I had been offered face-to-face counselling to start in a fortnight's time and we discussed the relative benefits of face-to-face and telephone counselling, both agreeing that the method is probably not as important as the counsellor and how you connect with that person. He stressed that the *relationship* is the most important thing, that I needed to feel comfortable and trust the counsellor. He suggested a useful website where I could find out more about different kinds of counselling to help make a decision but explained that I could not continue with him if I were to start the face-to-face sessions. He recommended that I should take time to think about it, but make another appointment with him now, which I could later cancel or postpone if I gave twenty-four hours' notice. I was pleased that he didn't seem in a hurry to get rid of me as a client and that I hadn't got to make an immediate decision, especially as my mind had been in such a state of turmoil ever since my first session with Caden.

There was a lot to think about over the next few days and it wasn't an easy time. I suppose I was very lucky that I had been offered two sets of counselling, both with very good counsellors, but having to make a choice was difficult, especially as I was finding it extremely hard to make decisions about anything. My inability to make decisions and the subsequent stress this caused me was one of the main symptoms of my depression. It was also one that I found particularly hard to cope with, as previously my ability to solve problems and make decisions had been one of my strengths. It added to my feeling of loss, that I no longer was the same person and that huge parts of me were missing.

Still very tearful in the afternoon, I left to pick up a friend,

Ann, as previously arranged to go to our Recorder Group. Ann was my other close friend who was to be very influential in my recovery, though I did not realise it then. She had been away on holiday so I hadn't seen her for a week or two and it was just lovely to see her and chat about her holiday, recorder music and have some general conversation. I realised time and time again over the next months how important friends can be, without them even knowing it, during times of depression. Ann invited me to go with her and several others to a satellite viewing at our local theatre about the Vermeer exhibition from London on the following Sunday. It sounded very interesting and I surprised myself by not only agreeing to go but also being very enthusiastic about it, with no fears. This was such a positive move forward that I was suddenly filled with energy and mowed both lawns when I got home! What a change in mood from the morning. This pattern of emotional highs and lows was to haunt me for many months, though I was told this is not a normal symptom of depression. I was over sensitive to everything that happened or was said to me, good or bad, and always seemed to be on an emotional roller coaster.

The energy and positive thoughts continued throughout the next day. I spent a busy and useful morning catching up with various tasks and going for a walk with my friend, Margaret, in the afternoon. Margaret was a great source of support and friendship and again we enjoyed a good walk and talk. In fact I was so positive that I became a little anxious that I was getting too 'high'. The high continued into the evening, heightened even further by receiving a lovely email from another friend and complimentary comments in the evening about improvement in my sight reading at Recorders. I was stunned by the huge effect that these small comments, whether made by email or in person, had on me. The effect was out of all proportion to the nature of the comment but they made me feel so alive, excited and worthwhile. By bedtime

I was so high that I couldn't sleep and I knew that there would be trouble ahead!

I was right! After a very disturbed sleep I was extremely tired the next day and was close to tears throughout the day all the time, even though I was not feeling unhappy at that stage. By this time I had discovered a method of controlling tears, which were still causing me great embarrassment if they occurred when I was out. I found that if I stopped and stared and examined something (anything) very closely and focused all my thoughts on how it looked, how it was made, patterns, texture, materials, weathering, dirt – any detail in fact – this intense focus and concentration on detail would stem the tears and, after a few minutes, I could then return to behaving normally. If I felt tearful when I was out I would use this method, concentrating hard as I examined brickwork on buildings, flaking paint on window sills, paving stones, flowers, weeds growing in cracks between paving stones, the bark on trees and all manner of things, whatever was nearby at a particular time of tearfulness. Many months later, I found that this is related to 'mindfulness', of which I was to learn much more, a method well known for helping to promote calm and reduce stress but at the time I thought I had invented this method for myself.

So the next week passed with lots of ups and downs. I coped with my normal everyday chores of shopping, cooking, cleaning, and managed to go swimming and to pilates. It rained every day, which didn't help, and Don was not feeling too well on several days – nothing specific, just tired and lethargic.

Frustrated at my ups and downs and lack of real progress, I decided on one Wednesday, to stop taking the citalopram anti-depressant tablets. This was the only way I would know whether my trembling and jumpiness was a side effect of the tablets or part of my depression/anxiety. I felt an overwhelming need to know this and to understand where I was. How different would I feel if

I were not taking anti-depressants? Would I still be over-sensitive in my emotional reactions to good and bad events? Or would I feel low and tearful all the time?

Looking back now, I know how unrealistic I was being in expecting results in just six to eight weeks but at the time it seemed that it had been going on for ever. In spite of what my GP and my counsellor had told me about being patient and giving myself time, this was not something I was good at. I was not used to being physically ill for more than a few days at a time, let alone being mentally unwell, and I needed to get back some control of my life. So I ignored all the advice and warnings of stopping the anti-depressants suddenly and just stopped taking them, determined to find out how I would cope and feel without the medication.

It was a foolish thing to do but, somewhat to my surprise, there were no side effects from stopping the medication, in spite of all the warnings on the packet. Nor did the lack of tablets seem to affect me as I still continued to be up and down, over-reacting to small events in just the same way. I had some tearful and agitated sessions and some periods of feeling quite good, notably when the sun came out, and when I managed to get out into the garden or for a walk.

On one afternoon, I had a long telephone conversation with my daughter who seemed a lot better herself. She was more positive and was picking up the strands of her life again, about which I was very pleased and relieved. It helped to lessen the guilt I was feeling about not going to see her and help her.

One Saturday afternoon, I went to a musical concert in the local church. As well as enjoying the music, everyone there was very friendly and I spent a lovely couple of hours relaxed and socialising with friends. I had started the day very tense, agitated and tearful, dithering around uncertainly, unable to decide whether to phone my friend, Ann, or not. But finally I did phone and that had led on to going to the concert. I realised that once I had taken control, things improved. I felt really good but not too high and, yet again, it became clear how important people are to each other and I felt very lucky to have such good friends. Their support was so influential in keeping me afloat. They didn't have to do anything special, just be themselves and let me know they still wanted to be my friend, even though I was not myself.

The following day, on Sunday morning, the weather was dull and rainy and the clocks had gone back from summertime to GMT overnight, so the day didn't start too well. Don was totally confused by the changeover; not only had he forgotten how to change the time on the clocks, which he found frustrating, but also he seemed to have no comprehension of what it was all about, why we were doing it. This was one of the key points in time when I realised just how severely his cognitive processes were declining. This realisation hit me hard and was something I found very worrying.

In spite of the poor weather, I went out in the afternoon to take Ann's dog for a walk, as she had to go out that day. Cari, an affectionate spaniel, was pleased to see me and not at all reluctant to go out in the rain. We didn't get too wet but found a lovely walk, with a stream rushing and burbling along after all the rain. As well as the beautiful countryside to look at, I was very conscious of the fresh air in my lungs and the wind in my hair and I realised how beneficial walking was for me, resolving to do more of it. It also felt good to have the company of an appreciative dog with me who ran about joyfully, making no demands but just having fun.

That night, a big storm hit southern Britain but, in mid Wales, we escaped the 80 mph gales and just had heavy rain. However, Monday turned out to be something of a strange day. It started when a police car drew up outside our house and a uniformed policeman arrived, wanting to take statements from Don and me about the car accident. I was due to go for my second face-to-face counselling session at eleven o'clock, but it took very little time to do my statement, as I still couldn't remember anything about the incident. The policeman then got called away to an emergency but said he would be back within the hour, so I left Don and went to keep my appointment with Caden.

By the time I arrived, I was in a dreadful state, trembling violently all over and extremely agitated with the shock of the policeman's unexpected arrival and the worry that I would be late for my session. When called in to the counselling room, I had to sit there for a few minutes until the trembling stopped while Caden just chatted to me about the storm and the previous big storm in the 1980s. He was his usual calm, professional self and, feeling safe and secure in his presence, I became calmer.

The policeman came back in the afternoon to take Don's statement. He was very good and patient with him and I think it did Don a lot of good finally to talk to someone about what had happened and to express his feelings, though he had always dismissed the idea of going for counselling himself. He certainly seemed much better afterwards and was pleased with the PC's attitude. The PC told us that they had decided to prosecute the driver and somehow, this news was a huge relief to me because it gave me reassurance that nobody saw the accident as my fault.

The counselling session had gone well and I felt very calm afterwards. Caden said that it seemed as if I was experiencing some of the symptoms of Post Traumatic Stress and we spent some time talking and thinking about my childhood and early life to see if we could find any potential events or experiences that might help us to understand why my reaction to the car accident had been so extreme. Nothing immediately came to mind but later that day I sifted through memories of my childhood and early life again, looking for any possible links from the past to the present.

I knew that I had been born in Kent during the Second World War in 1944 and that my birth was two months premature. My mother had been told that the cause of my premature birth was probably due to the stress of the bombing which was occurring all around her. Even if this were true, I thought it unlikely that as an unborn baby I would have been aware of such stress or of the dreadful effects that the bombs had when they landed, so I dismissed this event being linked to my present circumstances.

The only other event during my childhood that I thought might possibly be significant occurred when I was about six or seven years old. My father was the deputy principal probation officer for Kent and, from time to time, he brought children home to stay with us, sometimes for a week or two, sometimes for longer. I have no idea why or how this happened but, as a child, I just accepted these boys (they were always boys) coming into our home and usually enjoyed their company. One of them, Clive, was older, a teenager, and he stayed longer than all the rest. I was a very well-behaved, 'good' child, rarely in trouble, but Clive was the complete opposite, often in trouble with my parents, his school and the neighbours. I'm not sure what he did that was so bad but he was a daredevil and I secretly admired him for being brave enough to be so 'naughty' and to take his punishments, though not without loud protests. After some months living with us, he left school, was successful in finding a job and left us to return to his home in south London. Life was not nearly so exciting without him but worse, much worse, was to come when tragedy struck. One Sunday afternoon, we received the news that Clive had been killed in a road accident whilst riding his motorbike. It was hard to believe that this vibrant boy, so full of fun and life, always up to something exciting, my hero, was no more. It was a very sad day and a sobering thought that my father had been right when he said that motorbikes were too dangerous.

By the end of the evening I'd gone through most of my young life without finding any other traumatic experiences and had finally stopped thinking about it all but, during the night, I woke up, sweating and agitated with an experience from my early twenties flashing through my mind. It had been a dark November night when there had been a horrific train crash at Hither Green in south London. I had been on duty as a WPC in the Metropolitan Police at the time of the crash and was drafted to the major incident room at Scotland Yard where, along with a room full of other women police officers, spent all night collating information about the casualties and dealing with distraught relatives and friends of passengers on the train. Whilst on duty, there was no time to think, as the phones were ringing continuously and piecemeal information was pouring into the control room. It was a matter of getting on and doing a job as calmly and clearly as possible. I was surprised at how well I managed to cope for, although we had received some training, this had concentrated on how to use the equipment in the major incident room and what sort of details to find out and record. There was no training on how to deal with people in shock; people who were extremely agitated and anxious about missing relatives and friends but I found the words came naturally as I became totally absorbed in the situation, hardly conscious of everything going on around me. The drama of the situation kept us going all night until we were relieved at about 7.00 am the following day. It was then that the exhaustion set in and the full horror of the night hit home.

Now, forty years later, the memories of that night were still vivid in my mind. I was unable to sleep for the rest of the night and flashbacks haunted me for the next few days. I couldn't get these thoughts out of my mind however hard I tried. It seemed that I was more affected now by the horror of this event than I had been at the time. Although I'd been emotional and upset after I came off duty that night, I went back to work the following day and after a short 'debrief' session, took up my normal duties again. I was based at a busy police station in Brixton where there was always plenty going on, with no time for emotion or to dwell on what I'd experienced the previous night.

Now, all these years later, I wondered whether I had never properly dealt with the feelings from that night. In the world today, no doubt some sort of counselling would be available but, in the 1960s, police officers were expected to deal with anything and everything in their stride. Showing emotion or being upset would have been scorned as weakness.

After several days of re-living this experience in my mind, it was walking that finally calmed me down. I had recently seen a poster about a group, 'Walking for Health', run by our local Mind organisation. The group met once a month for a two-hour walk. I had contacted the group leader, a volunteer with Mind who was very knowledgeable and experienced in organising walks in our local area, and she had offered to pick me up in her car to drive to the starting point. Seeking a change of scene, I was pleased to accept her offer to join this small group of people, who all had some sort of mental health difficulty. It was a friendly, relaxed group where people understood the benefit of walking and talking together, with no pressure to discuss our individual problems but the opportunity to do so was there if we wished to share information about ourselves. I found the experience of walking with this group very useful as it gave me the confidence to explore new places in the company of others, under guidance of the group leader, some places that I did not know about and others where I would not have walked on my own.

The walk that week was in the Elan Valley, about fifteen miles from home. It is a remote and beautiful area where several large reservoirs were built in the nineteenth century to supply water to the fast-growing population of Birmingham. Three huge dams were constructed, and a village flooded to achieve a system of conserving water in the reservoirs which was then piped by gravity all the way to Birmingham. It is an amazing feat of civil engineering, particularly as it was achieved without the aid of the tools and technology available in the twenty-first century.

Today, the valley is a wonderful place for walkers, with many different routes to explore in the spectacular countryside of mountains and lakes. The most popular foot/cycle path follows the line of the old railway which used to transport the building materials for the series of huge, staggered dams, the highest one up in the mountains leading down to the lowest on the valley floor. On the day of our walk, amidst sunshine and showers, we were treated to a myriad of rainbows. Our leader took us on a circular walk around and across the lowest dam. All we could hear was the sound of torrents of rushing water pouring frantically down the dam wall, drowning all other sound and throwing up curtains of spray in the wind.

It was an exhilarating experience and one which helped to calm my feverish brain. Being confronted with the elements, the wonders and power of nature and the amazing feat of engineering evident before us, all these gave me a different perspective on the world. After this walk, I was able to park the old memories which had been haunting me and to return to coping with the present.

Chapter Six
FACING UP TO CHALLENGING DECISIONS

I now had to face up to four challenging decisions which could not be put off any longer, all of which were causing me considerable anxiety. Since the accident, I had found making any decisions difficult but these were all important ones so the pressure was even greater.

1. The first one was regarding the accident itself. The solicitor from my insurance company had informed me of an offer of compensation from the other driver's insurance company. She stressed that *only I could decide* whether to accept it or not.

2. The second decision was what to do about the counselling sessions. Should I continue with the telephone sessions, with a counsellor whom I had grown to know and trust and who had helped me a lot, or should I change to the face-to-face sessions with Caden, where the relationship was proving much more intense and the effect much more tumultuous?

3. The third challenge and the most difficult and demanding one was how to progress my relationship with my daughter and grandchildren. I was trying to accept what Brian had stressed, that the issues about my daughter's life *are not my choice*, however much I might want to influence her. I had been a little reassured by Brian's calm acceptance of my feelings about my baby grandson but this didn't make it any easier to face up to seeing him.

4. The fourth and final decision was whether I should go to the annual Recorder Workshop. This was held in the autumn of every year when three or four Recorder groups from neighbouring U3As met together for a whole day's playing, tutored by the National Adviser. I had been to previous sessions and found them extremely enjoyable and inspiring but this year I was not at all sure that I could cope with engaging with a large group of people.

Challenge 3 was by far the most important and, as half-term was approaching fast, I needed to face up to it urgently. I talked to my daughter on the phone and arranged to meet her and the grandchildren in Hereford on the Thursday of that week, where we could go swimming and to the park or the shops, so there would be plenty to keep everyone occupied, whatever the weather.

Taking Brian's advice, I warned my daughter that I may appear different. This seemed to worry her as she didn't know what to expect and I found it impossible to explain, so I think we were both tense and apprehensive about the meeting and I was very stressed and close to tears on the journey there. We had arranged to meet at Asda and, as I parked my car, my twelve-year-old grandson suddenly appeared at the window of my car, making me jump out of my skin. He had been waiting outside for me whilst my daughter and granddaughter were in the café eating breakfast. In spite of the fright he gave me, I realised that I was very pleased to see him. We had always had a close relationship and, since he was a small child, he would wait for me eagerly in anticipation of my visits. It was reassuring that he hadn't changed, even if I had. Still trembling and shaking, I went into the café with him, ordered some drinks and joined the others. There were no awkward silences, not knowing what to say, as both grandchildren were intrigued and fascinated by the memory loss that I'd experienced; they kept talking about it and asking questions. Far from causing me distress, I found it helpful that they were so matter of fact about it all and we had some interesting conversation. My granddaughter cheered me up by saying she couldn't believe I had been in such a state as, 'Usually you're so clever, Grandma!' My grandson showed surprising insight and said he thought it was because I was worried about Grandad and whether he was hurt – this was much the same as the possible explanation that my counsellor Caden had put forward on my last visit.

When breakfast was finished, we all decided to go to the swimming pool and, with the two older grandchildren both begging me to go in swimming with them, we all had a brilliant time for the next two and a half hours. My daughter took the baby to the small pool so I didn't see very much of them, as the other grandchildren took charge of me and even got me on the flume. I was somewhat surprised that a twelve-year-old boy, in particular, should be so keen for his grandma to go swimming with them but it was very good to mix with young people for a change and to share their energy and enthusiasm. We enjoyed ourselves tremendously that afternoon; after swimming we all went to the park and then to the shops to buy trainers. By the time I left them, I felt quite high but not over the top and I even enjoyed the drive home. I had found the company of the grandchildren delightful. We had lots of uninhibited *fun* in the pool and I realised afterwards that I felt younger, or at least not so old any more! I think this was an important development in the long process of my gradually fitting bits of myself together again.

I was a little concerned and guilty that I hadn't related much either to my daughter or the baby but at least a first step had been taken in seeing them again. Rather to my surprise, I was exceptionally jumpy all evening when watching TV and then when in bed for an hour or so but I wasn't shaking or trembling. I wondered whether the jumpiness might be a mild form of epilepsy or just another example of hyper-anxiety.

A programme I watched that evening dealt with 'Bedlam', the original Bethlehem Hospital and how it works in the present day. The first episode that evening concentrated on 'anxiety'. The cases in the documentary were all really serious ones, nothing like my symptoms, but I noted that 'intrusive thoughts' are a little known feature or symptom of OCD. The psychiatrist on the programme said that everyone has intrusive thoughts – which may sometimes be shocking – but the difference is that normal people don't act on them. He gave a personal example in which he was driving his car along a road where a group of young children were crossing. His intrusive thought was that he could drive on and run them over but, of course, his actual behaviour was quite different – he stopped and let them cross safely.

At the time I was very shocked by the fact that he had such a thought and just as shocked that he was prepared to admit to it so easily. Much, much later, after I had done a course in Mindfulness, I came to understand that we cannot control our thoughts – they come and go of their own accord. We have to learn not to be shocked, upset or worried about them but just accept them and let them drift away again. This was such an important lesson to learn, though it did not come easily.

Now that I had faced up to the most difficult challenge and that had gone well, I decided to make the decisions about challenges 1 and 2. I had changed my mind backwards and forwards many times in the past days about both these decisions but now was the time to act on them. That Friday it rained and rained all day and, by the afternoon, I was tired and on the verge of tears with indecision and anxiety about making the wrong choices, and I was probably suffering from some anti-climax after the previous day which had gone so well.

First, I tackled Challenge 1 – whether to accept the offer of compensation for the car accident.

I had never sought or expected financial compensation for the car accident but, because I had added the option of legal expenses to my insurance policy, this was something that my insurance company's solicitor had instigated. I had no idea of what would constitute a reasonable offer but it was the necessity of making the decision that was causing me stress. I kept changing my mind but eventually I did decide, as I couldn't live with the anxiety of indecision and accepted the offer just to avoid further stress. Once I had posted my acceptance form off to my solicitor it gave me some relief and I was glad to have this problem dealt with. It was something that I no longer had to worry about and seemed so easy once it was done.

Then I tackled Challenge 2 – whether to continue with telephone counselling or change to face-to-face counselling. I had already arranged the next session with Brian so I rang the telephone counselling service to postpone this. I was told that I could also postpone the two further sessions to which I was entitled indefinitely but, after ten days, my file would be closed and after that I would be placed on a waiting list to resume sessions, which may be with Brian but could be with another counsellor. This postponement gave me a breathing space in which I could see how the face-to-face counselling with Caden would progress. Initially, I felt pleased to have taken control but, later that evening, I was panic stricken, wishing above all else that I could speak to Brian again. I knew that I would miss him. He had become something of an anchor, holding the pieces of my precarious wreckage safely together, while the salvage operation was progressing slowly. But I had made my decision and knew I would have to live with the consequences for the time being.

Only the Final Challenge remained – whether to attend the

Recorder Workshop. It was Friday and the workshop was to take place the following Monday so this final challenge, too, had to be tackled without further delay. Although I had very much enjoyed the previous workshops, now I was suffering from a crisis of confidence. Could I cope with joining a large group, many of whom were very competent players? Could I face mixing with all those strangers? Would I be able to play the pieces? How would I react if I failed? Would I let our Recorder Group down? An added stress factor was that, until this year, I had played descant recorder but recently had changed to playing a tenor. I had it in my head that there would be a greater expectation for a tenor player to do well. This I now know to be complete rubbish but it was very real in my head at the time and showed up my own expectations and the pressures that I put myself under.

On Saturday, I woke early at 5.00 am with my brain very active, so I spent some time writing down everything that I'd been through during the past week. I had my plan ready for Monday; I would drive myself to the workshop giving me an 'escape route', as I would be able to turn around at any point or, if I made it to the workshop, I would be able to leave whenever I wanted to and would not have to wait until it finished. By Saturday afternoon, I had plucked up the courage to phone our Recorder Leader to explain my situation and my anxieties. He was very kind, reassuring, and encouraged me to come along, even if I wanted to leave early. So I had a session practising my recorder and felt a little more confident, though I was very jumpy in the evening, especially with fireworks going off now and then, being 5 November. I had been off the Citalopram tablets for a week now, with no noticeable effects.

On Sunday I was tense and on edge all morning but decided to take an elderly friend out to a Winter Craft Fair in the afternoon. She enjoyed herself and I felt much better for going out and for doing something positive for someone else. It made me distance myself from all my worries and anxieties for a few hours. That evening my escape plan started to disintegrate when a friend rang to ask whether she could travel with me the next day, as she had a problem with her car. Very reluctantly, I agreed to pick her up at 9.50 am, having explained that I may leave the workshop early, but she thought she could get a lift back home with someone else if necessary, so there was no getting out of it!

Later still, I had an email from my friend, Ann, asking if I would like to travel with her. She had decided to take her dog, Cari, with her so she was taking her own car. It had become clear that I wasn't going to be able to travel alone as I'd planned, and I thought it might be a good option to travel with Ann and her dog. If I needed time out from the group, I could always take the dog for a walk and I knew that would calm me down. She was happy to pick up the other friend as well and it made sense for three of us to travel in one car.

On Monday morning I got up early and attended an appointment with my GP at 8.30 am Once again, I felt that Dr Alice was very kind and seemed genuinely interested in me. I had been worried that she would be annoyed that I was no longer taking the anti-depressants she'd prescribed but she seemed to understand my explanation of why I had come off the Citalopram, that I needed to know where I was, how I really felt. She was just relieved that I hadn't had any unpleasant withdrawal symptoms which can occur when ceasing anti-depressant medication suddenly. She mentioned that my counsellor, Caden, had been very concerned about me. He had told her about my suicidal thoughts and, although I assured her that I was feeling very different now, she emphasised that if I were to get low again I must ring her or talk to Caden. Above all, I must be honest with them.

I mentioned my concerns about the trembling and jumpiness and whether they could be symptoms of epilepsy. She asked me why I thought of a possible connection to epilepsy and I explained that my son, at the age of seventeen, had developed four types of epilepsy and that one of the first signs, which we didn't recognise at the time, was a shaking and jerking of his limbs when under stress. It was not until after he had major seizures which rendered him unconscious, that investigations in hospital diagnosed the less serious myoclonic seizures which had resulted in the muscle jerking. Dr Alice thought it unlikely that what I was experiencing was related to epilepsy but, nevertheless, offered to refer me to a consultant if I was concerned. She also offered me different medication, such as diazepam, rather than anti-depressants, to calm me down and help with the jumpiness. By this time, I had great trust in Dr Alice and was reassured by her view that I was not developing epilepsy, so I decided to decline both offers for the present and said I would see how the counselling went. She told me that she had been reading up on TGA and, depending on the underlying causes, thought it might take many weeks, even months, to make a full recovery. I was so impressed and grateful for this doctor's genuine interest and care for me. It made such a difference, making me feel valued, less worthless than my own view of myself, and I left the surgery feeling much more confident and able to face the challenge of the day – to attend the Recorder Workshop.

The car journey to the workshop went well. I sat in the back of my friend's car with her dog, Cari, and found that stroking the dog was a very calming and relaxing thing to do. It gave me an excuse to opt out of having to make conversation and took my mind off coping with the workshop. As we arrived and went in, I was trembling all over, shaking like a leaf and feeling sick with nervousness. But other friends were arriving too, greeting us eagerly. They were so pleased to see me there that, after a cup of coffee, a biscuit and lots of chat, I calmed down again.

Once we started playing, the time flew by. I could manage the pieces of music quite well and my playing was fine, with the recorder behaving itself in spite of being cold. At lunchtime, very much to my surprise, I found that I could talk easily to the tutor and people from other U3As and was very interested to be shown a large contra-bass recorder, with a demonstration of how it worked. The afternoon session was more difficult. I got lost following the music once or twice but didn't panic and actually managed to play it properly the second time we did it. There were five of us playing tenor recorders and we all did well. The tutor was impressed at how much we had all improved since the previous year's workshop and we ended the day feeling very pleased with our achievements and his praise!

That evening I was tired but feeling very good and, once more, felt so lucky that I had such great support and care from my doctor, my counsellor and from my friends who were all looking after me so well.

I was still 'walking on air' all day on Tuesday and actually felt that my participation in the Recorder Workshop had been a REAL achievement, not just a pathetic one, like my daily targets of the past few weeks. Playing the recorder together with everyone else was much more than just a 'sum of the parts'; the music we made was something really to be proud of and I had played a part in this achievement. I felt *valued* for the first time for weeks. It did wonders for my self-confidence and this, together with my relationships with my grandchildren, made me believe a little bit in myself again and that life may be worth living after all. Even though there were still many challenges to face, it may be worth the effort of dealing with them.

I felt stronger and that, maybe, I would be more able to face up to some problems that I knew I must deal with but hadn't yet begun to tackle. These included my relationship with my daughter, and facing up to the problems of old age for my husband and myself, being very aware that my seventieth birthday was only a few months away.

My good mood from Monday and Tuesday was still with me on Wednesday morning but was not to last much longer! On Wednesday, I attended my next face-to-face counselling session and that's where more problems arose. I went in to the session feeling good, still high from Monday, and started off well by telling Caden that I was feeling different and had stopped taking the Citalopram tablets, and so I felt that I was really making good progress, especially as I had tackled all the challenges successfully. He seemed to understand my reasons for stopping the anti-depressants and made no criticism of this decision. He thought I looked different – better – and could see glimpses of the 'old me', though he pointed out that I would never be exactly the same again, after all my experiences. He commented that I seemed full of a restless energy rather than anxiety, eager to get on with the session. I think this was in response to me seeking clarification of what we were supposed to be doing in these sessions.

When he asked me how the Recorder Workshop and meeting my daughter and grandchildren went, I couldn't help but launch enthusiastically into a full description. I explained that my 'escape plan' fell apart but he showed me that, by travelling with my friend's dog, this became a new escape route. This led on to discussion about the therapeutic value of animals but I was adamant that I had enough responsibility already, without looking after a dog of my own. Rather than just listening passively to my glowing accounts of the day out with my grandchildren, Caden probed quite a bit but he seemed to agree with my feelings and interpretation of everything that had taken place. We really seemed to be on the same wavelength and he 'got' the points I made, which made it easy to talk to him in an honest, uninhibited way. He told me that he had planned to start some Cognitive Behavioural Therapy (CBT) with me today but he had realised, as we talked, that I was 'doing it myself'. I was already challenging my thoughts to see if they were based on reality or on something in my mind which would skew my perception in an unhelpful way.

He asked me how I was finding the night times and I admitted these were still often difficult. I told him about searching my memory for events that may have influenced my reaction to the car accident. Then, although I found it very hard to put into words, tearful and choked with emotion, I managed to give him a brief version of my involvement in the rail disaster in the 1960s. I was no longer angry with Caden but still shocked at my reaction to those memories now, how they were now haunting me, and asked him what was the point of reawakening these events from the past.

We discussed this for some time and he said that it can help to share painful memories with someone, even to write them down and give them to someone you trust. By sharing, you may feel that you do not have to bear all the pain alone. Eventually, we agreed that, having faced them, I would try to pack them away again and leave them undisturbed, as they had been for the past forty years.

At least I had dealt with the issue, opened the memories up for examination, addressed my feelings face to face with Caden, and the world did not fall in. I was learning, slowly, to talk about very personal, sensitive thoughts and feelings, even when I found this extremely difficult.

I also tried to explain how I often felt isolated for, even though I have friends and family who cared about me, they didn't really understand what I was going through. Watching programmes about mental health on television, such as *Bedlam*, had helped a little and made me realise that other people do experience what I am feeling and some are even a great deal worse.

The session continued productively and positively until close to the end, when Caden told me that he would like to see me again next week, as today we had concentrated on how well I had been doing but he felt that was not the whole picture; there may be still be some underlying issues that needed to be addressed. He arranged for me to see him again in a week's time.

At the time, I accepted this arrangement but, by the evening, I was unable to concentrate on anything and became increasingly upset, angry and depressed. I became very resentful towards Caden for ruining my good mood and undermining my feelings of progress, achievement and the regaining of some control over my life. I questioned myself, 'What did I say to make him doubt me so much?' Although I was able to recognise that there was some truth in what he said, as I knew I was still very vulnerable and my husband agreed, dark and despairing feelings overwhelmed me. The questions wouldn't go away, just round and round in my brain. 'Did Caden somehow resent that I was feeling so much better and beginning to take control of my life again? Did he not like me asking, "What are we doing today?" being impatient to get on with the session? Did he want to stay in control? Why did he need to undermine my feelings of success and happiness so quickly?'

I spoke to my daughter on the phone but she couldn't understand why I was so upset and it is inconceivable to me now why I reacted like that and entertained such malevolent thoughts about Caden's motivation. I knew I couldn't go on like this, yet could see no way out.

As I became more desperate, I got out a sleeping bag, curled up right inside it, in the dark to shut out the world. I was aware that this was strange behaviour but was past caring, just seeking some means of blacking out the world, to stop worrying and thinking. This worked for an hour or so but I cried so much that I felt very sick and developed a bad headache. Still feeling tired and exhausted, I went to bed early but then couldn't sleep. I just kept crying until at least 2.30 am and then drifted off to sleep for a while but was woken again at six o'clock by dreadful dreams that I was being taken to an asylum, then hung up by my hands from a tree. This started me off into floods of tears again.

By this time I was feeling so angry with Caden. It was as if he had burst my bubble of happiness; I was devastated that he could do this to me and leave me in this state. I suppose I knew that it wasn't really his fault and really I was angry and disappointed with myself but it was easier to put the blame on someone else. At the same time, I wondered how I would cope without Caden when the counselling sessions finished, for these sessions had become so important to me and I couldn't bear to think of living without this lifeline. But I also had another fear, that of becoming too dependent on Caden. I knew I would miss talking to him, as I had come to view him as a friend as well as a professional counsellor. Maybe this was wrong but we seemed to share the same views and values about many things and I was dreading feeling rejected and abandoned by him when the sessions came to an end. In such emotional turmoil, I even considered phoning Brian to discuss my feelings with him and to ask him whether he thought I should end the counselling with Caden now, so that I would retain control and he wouldn't be able to 'reject' me.

Still feeling angry and distressed in the morning, I went outside after breakfast to work in the garden and used the opportunity to vent my feelings on the poor plants, in a frenzy of autumn tidying. Slashing and cutting everything down viciously helped to get rid of some of my angry feelings but I came to the decision that I would not go back to see Caden again. I felt he had betrayed me by wanting to probe behind my version of events and I suppose that I was afraid of what he might uncover next, just as I thought I was beginning to cope and put pieces of myself back together. Up until then, he had seemed benevolent and a fairly passive listener to whatever I told him but now he had become a threat, which made me feel I didn't really know him at all and was very fearful of what I might discover.

In the cold light of day, it did not seem a good idea to discuss these thoughts with Brian who, I'm sure, would have thought it inappropriate. No doubt this is one of the reasons why you should engage in counselling with only one person at a time; a counsellor cannot properly deal with criticism or angry feelings about another counsellor. This would interfere with the relationships and trust. I had made my decision and would have to battle on alone without the help of either counsellor.

That afternoon, I was still feeling extremely unhappy so I persuaded my close friend, Margaret, to come with me on a walk, suggesting we tackle the local castle, which was situated at the top of a long, steep hill, as I was in need of a challenge, not just a walk! Poor Margaret suffered bravely with the difficult terrain, not helped by being soaked in a heavy shower soon after starting out, but she accepted the strenuous activity without complaint, recognising my need for vigorous exertion. We were rewarded for our efforts when the sun came out and lit up the afternoon. As we climbed, the view was marvellous and we saw some interesting and beautiful fungi. While I was in Margaret's company, I felt much better as we walked and talked but, in spite of this respite, I knew that tears would still be there if I let them.

In this vulnerable state, that evening I watched the second part of 'Bedlam' and found it very upsetting, as it was about a man attempting suicide by overdose, which was the substance of my plan. It made me fully recognise the dreadful effect his actions had on his family, especially his children.

With a terrible headache, feeling physically ill and totally gutted, I took some Paracetamol and went back to bed. I must have drifted off to sleep for a few hours but then woke again still in turmoil.

Wanting to phone Brian but realising this was not possible, as I had now committed to the face-to-face counselling with Caden, I went on the internet hoping to find a way of relieving my distress. One website, Sane, looked promising but their helpline had closed at 11 pm and it was now the early hours of the morning, so I went onto their online Forum. This was good in a sad way because I realised that I was not alone in how I was feeling. There were many others feeling the same and saying exactly the same things as I was thinking and feeling. I was profoundly shocked at their pain and suicidal thoughts but felt unable to comment or support anyone because I was in such a bad place myself. I was afraid that I would say something along the lines of 'If you feel that bad why don't you just go and do it?' That clearly wasn't the aim of the Forum on this website but I couldn't see any positive way forward for them or for me. It was a shocking and saddening experience to realise that there were so many desperate people suffering out there. Many were in a worse situation than I was, as their friends or family had had enough and were no longer supportive, or their GPs and counsellors hadn't helped them. I felt for them in their desperation but was quite unable to offer them words of comfort or support, as their situations seemed so much more hopeless even than my own.

The next morning, Friday, I was still tearful and miserable but managed to get up and get ready for my weekly pilates class. As I walked from the car park to the hall, I was struggling to hold back tears. When I looked through the glass doors, I could see that my two good friends, Margaret and Mercia weren't there.

This was the final straw; it was all too much. I walked back to the car park where I met Margaret coming down the path. She took one look at me, opened her arms wide and we stood there in the rain, with me clinging to her and sobbing. After a few minutes, as I let my emotion out, she offered to take me home or go for a coffee but I felt too guilty to allow her to miss the pilates class which we had to pay for whether or not we attended, so I convinced her to go in, put a mat out ready for me, assuring her that I would join her shortly. I went back and sat in my car for several minutes, where I managed to compose myself sufficiently to go in now I knew that Margaret was there.

I got changed outside the room and just slipped in quietly. The instructor didn't make a fuss; I think she could see there was something wrong. By concentrating very hard on the exercises and pushing myself to do everything perfectly at a higher level than normal, I managed to control my emotions and hold myself together. This had a calming effect and I surprised myself at how well I could perform in these conditions.

At the end of the session, Margaret and I went for a coffee in a nearby café and I unloaded all my feelings about Caden. Tactfully, she suggested that my perception of what he'd said might not be quite accurate and his intentions may have been very different from how I was perceiving them. She thought I should talk to him about it or, if I couldn't talk to him, write my feelings down, which I did later. I explained that the thought of going back and walking up the long corridor to the counselling room was terrifying, like going to the guillotine, so Margaret offered to come to counselling with me next week; she would push me up the corridor and shove me through the door if necessary! She also suggested that I see my GP again, with a view to re-starting the Citalopram, but I refused to consider this, quite adamant that I did not want to take anti-depressants again.

Feeling a lot calmer and more in control by then, I was able to go home and prepare lunch. Later, after a long bath, I wrote down everything that had upset me, which I thought I might give to Caden to read. I went on the Sane website again that evening but avoided the Forum which I'd found so distressing the previous night. I was more interested now in finding out all I could about mental illness and its various forms.

Saturday found me very flat and emotionless, no tears but no positive feelings either. Feeling in great need of support, I decided to try to speak to my telephone counsellor again. I phoned at 6.00 pm but no-one phoned back until 10.30, so I spent a very tense evening on edge, waiting for a call and hoping to be able to speak to Brian, only to be told then that he was on nights this week and wouldn't be available for two weeks, which left me feeling very emotional and alone. I think, by this time, I was so emotionally exhausted that I just collapsed into bed and I don't really remember any more about that night, so I must have slept.

On Monday, it was Margaret's birthday so I decided to make a big effort and attend our U3A meeting. This was the first, full monthly meeting I'd been to since becoming unwell and was a huge step to take. Feeling very nervous, trembling and shaking all over, I met Margaret outside, as we'd arranged, and walked in together. We had a coffee and my coffee cup was rattling in its saucer as I carried it to my seat but I made it into the hall, sat down among the two hundred people and managed to pay attention to the lecture which, fortunately, held my interest. Sitting there, at the back, and concentrating on the lecture enabled me to relax and calm down sufficiently to be able to stay on afterwards with Margaret and two friends for a drink and lunch. I know I wouldn't have done this if it hadn't been Margaret's birthday but I felt it really important to make the effort for her, especially as she had been such a good friend to me. Doing something for someone else, rather than concentrating on myself and my own feelings, made a change and had the added benefit of making me feel better.

Later that afternoon, Margaret and I both went swimming and had a long chat whilst getting dressed afterwards. I felt that I had completed another challenge and would be able to manage U3A meetings in future. I was pleased with how well the day had gone and interested to realise how close to both laughter and tears I'd been all day, thinking that these must be very close on the emotional spectrum and both act as some sort of release mechanism.

Chapter Seven
CRISIS

Two days later was the date for my next counselling session, which I approached with considerable anxiety. I had listened to Margaret's words of advice and decided to go to the session, very tempted to take her up on her offer to come with me, at least as far as the door, but I knew this would mean her missing a Shakespeare Workshop, an activity she loved, and felt I couldn't ask that of her. So I tried to be brave, telling myself that, if I could manage the strenuous walk up to the castle the previous week, then I could surely manage a few yards along a corridor to Caden's room at the surgery.

Wednesday 13 November: the Session

I kept busy all morning to take my mind off the approaching counselling session and took myself there in good time for my appointment. The walk along the corridor seemed a long way to my trembling self and anxious mind but I forced myself to do it, feeling as if I was 'walking the plank'. I entered the room with some trepidation but Caden soon put me at ease with his calm, professional attitude, yet somehow still exuding a warmth and compassion. I began to feel safe there, in this room where we had shared so much already. He could see I was anxious and upset and asked me to tell him about some of the bad times over the past week .

I started by telling him about hiding in the sleeping bag and how shocked I'd been at my own behaviour. He accepted this as something quite normal and reassured me by saying that it was actually quite a good idea to find some comfort in blocking out the world for a while and to have space and time just to be myself in a safe, undemanding place. He explained that it would be worrying if I'd stayed there and hidden away, never going out, but as a short-term behaviour it was nothing to be concerned about. Up until then I had thought it was a very weird thing to do but I could see his point and began to feel slightly better about myself. He was also not concerned about me breaking down in tears, unable to face going in to pilates. In fact, he took a more positive view and emphasised the point that I was strong enough to go in and, once inside the class, I had challenged myself to work at a higher level. He thought this showed how strong I was and it was that which I should concentrate on, not the tearfulness.

Caden's encouraging words and positive view made me feel a little more confident, so I then took the bull by the horns and managed to tell him how upset I'd been after the last counselling session. I explained how I thought he'd lost trust in me and how important that trust was to me, as it had been he who had enabled me to put the first piece of my smashed-up self together again, by trusting me in the first session with him. Caden was obviously surprised and taken aback about how I'd perceived what he'd said to me about there still being some underlying issues that we needed to work on. He went to great lengths to explain that he thought I'd made significant progress in a short time but that was not the whole picture and it was important to use these sessions to explore everything. Once he had explained, I believed him and could accept this but I was glad that I'd raised my reaction with him.

We then moved on to explore why I'd had this breakdown. Caden had been reading up on TGA and thought there may be things that had built up over a period prior to the car accident and that was just the trigger. I told him about a conversation I'd had with Dr Alice, who had suggested the same thing, that stress had been building up over a number of months and then my brain and body were saying, 'That's enough, I'm shutting down now.'

I then told him about the very stressful five months that I'd experienced from April to August and, the more I talked about all this, the more I realised how exhausted I'd become, both physically and emotionally, during that time. It all began to make sense. Both Caden and I thought this was a very useful session and we'd made some real progress but I recognised that there was still a good way to go.

I remained positive for the rest of the day and realised that my brain was working a lot more effectively now. In the evening I enjoyed going to Recorder Group but, as usual, my positivity didn't last very long. By Thursday afternoon I felt tired and tearful, unable to settle to anything and I was very tempted to curl up in the sleeping bag again. I resisted this as there were practical things I had to attend to. Maybe this was not a good thing and I should have given myself some time out, as things were going to get much, much worse over the next few days.

Unable to sleep that night and emotionally distraught, I felt my panic and anxiety developing into complete despair once again. In a desperate attempt to gain some control, I got up and started to write down everything I was feeling and thinking. I couldn't understand why I kept reacting like this; every time I thought I was making progress, as at the last counselling session the previous day, from which I came away feeling very relieved and 'at peace', then I seemed to flounder and sink and become a complete wreck again. This seemed to happen time after time; I would come away feeling good but my brain would explode with thoughts and feelings which I couldn't catch hold of, resulting in turmoil and distress.

That night, I wrote six pages of notes, trying to reflect on what had happened and what it was that was happening to me. The notes begin:

I'm going to try writing in an attempt to stop the feelings of panic and anxiety developing into something worse – despair – again. I just don't understand why this keeps happening. There was no apparent reason tonight, as I have felt generally much better since my last counselling session on Wednesday which resulted in me feeling very relieved and 'at peace'. Things seemed to be going well after that so why has it all gone downhill?

First, I thought about the session with Caden, from which I'd come away very positive. I knew I was pleased that he just seemed to accept me as I was or wanted to be, without labelling me as obstinate, arrogant, difficult or always knowing best. That meeting was good and there was nothing there to upset me or to blame him for this week.

Then I had enjoyed a walk with Margaret in the afternoon. We enjoyed seeing the wonderful colour of the beech trees in the park and were quite at ease with other, chatting and laughing, enjoying each other's company. In the evening, I'd gone to my recorder group and that had been a good experience too, with new music to play which I tackled quite confidently. I'd felt very alive there and back to being 'Jupiter' – my nickname for being the one who organises things. But I didn't get too high, just organised, so was pleased about that.

On Thursday morning, at the invitation of another friend, I had driven Margaret and myself over to her house for coffee. This friend is a retired GP and she thought it might be helpful for me to do this drive – about twelve miles each way – in the company of a good friend, and to enjoy a morning away from home. The plan worked and it had all gone well; it was a very enjoyable morning.

It was that afternoon when the trouble started; I became so restless but couldn't concentrate on anything. Not able to work outside in the garden as it was raining, I tried a few things indoors but gave up on them all. I wondered whether the lack of exercise over the past two days contributed to my low mood. Finally, I concluded that it was the same pattern of a crash landing into a sea of turmoil, after the counselling on Wednesday. Although I had come away feeling fine, my brain was by now exploding, with thoughts and feelings milling around, and once more I found it hard to catch hold of any of them; they were just washed away in the currents, out of reach, like pieces of loose wreckage again. I knew I was in desperate need of sorting them out. I needed to take control and make sense of things again.

Writing everything down helped. Just being able to recognise what the problems were felt like a first step and, as I wrote, several things slotted into place. I realised that, now I'd completed the two final challenges previously identified and sorted out the immediate issues, I knew that I had to start facing up to tackling properly the more in-depth, complicated family issues that are fundamental to my real life, not just the 'frills' around the edge. So far, I had immersed myself in these challenges, blocking out everything else, and now my 'holiday' from all this was fast coming to an end and panic, panic, panic was welling up. At this point I became overwhelmed by panic and had to stop writing.

The next evening, I forced myself to return to the writing task, determined to try to think more rationally, as I couldn't face another crisis in the middle of the night. I knew that I had two choices; one, I could start to take control and deal with things or, two, that I should just give up and carry out my plan to end it all. So which way should I go?

That day I had felt alright – not great, but stable. I'd really pushed myself in pilates and did things I didn't think I could do, which was remarkable. So I thought, if I can do this by putting my mind to it, really concentrating hard, perhaps I could tackle other things successfully. What had become obvious to me was that there was a lot of 'stuff' – thoughts and feelings – that were just a product of my mind (or brain) and maybe there is no such thing as 'reality'. It all just comes from inside us and the only things that exist are our perceptions. So, having come up with this deep thought, I kicked myself into actually facing up to what I needed to sort out.

First and foremost was the maelstrom of feelings surrounding my daughter, her baby and the baby's father, a man with whom she'd had a tempestuous affair but with whom she no longer had contact, as he had refused to acknowledge the baby as his and wanted nothing more to do with my daughter or his child. I recognised with some surprise that I had managed to say their names to myself. Previously, up until then, I was just referring to 'the baby' and to the father as 'that slimy scumbag', as I thought he didn't deserve to have a name.

I'd been reading a book, *The Hare with Amber Eyes* and, at Book Group earlier that week, we discussed the ultimate humiliation of the Austrian Jews during the Nazi occupation, when their real names were erased on documents and all males were recorded as 'Israel' and all females as 'Sara'. Not only did the Gestapo take away their jobs, property and possessions but also their identity, their very being. And I questioned myself, 'Is that what I'm trying to do with him? by never speaking of him by his name, even to myself?' I felt so ashamed. I'd never felt such feelings of hatred for anyone like this before in my life and now felt dreadful about it, both physically – hot, sweating, sick, breathless, and emotionally – guilty, angry, overwhelmed, desperate. Once again, I couldn't write any more; it was too painful.

In floods of tears and racked with guilt, I felt that I was such an awful person to have these angry, bitter feelings and I thought that even the professional Caden might have problems in not judging me now. Caden had been so important in helping me start to find bits of myself again that the thought of him judging me badly was devastating. Experience had shown me that he didn't react to my tearfulness or actions like hiding in a sleeping bag. I knew that he must relate to some of the things I'd told him, to be able to understand what I was thinking, which he did so well. In fact, sometimes he seemed to know what I was thinking better than I did. I knew that I couldn't afford to lose him as an anchor, secured to the bits of me that were left in this wreckage and the tumult of emotion I was now experiencing. Absolutely exhausted after these thoughts and a tirade of tears, I was unable to write any more and put myself to bed at about ten o'clock, though I was unable to sleep.

Just after midnight, I tried to write again, feeling a little calmer and thinking that some of my feelings of self-disgust were perhaps an over-reaction. I wondered whether my feelings about 'him' not being deserving of a name were 'intrusive thoughts'. Although I couldn't and didn't want to call the baby's father by his name, I was not actually trying to erase his identity – in fact it wouldn't affect him at all, as he wouldn't know anything about it. So, although my feelings were still there, I was not going to *act* on them and I didn't have any power over him, anyway. Also, I felt that he did deserve some anger against him for the way he had behaved and treated my daughter and his son by refusing to take any responsibility for them when they needed him. At this point, I decided consciously to put him away for a while and to concentrate on how to rebuild and manage my relationship with my daughter and baby grandson.

Having established this plan in my mind, I then managed to sleep and missed the dreaded early hours slot of wakefulness between two and three o'clock. At about five o'clock I was awake again but decided to try to read some of my new book, *The Goldfinch* by Donna Tart. The opening lines of chapter one immediately gripped me, as they describe how Theo, a thirteen-year-old boy, confined to a room in a hotel in Amsterdam, was afraid to telephone anyone or to go out, and reacted with fear and anxiety to even the most innocent noises around him. His feelings described my own so exactly that I totally identified with this young teenager, in spite of the completely different place, age and the circumstances which had brought this state about. I had no idea then what had brought Theo to such a low ebb but I knew keenly how he felt at that point in time for I, too, was extremely sensitive to all noises. I would jump if the phone rang, if the clock struck the hour, a lawnmower suddenly started – all manner of noises, that normally I wouldn't even notice, would start my heart palpitating and cause my breathing to become rapid and distressed. At home this didn't matter too much but sitting in the cinema or theatre had become embarrassing, as I would jump and jerk violently at any sudden noise, my reaction quite out of proportion to what was happening in the film or play. It was the same in the doctors' waiting room, where an electronic beep draws attention to the next patient to be called. I was a nervous wreck.

Theo's story is very poignant and moving and he suffers some dreadful experiences. There is no similarity in our stories, except for his reactions to extreme stress, but his feelings at that point fitted mine so exactly that I couldn't believe it. Being so identified with Theo, reading the first chapter had me in floods of tears again, so much so that I had to stop reading for a while. Yet this was a different sort of crying, more that of a *grieving* for Theo who lost his mother after a bomb explosion in a New York Museum and Art Gallery. It made me wonder what *I* was grieving for – maybe the lost Me? Whatever, it felt alright, permissible, to cry like this and somehow a great relief. I reminded myself of Caden saying it was a normal human reaction to cry, and I knew that had felt like him giving me permission to cry. I'd certainly exploited that lately, having done more crying in the past three months than in the past three or more years!

The other thing that struck me was that I didn't have to worry about not being able to relate to fiction books any more, as I'd become totally involved in this book; I'd have liked to stay in bed all day reading it but knew I had to get up and face the day. Reading back over my late night entry, I felt like I was a different person the next morning. All those violent feelings of the night seemed to have evaporated but I knew, really, they'd just been hidden away for now and I would have to face up to them again.

I hadn't really done what I had set out to do with this writing the previous night and was not at all sure that this was what Caden had meant, but at least it had prevented the dreaded total panic and desolation in the early hours of the morning. What had surprised me was that people in crisis all seem to have the same feelings, however old or young they are and whatever the cause of their suicidal feelings. There seemed to be very little logic in why someone might feel suicidal. I was conscious that people in the Philippines Disaster were there struggling to survive in the most appalling conditions at the same time that I (along with others in this relatively wealthy country) was thinking about how not to survive – how to end my life – when I had everything they had lost or maybe never had. I found that contrast so terrible and sad that it made me feel extremely guilty.

Although I would have loved to have stayed in bed and read more of *The Goldfinch*, I managed to get up and busy myself with various jobs around the house and garden, then went for a walk in the afternoon. By chance I met my friend, Ann, who was walking her dog and we walked together for a while, then became engrossed in conversation whilst standing on the bridge over the local river. We stood there for some time, idly watching the water flow by peacefully below us as we talked. Ann was telling me about the weeks leading up to her husband's death, some years previously and I was listening, gazing at the water as she talked. Even her dog stood still, patiently, mesmerised by the river as it flowed gently over the rocks, not rushing or swirling as it did sometimes, but emanating a feeling of calm and peacefulness.

That evening I decided to try writing again but this time my aim was to order my thoughts about the meeting with my daughter planned for the following Thursday. These are things that I wrote down as wanting to achieve during that meeting:

• Show my daughter that I love her and value her still, whatever has happened

• Make a real effort to relate to my baby grandson again;

• Try not to be too vitriolic about the baby's father but at the same time don't go along with any fantasies she might have;

• Maybe try to explain my feelings about him and what he's done to her and to the family;

• Do something enjoyable together . . . perhaps buy some clothes for the baby;

• Try to involve myself in the baby's first Christmas and get him a present or some ideas from my daughter by looking around the shops together;

• Make sure I give my daughter praise and encouragement for her decision about the house;

• Remember that she is Menna, my daughter, so don't try to talk to her like I would to Caden. We are highly emotionally involved. I am her *Mum* and we both have emotional needs in a complicated situation;

• Be careful – listen carefully, don't get wound up or upset (or at least don't let it show). Remain calm and non-critical of her, if not of him, and try to recognise that it is her life, not mine.

Whether it was the sense of achievement of writing down these thoughts in an ordered way, or just physical exhaustion, it worked and I had a good sleep on Saturday night.

Sunday 17 November

I woke about seven o'clock and read more of *The Goldfinch*, which started me off crying again about something on almost every page. I seemed to have totally identified with the thirteen-year-old boy, living every step of the way with him as he struggled over the weeks and months to regain some state of 'normality', though in his case his world had totally changed. I finally tore myself away from the book at 9.00 am but it left me in a very emotional state, with tears very near the surface and Don commented that I seemed 'far away'.

By the afternoon, I felt in need of finding some peace and decided to walk to a remote place I knew up in the hills where I'd found solace before, hoping to feel secure there. Unfortunately, in spite of tramping around for ages, I was disappointed and unable to find the sheltered spot, though I think the walking did some good and I returned home feeling a little better.

That night, though, things really deteriorated. I woke about two o'clock feeling hot, agitated, restless, anxious and desperate. I stayed in bed, tossing, turning and struggling for an hour or more, becoming more and more despairing; then suddenly, I felt full of a compelling energy, leapt out of bed, pulled on my jeans quickly over the top of my pyjamas, thrust my feet into trainers and, taking a torch from my bedside table to avoid putting on lights, ran quietly downstairs. It was as if my body had a will and energy of its own and, grabbing a jacket in the porch, I was propelled outside into the night and found myself hurrying down the road towards the river by the bridge where I'd been standing the previous afternoon. It was as if I had been taken over by some violent force with just one objective – to find peace in the river. The image in my fevered mind was vivid – I could see myself lying face down in the water, with arms outstretched, finding oblivion by drowning.

At 3.30 am this November morning was dark, quiet and calm. It was dull and slightly misty, with no hint of wind or breeze, surprisingly mild for November. Everything was totally still and quiet, not a soul about, no lights in the houses, no traffic, no planes in the sky, no rain, no sounds. Even the sheep in the field next to the river were as silent and still as statues as they slept. I walked quickly, still hot and flushed but filled with one purpose.

As I neared the river, everything was covered in low cloud, the mist hanging like a curtain over the motionless sheep, masking the trees and hedges. It was like entering another world... ethereal, mystical. I reached the bridge and could just make out the dark river below, still flowing gently and peacefully, like an old friend waiting patiently for me to join it, to float on its surface, become one with it and drift away for ever.

Finding a gap in the hedge, I pushed my way through and clambered down the steep bank to the water's edge, discarding my jacket on the way, and stepped off the bank into the water, which seemed so inviting. Relief flooded over me as I felt its inky coldness swirl gently round my legs and I vaguely hoped that hypothermia might help to hasten the end.

I stood there in the stillness for a few moments, breathing in the scene, contemplating the next step, when I was overcome with the strange beauty of the night. There were no stars sparkling in the sky, nor a moon shining down benevolently, no frost glittering on the grass, yet the damp, misty stillness and silence brought a feeling of such calm and peace that it had a beauty of its own; not a sound nor a breath of air disturbing the stillness, no nocturnal animals making a sound, no busy human activity, even the water was cool and calm. The world slept in total quietness. I felt myself slowly deflating like a hot air balloon, as the heat of my frenzied energy left me. As it all washed over me, I too became cool and calm, while reason crept back into my brain, taking over from the turmoil of emotion. I became aware of why I was standing in a river in the middle of the night, of what I was intending. At this point I knew that this was not the way to go. I began to think of the effect my suicide in this way would have on those close and dear to me. This wasn't how I'd planned it. I'd not even written them letters to try to explain, and this seemed wrong. I knew I could not do this to my family, just disappear into the night with no word, no explanation. At least I owed them that. The urgency to end my life seeped away and I decided to wait and return to my 'plan' which now seemed a far better way to end it all.

I turned away from the river and climbed back up the bank, retrieving my jacket from the bushes, glad of it now that I was no longer full of a burning heat. I crossed back over the bridge, leaving the river behind, still there flowing calmly but relentlessly on its way. It still filled me with peace to see it but I no longer wished to join it.

The sheep were still there, sleeping quietly in the field, just indistinct mounds in the misty darkness.

I crossed the road and walked into the cemetery where I sat on a bench among the still trees and the quiet graves, absorbing the peacefulness of this place, the gravestones' dark silhouettes scattered among the tall trees and thick bushes. I sat for some time, thinking, just letting the quiet stillness envelop me and do its calming work. It didn't seem a scary or ghostly place, just a natural resting place for those whose time on earth was over. All these people, amongst whose gravestones I was sitting, had lived their lives but had now passed on. They were no longer alive; the stones were all that remained to mark their lives. I realised then how short a time our life span is when measured against the past or the future; that it would soon pass in time, without the need for any drastic action from me. Feeling strangely at peace with the world and even with myself, I walked home slowly, left my soaked shoes and jeans in the garage, dried my feet and went back to bed where I slept until morning.

Chapter Eight
AFTERMATH

Monday 18 November

When I woke in the morning, I found it hard to believe the events of the night before. It was as if a different person inside me had taken over. I could no longer feel the depths of despair that I'd felt only hours previously and I was very shocked at how rashly I had acted and how close I'd come to ending my life. I was unable to understand why this had happened, especially as nothing in particular had gone wrong on Saturday or Sunday, so what was it all about? I was also scared, filled with terror, of how I might react if something did go wrong. This was bound to happen at some point; how would I cope then? It was one thing to have a carefully thought out plan that I could use at an appropriate time but quite different to feel invaded by some sort of force that galvanised me into ill thought-out action. It made no sense. Why had I been driven to go to the river with the intention of drowning? I am a strong swimmer and even gained a lifesaving Bronze Medallion many years ago, so it would go against all my natural instincts and learnt behaviour to drown myself. I had spent hours researching the best way to commit suicide but none of this even entered my consciousness at the critical moment. All of a sudden, I felt very fearful of being abandoned to face all this alone and it was very clear that I needed help. This had been a real crisis point and I had to decide what to do about it.

It was a strange day. The shock had made me feel quite numb and very subdued. I went about tasks like an automaton, keeping busy all day so as not to have to think about it or dwell on it. I could function quite well physically, doing some final tidying up in the garden, and I went swimming in the afternoon but I was unable to talk to my friend, Margaret, or anyone else about what had happened. I seemed to be living in a kind of suspended world, knowing what was going on and even participating in it but as an observer of myself.

Tuesday 19 November

I got up early as I had a pre-arranged appointment with Dr Alice at 9.10 am. These appointments are supposed to be for only ten minutes and I had no intention of telling her what had happened. Instead, I told her about the recorder workshop and my considerable progress during daytime hours. She is such a good listener and seemed so pleased and caring that, as I talked, I found myself relaxing and emerging from my numbed, shocked state, gradually becoming myself again. I found myself suddenly opening up and telling her a lot about my feelings and anxieties regarding my daughter, my baby grandson and his father.

I was very surprised at myself, as I had never dreamt that I would be able to vocalise these thoughts out loud to anyone, let alone to my doctor, but she listened attentively and patiently, without rushing me and was very understanding and sympathetic. Just when I thought this outpouring had finished, and encouraged by Dr Alice's patient listening, I decided even more surprisingly, to confess what had happened on Sunday night.

Dr Alice remained calm and composed and the world didn't fall in around us but she was obviously very concerned and anxious to keep me safe. This time I found that I was relieved, rather than angry, that someone did want to keep me safe. She suggested trying a different anti-depressant, Sertraline, for a few weeks and also recommended a referral to a psychiatrist and the local mental health team. Knowing that I could be in real danger unless I accepted help, I agreed to both these suggestions. When I came out of the surgery I found that I had taken up half an hour of Dr Alice's time but felt hugely better and relieved that I'd found the courage to admit some of my underlying deep-seated anxieties and fears. I was so grateful to this doctor for giving me the time and space to seek help, without pressuring or judging me. I felt she really understood and so I was ready and willing to accept the help she offered.

The rest of the day passed in a sort of daze, during which I functioned well enough on the surface but without any real thought of what I was doing. Apart from getting upset and tearful about a problem with the U3A website, for which I was responsible, I managed to appear normal, to observe social niceties and even to go to a recorder practice. Although I was still acting automatically, without any feeling or commitment, the day was more pleasant than the previous one and, underneath the surface, I could feel something of 'me' being present, well-hidden down in the dark depths but not entirely missing.

I collected the prescribed anti-depressants from the pharmacy and took one in the early evening, before going to the cinema with a group of friends to see the film *Philomena*. I didn't have to drive so was able to relax. Even though it was a sad story, the acting by Judi Dench and Steve Coogan was great and I found myself laughing out loud at much of the humorous script, appreciating the company, and being part of my group of friends. Somehow this made me feel wanted and safe. I doubt if the Sertraline would have acted so quickly to achieve this better frame of mind but it seemed as if these new tablets had really made a difference already. I am sure the change was much more related to my doctor's care and compassion. I knew she was there for me and would support me through these difficult times.

That night my sleep was much better and, although I woke at

2.00 am and only dozed then until 4.30, I felt completely different from my usual frenzied self at that time in the early hours of the morning. I was just pleasantly warm and very relaxed, except for a dreadful headache, but even that was preferable to the doubts, fears, worries and feelings of self-loathing that I would normally experience on waking during the night. I was not agitated, restless or on edge but managed to stay in bed resting even when awake. It was wonderful to sleep without being haunted by angry, sad or despairing feelings, though it made me feel very weak that I had once again let myself down. I could understand – for the first time in my life – why or how people get hooked on drugs to block out their real lives and I felt ashamed that I'd not been able to appreciate their addictions with more empathy. It was a humbling experience.

Thursday 21st November

A day or two later, I got up early as I was due to go on a coach trip to Gloucester Christmas Market, leaving at 8.30 am. I'd been doubtful about the wisdom of starting new anti-depressants the previous night but need not have worried as there were no apparent side effects, except for my headache which disappeared after taking a couple of paracetamol.

The journey on the coach was good. I sat with my friend, Margaret, and we chatted easily all the way, the miles soon passing. In spite of taking the anti-depressant tablets, I felt as if my brain was in gear and that I was fully engaged in what was happening, no longer viewing the world with blurred vision or feeling disconnected. I'd arranged to meet my son and daughter in Gloucester and, after a stroll through the Christmas Market, we all went for an early lunch to Pizza Hut where I was able to relax over the meal and fell in love with the baby all over again. He was delightful; a very happy baby, with lots of smiles, looking at everything that was going on and even laughing through lunch, and I felt sure that he liked me too! We had bonded again.

After refuelling ourselves with a good meal, we managed to attack the crowded shops where we were successful in buying Christmas presents for all the grandchildren. Against my will, I found myself agreeing to contribute towards a new Xbox and game for my grandson as, although I hate buying this sort of gift, I recognised that I have to accept how children live and play now in the twenty-first century. I also knew that he would love this present.

My son and daughter had to leave soon after this to get home for the older children coming home from school but I enjoyed a leisurely wander around the market before meeting a couple from the coach whom I joined for coffee in one of the many restaurants, before the coach left to come home. After a busy afternoon it was good to sit down in the café, to relax and just watch people going busily about their business. Living in Mid-Wales, I don't often go to large towns or cities like Gloucester, so it was a very different experience but one which I found myself enjoying. The day had gone well, at least on the surface. When we got home, I was tired but very pleased that, not only had I managed the day successfully – joining a large group of people, relating to my daughter and baby grandson – but I'd also actually enjoyed myself and felt as if I'd achieved quite a lot.

There was, however, one thing that had upset me and, although I'd not reacted at the time, I now allowed my feelings to surface, and felt devastated. During conversation over lunch, I had deliberately not made any mention of my daughter's husband or of the baby's father but they had come up incidentally when we were discussing arrangements for Christmas. My heart had plummeted when my daughter explained that, on Christmas Day, the two older children would go to their father and she would have them on Boxing Day. I had been hoping that at least they would all spend Christmas

Day together but now there were to be none of the usual family traditions – no stockings, no family Christmas dinner together, no visits to or from us, the grandparents. It seemed as if everything was to be smashed up. With my heart in my mouth, I'd managed to ask the question 'What will you do on Christmas Day?' and the answer was something I'd dreaded, 'Take the baby to see his father'. It had become obvious during our conversation that my daughter was now in regular contact with the baby's father and also with his family. When I'd suggested buying clothes for the baby, my daughter said nothing was needed, as his father's sister had given her a sackful of baby clothes. It had become clear that his father was now showing some interest in his baby son. At the time, I'd kept very calm and made no comment, enabled only perhaps by the new anti-depressant tablets which seemed to have kept me very stable all day. Whilst I knew that a relationship with his father was probably a good thing for the baby, I had no trust in him sustaining a meaningful relationship either with the baby or with my daughter. It also left little hope of a reconciliation between my daughter and her separated husband, something I found very sad, heart rending, in fact.

At least I'd come to terms with contributing towards the Xbox, as I felt that a joint present from my grandson's mother, father and grandparents might perhaps demonstrate to him that we are still all a family, working together for him and his sister. Not everything was smashed to pieces, even though Christmas would be very different from usual this year. Viewing it all like this made me feel a little more positive.

Friday 22 November

After the excitement of the previous day, I felt exhausted the next morning and, by the afternoon, my mood was very low: *totally blue and in danger of sinking into black* was how I recorded it in my diary. This was in spite of another restful night and a reasonable amount of sleep, without any anxiety or distress in the early hours. I had been very affected by scenes in a documentary programme on television, the final part of *Bedlam* which dealt with mental illness in the over-sixty-fives. The patients had suffered such dreadful breakdowns; the programme focused on terrible cases that just happened so quickly. A psychiatrist explained that today we live in a society that values perfection and as we get older, it becomes harder to remain perfect. As I listened to his words and watched the case study of one woman in particular, my chest became tight, my heart palpitating, my stomach in knots and my body tense. This woman had become totally confused and was unable to recall anything about her past. 'I'm not me,' she kept saying, 'I can't stand it any more.' I knew exactly how she felt. Her state of confusion had happened very suddenly, overnight, and she'd been admitted to hospital with depression but had now been diagnosed with an extreme case of dissociative disorder (which used to be known as hysteria), in which you don't recognise yourself any more.

The psychiatrist explained, 'We all struggle as we go through life with things that we find difficult but sometimes life can throw something at you that sends you into a fantastic spin. It throws you into conflict with yourself and you can't deal with it so the way you cope with it is by escaping to a different state.' This seemed so pertinent to my own experience in spite of different circumstances. The positive thing was that this patient made a remarkable recovery after nine months of not speaking or sleeping. Eventually, it was ECT treatment that gave her the belief she needed to get better. The psychiatrist warned though that the danger now was that she would want to get back to normal by keeping busy, to get her sense of self back but, by avoiding the pain of peeling back the layers to think about who she really was, she would be in danger again. She had disappeared into the dissociative state because she was unable to cope with the pressures and strains of her life; by coming back into life she would expose herself once more to the anxieties and difficulties that drove her into that dreadful state. To help avoid this and to support her, she would be discharged as an in-patient but would be encouraged to come back as an out-patient for psychotherapy and counselling.

I found the life stories, and this patient's in particular, so terrifying and moving. So much of what she was feeling was relevant to me – the dreadful void of not knowing who I was any more, how I felt what was the essential 'me' had been smashed up into tiny pieces. I was aware that I was gradually putting some of these pieces together again but now I was not sure that I wanted to become entirely the old 'me' again. I thought I would like to change in some respects but I had no clear picture of what I wanted to change or who I wanted to be for the future. It was all so confusing and frustrating.

Over the next few days, the pattern of my moods changed completely. The new anti-depressants helped me to sleep well at night and I was no longer experiencing those dreadful early morning hours but, strangely, the night-time terrors were replaced by dark, dreadful days. When I woke in the morning I felt rested and able to get up to face the day but, before long, each day became a trial. I felt so terrible... dark, negative, gloomy, unable to settle to anything, tearful all the time, not wanting to do anything or to or talk to anyone, just withdrawing into myself. I still managed to cook meals for my husband but had no appetite and ate very little myself, feeling nauseous at the sight or smell of food. My husband was very concerned about the change in me for, whilst I could keep my night-time difficulties to myself, I could not do this during the day. One afternoon, I found a brief release after going swimming, and forcing myself to swim very aggressively up and down the pool. That evening, I was calmer but this relief was short-lived and the storms soon swept over me again.

I was really struggling to manage even routine tasks, feeling that nothing was worthwhile any longer. I spent many hours lying on my bed, trying to doze and shut out the world. Thoughts of suicide kept coming into my mind. Lying in the bath, I thought of drowning myself there but I knew this wouldn't be fair on my husband who would no doubt find me. At one point, I felt so bad that I thought of taking the tablets that I'd collected together as part of my suicide plan but knew that I would be discovered too soon if I took them there and then at home and so, robbed of all energy and motivation to do anything, I was unable to collect everything together and walk to my chosen place. Constantly tired, not eating properly and unable to concentrate on or enjoy any activities, it seemed as if I'd sunk to unfathomable depths, even deeper and darker than my previous experiences. I wrote in my diary:

> I wish Caden could tell me what to do to make this go away. I feel so dreadful, not wanting to do anything, go anywhere, see anyone. All I want is to end my life and I don't even have the energy to do that. When will it all end?

Saturday 23 November

I slept well, from 9.30 pm–5.00 am and then again until 8 am – over ten hours sleep and no lying awake during the early hours! But the trouble now was that I was very, very low and was tearful all day. I tried a walk in the afternoon, which helped a little, but still I was tearful again in the evening.

This pattern continued over the next few days – a complete turnaround from what I had experienced up until now. It was clear that the Sertraline tablets were making me sleep much better at night but now I felt dreadfully low every morning, whereas previously I had made such good progress during daytime hours and my bad times were at night.

By Tuesday, I was so depressed and full of self-disgust that I lay down on my bedroom floor and shut my eyes to try to shut out the world. I felt so bad about myself that I didn't feel worthy to lie on the bed. After some time, I was brought back into the world by the phone ringing and the need to prepare some lunch for my husband. Feeling heavy and sick, in both mind and body, I dragged myself up off the floor and somehow forced myself to do what was necessary, conscious of the need to appear normal, even though my state of mind was dark, dismal and desperate.

That afternoon, a friend called to pick me up to go to recorder practice. Once again, I forced myself to appear 'normal' and go along. I was aware that I was plunging to new depths but I felt it was important to prevent anyone from knowing just how low I was getting. There were only four of us there that afternoon and our leader worked us really hard on some difficult new pieces. I had to focus entirely on the music, learning some new notes and mastering the difficult phrases but it seemed that this total concentration seemed to do me some good as, although I was exhausted mentally, my mood had lifted and improved slightly by the end of the afternoon and remained stable all the evening.

Somehow I survived until the following week when I had an appointment with my counsellor, Caden. Although I was doubtful that it would be of any benefit, I made an effort and managed to attend.

Wednesday 27 November

Trembling and very agitated, I made it to the surgery and approached the session anxiously, knowing that I should tell Caden about the events at the river. Shaking all over and feeling as if I was choking, I found that I was unable to speak in answer to Caden's opening question 'How are you?' but he recognised my distress and began the session by telling me what he knew from Dr Alice about the events of the previous week, the referral to a psychiatrist and trying some different anti-depressants. He asked me how I was finding those and I told him that they had totally transformed my night times. I was sleeping really well and, even if I woke during the night, I felt relaxed and content and would soon fall asleep again. But the daytimes had turned into a nightmare; I was always tired, didn't want to do anything or go anywhere, just wishing I wasn't there any more. I couldn't understand how, when previously I wasn't sleeping well at night, I was full of a nervous energy during the daytime, pushing myself hard to overcome challenges and achieve the goals I'd set, often having more energy than I knew what to do with. But now, although I was sleeping well at night and therefore should have had more energy during the day, I was constantly tired, lethargic and unmotivated. All I could think was that I didn't want to be here any more but sadly I didn't even have the energy or will to do anything about it.

As usual, Caden remained very calm and composed as he explained that the Sertraline has two effects; the first, a sedative effect, had obviously kicked in at once and was making me sleep better at night and may also explain why I felt so tired during the day; but the anti-depressant effect has to build up in the brain for a while before it takes effect. In the meantime I was likely to become more anxious and depressed. He reassured me that the depression I was feeling now was, in fact, more 'normal'. The euphoric part and huge mood swings that I had experienced up until then were more uncommon and puzzling. In the meantime, he assured me that he would continue to see me and, together, we should try to unravel any issues or worries that had been present even before the car accident triggered the depression.

Having this explanation and reassurance that things would get better helped a lot and I was then able to move on to a discussion about underlying worries and feelings that may have contributed to my reaction to the accident. He felt that, although this had been the trigger, the cause was probably much more complicated. I was able, at this stage, to admit that I thought there were underlying reasons and I offered to read him part of my night-time writing, when I was trying to clarify in my head what I was feeling but, first, I extracted an assurance from him that he would try to understand and not trample on the very personal feelings that I had expressed. He stopped me then and asked me to think how I would feel after I had shared this with him. I knew that how I would feel would depend on his reaction but decided to trust him and go ahead. I read the section about my need to sort out my relationships with my daughter, my baby grandson and his father; my feelings and my difficulty in calling them by their names; about my guilt and shame, how I was comparing myself with the Nazis in the book, *The Hare with Amber Eyes*.

I was amazed that I was even suggesting sharing these thoughts by reading out loud what I'd written, something I could never have done even a few weeks earlier, but I was learning slowly to trust both my GP and my counsellor which, in itself, was a huge step forward. Caden listened very carefully and immediately grasped that there were two themes: one was my hatred of Evan and that the strength of that feeling was shocking to me; and, two, my distress and horror at thinking my feelings were similar to the Gestapo. I then had to explain and outline the events over the past year and particularly the past six months that had led to this state of affairs. As I had already explained this some days previously to my GP, this was not so difficult.

My daughter was married with two children when she had an affair with Evan and decided to leave her husband. Some months later, her relationship with Evan deteriorated and came to an acrimonious end. Menna then returned to live with her husband, only to find that she was pregnant with Evan's child. It was a difficult pregnancy, with physical complications and much emotional turmoil. Evan made it clear that he had no wish to resume any sort of relationship with her or to accept that the child was his. Menna stayed living at home with her husband and children but it became clear after a few months that the family was in crisis. I started to spend a great deal of time at their home, helping the family to function, and caring for my daughter who was suffering greatly. There were many problems to sort out and plans to make for the future but we all worked hard together and kept things going fairly well. Aware that my husband had his own problems, I didn't share all of my concerns with him but kept the full picture to myself.

After the baby was born, I spent the weekdays at their home, looking after the grandchildren and, of course, my daughter and the baby, once they were discharged from hospital. It was hard work looking after her family, with the two older grandchildren on holiday from school and their dogs, chickens and a pony to care for each day. I was up, working constantly from seven in the morning until ten at night, with very little rest or relief. Every Friday evening, my son-in-law would take over and I would return home to my husband, where I would spend the weekend catching up with everything there, and preparing for the following week. Having had a Caesarean section, Menna was unable to do very much physically or to drive for six weeks. This period was just due to come to an end when my husband and I were involved in the car accident.

Caden listened carefully as usual and we agreed that it was clear I had become physically and mentally exhausted during that six month period. It was likely that the car accident was the final straw. I felt relieved that I had now shared the whole story with him and gained some reassurance from his acceptance of my feelings. Having put all my thoughts and feelings into words helped to put them to rest, at least for the time being.

We then explored the depth of feeling I was experiencing; for me, to feel hatred was unusual, for I may like or dislike a person but I never hated anyone. We spent some time considering this very powerful emotion of hatred and the need to let it out somehow, not to let it fester inside you. I wasn't sure how I wanted to do this but promised to think about some of Caden's suggestions that might help to release my feelings – perhaps doing something violent, like using a punch bag, or slashing down weeds and brambles in the garden, or maybe writing a letter to the baby's father telling him how despicable and abhorrent I found him. Caden stressed that I wouldn't have to send the letter or even show anyone else what I'd written but the act of writing it may prove to be cathartic and beneficial to my state of mind. We also explored my feelings of powerlessness to do anything about the situation between Evan and my daughter. We worked through how I had blamed my baby grandson for the accident and I agreed that my wish to reject him was more about who his father was. I was relieved that I still felt I had worked through those feelings now; having spent a good time with the baby during the previous week, I was now able to relate to him as a person in his own right.

Caden then took some time to prepare me for the approaching appointment with the psychiatrist and the mental health workers. He warned me that they would want to talk about my safety and that I may find the retelling of events stressful but it was important to tell them everything. I found that I was able to talk to Caden about the events that had prompted Dr Alice's referral, telling him about what had happened on that Sunday evening at the river. Having already told Dr Alice, it was somehow not only easier to speak about the situation again but also a relief to put it all into words.

Over the following months and years, I found it helpful to tell this story time and again to various medical professionals and, on occasions, just to myself. The telling and re-telling of the story seemed to have some healing property. It wasn't enough to tell it once; I had to keep telling it until it ceased to hold its horrors. Again, Caden did not over-react to anything I told him; there was neither judging nor blaming, just careful listening and support. He knew that Dr Alice had referred me to see a psychiatrist and encouraged me to take advantage of the help that would be offered quite quickly from the Primary Health Care Team. He insisted that he would continue to see me on a regular basis until such time as the appointment with the psychiatrist took place, which he thought may not be until the New Year, although he would expect a Community Psychiatric Nurse (CPN) to be in touch before then. I found this very reassuring and I also felt that he cared sufficiently about me to want to see me again, even though other arrangements were being made. This helped to relieve my guilt, as I'd had a vague worry that he would feel that I'd rejected his work with me and had wanted to move on to someone else, which certainly wasn't true. After the session, I felt quite a bit better and my self-loathing diminished, as Caden had made me feel worth something again. He had persuaded me that it was worthwhile to hang on and give the new anti-depressant tablets a chance to work properly and to find out more about how I could be helped by mental health professionals.

That afternoon, I went for a long walk with Margaret. We took a different route from normal, through some woods, high above a deep, narrow gorge. It was a spectacular rocky place with a stream at the bottom and the path covered in a thick layer of dry autumn leaves. Remembering from childhood the fun of kicking autumn leaves, Margaret and I had great fun in rediscovering this pleasure. As I thought about what Caden had said about letting some of my hatred out, I indulged in some particularly vigorous kicking, a very therapeutic activity. This culminated in my kicking a lump of rotten wood down into the gorge, where it shattered into minute pieces on the rocks below and tumbled away into the rushing stream. That was very satisfying; it got rid of Evan symbolically and purged me of some of my hatred in a safe and controlled way!

Sadly, the feeling of relief and hope didn't last. The following morning I was so low and tearful that I went back to bed feeling very suicidal but without the energy to do anything about it, and just lay there, dozing, to shut out the world until lunchtime. By mid-afternoon I felt slightly stronger and less miserable. Later, I found out that this is a classic pattern for people suffering from clinical depression; very often their worst time is during the morning, with an improvement as the day wears on. But I didn't know this at the time and found it very difficult to take a step or two forward each afternoon, only to find I had then slipped back each morning.

The same pattern occurred on Friday morning. I forced myself to get up and go to pilates but deliberately arrived late, so that I didn't have to interact with people. Afterwards, I found it impossible to talk to people, so I went straight home. I managed to have a long conversation with Don about how he was feeling, with both physical and mental problems affecting him, and discovered that he had fears that I would have him 'put away'. Having spent time focused on someone else's feelings, rather than my own, for a bit and having reassured him that I had no intention of doing anything like that, we both seemed to cheer up a bit and the world looked a little more promising.

The next day, during the afternoon, I found the energy to take my old microwave to the recycling centre a few miles out of town and was pleased to get rid of that successfully. When driving back, I had just approached the town outskirts when my brain seemed to click and suddenly I was aware that I felt good, not tearful or depressed but active and alive. This was such a sudden and massive shift that it was hard to believe. I was euphoric! I had not experienced anything like this for several months, even on my good days, and had forgotten how it felt *not to be depressed*! It was incredible.

My mood improved during the rest of the afternoon and evening. I felt happy and exhilarated but didn't get too high, though I was so excited it took me a long while to get to sleep that night. I had mixed feelings of apprehension about whether it would last on the one hand, whilst on the other hand I was concerned that if I was alright now, was it a waste of time for me to see a psychiatrist and CPN?

Over the weekend, I continued to feel a lot better, although not as good as the epiphany on Friday afternoon. On Saturday, I was tired after a restless night but still alert and positive. I enjoyed planting some bulbs in pots outside, ready for the spring, and realised this was a very forward- looking thing to do, looking to the future and even accepting that I would have a future.

I was still apprehensive that this improvement wouldn't last and was rather tense and on edge all day on Sunday but recognised that this was anxiety rather than depression, so I still had some hope.

Monday 2 December

I had an appointment with Dr Alice at 9.10 am and once again, she was so supportive and helpful. I told her about the effects of the Sertraline and she gave me a prescription for another fourteen days. Afterwards, I wondered whether this limited supply was deliberate, as I had mentioned my suicidal thoughts again during the previous week. We talked for some time about this and she, like Caden, encouraged me to hold on, as I was doing really well, but she warned me there could be difficult days ahead and stressed that I needed to recognise this and look at the overall picture. It may seem like three steps forward and two back and, although this would be hard to cope with, I must see this was still progress.

She updated me on progress with the referral to a psychiatrist and explained that, due to my age, I would have to see one of the psychiatrists who specialised in older people. This had caused a slight delay but she would follow it up. I suggested that maybe I didn't need to see anyone if the new anti-depressants were working but she definitely thought it would be worthwhile because of the strange pattern of my depression and how it had all started.

We also discussed my husband, Don, and she explained the procedure for assessing people with suspected dementia and suggested that I try to get him to come in to the surgery to start the process, as there was medication which could help.

This was another lengthy appointment during which we covered so much ground. I was amazed at how easily and comprehensively I could talk to her about anything now. I found her so understanding and encouraging; she never made me feel stupid for my anxieties and fears, acknowledging how difficult it all was with such sincerity.

Feeling good, I worked in the garden for a while and then went swimming in the afternoon. Unfortunately, I went deaf in one ear after swimming and was very frustrated by this as it made me feel physically unwell for the next few days. I also became very restless, agitated and depressed again as the week wore on, as I knew I had to see Dr Darius, the psychiatrist, on Friday and this was preying on my mind. *What would he be like and what would be the outcome of this visit?* The uncertainty made me very anxious and apprehensive. I tried to keep active but found it impossible to settle to anything.

Chapter Nine
THE PSYCHIATRIST

Friday 6 December

The morning of the psychiatrist appointment dawned at last and I left in good time to drive there, at a Health Centre a few miles away. To my disappointment and concern, I was told that Dr Darius had been called away to deal with an emergency and was running one hour late! Not only was this a big anti-climax, having psyched myself up to face him, but also I was worried that my husband would be anxious about me if I was away for such a long time and I wasn't at all sure that I should wait. It would be no use calling Don as, by this time, he never answered the phone and the phone ringing would only serve to frustrate him and make him more anxious.

I sat down in the waiting area, obviously looking very worried. A Community Psychiatric Nurse (CPN) came out, introducing herself as Ellie, and she sat with me chatting, trying hard to ease my anxiety. She explained that she was due to attend my appointment with Dr Darius as well. After about twenty minutes or so, he rushed into the building but there was another patient also waiting whom he had to see before me, so the waiting went on.

Dr Darius asked Ellie to do a couple of memory tests with me while we were waiting, and so we went into a consulting room to complete these tests, which at least gave me something to concentrate on. Once these were finished, we also talked some more, not just chatting this time, but serious talking. Ellie asked me some questions about my background, about self-harming and about how I would feel about having contact with her on a regular basis as a CPN. Until this point, it had not occurred to me to think of suicide or attempted suicide as a form of self-harm and I realised that I had answered incorrectly on various previous occasions when this phrase was used. I found it strange that even professional medical people often talked in euphemisms such as 'dark thoughts' or 'self-harm' and seemed reluctant to mention the word suicide or to ask if you had thoughts about killing yourself.

At long last, Dr Darius was ready to see me. As we were introduced, he said jokingly that he would put me in the 'hot seat' but assured me that he wouldn't put me through it. In spite of his assurances, however, it felt to me as if he did 'put me through it' and I found the long session gruelling and disturbing, as if he'd put me through a mangle to squeeze all sorts of information out of me.

First, he asked me many questions about my background and my life history, all the time taking copious notes. I wasn't at all sure what was relevant and what was not but we started at the beginning and worked our way through birth, parental background, early childhood, schooling, relationships with parents, teenage years, work and so on into adult life. He encouraged me just to talk, only interspersing with a few probing questions here and there. This part was fairly easy.

I told him that I was born in 1944, during the last year of the second world war in a private nursing home in Kent, in the days before the NHS came into being. My parents had married a year earlier, in 1943, on completion of my father's training as a probation officer and his first posting to Kent. Prior to that he had owned a clothing factory in the West End of London but after this was destroyed by bombing in the air raids, he took a new career direction.

Upon marriage, my mother became a 'housewife'. An intelligent woman, she had previously worked in the Civil Service in London, being transferred, at the outbreak of war in 1939, from the Board of Education to a responsible position in the Admiralty in Whitehall. She often had to work all night in the basement of the Admiralty Office there. When she married, she had to retire from her post, as the civil service marriage bar, which was still in existence until 1946, prohibited married women from joining the civil service and required women civil servants to resign when they became married. My mother never complained and seemed just to accept her lonely, unpaid position as a housewife but I'm sure she must have found it isolating and often boring to be at home all day, spending her time and energy on cleaning the house, washing, cooking and shopping with no adult company for hours on end. In those days, housework was hard manual labour without central heating, vacuum cleaners, washing machines and, with no refrigerators, shopping had to be purchased every day or two.

Three months after I was born, my father obtained a post as principal probation officer for Palestine and he left on a ship in June 1944, along with soldiers bound for the D-Day landings, or so I have been told. Consequently, for the first year of my life, I only knew my mother but, when we joined my father in Jerusalem a year later, he and I soon bonded and enjoyed a close and happy relationship throughout the rest of my childhood. I have no real memories of our time in Palestine, though apparently I was a sociable, happy child who, as I learnt to talk, was bilingual in Arabic and English, being cared for much of the time by a young Arab woman.

We returned to England in 1947, during the long cold winter of that year, and for the first few months we all lived with my maternal grandparents in south London, until my father, who had obtained a position as deputy principal probation officer for Kent, bought a house in Maidstone, the county town. We moved there shortly before my brother was born in the summer of that year, when I was three. At the time of his birth I was again sent to stay with my grandparents for a fortnight but, having lived with them earlier that year, I settled well and enjoyed the company of my aunt and two uncles, all younger than my mother and all of whom still lived at home with their parents at that time. There was no traumatic separation and I had fun with my uncles who often played rough and tumble games with me, whilst my aunt would take me to different parks and playgrounds with wonderful swings, slides and roundabouts. Visits to London parks remained a big treat throughout my childhood.

Although I have been told that, after a couple of weeks of my mother coming home with my new baby brother, I asked if we could take him back to the nursing home, I don't remember any lasting feelings of jealousy or resentment about my brother, and life soon returned to normal. My brother and I shared many happy times together as children and, whilst we were not very close due to the three year age gap, we rarely quarrelled or argued.

Our home was a semi-detached 'chalet' style house in a pleasant, suburban avenue, bordered with grass verges and trees and it had a large garden in which I spent many very happy hours playing with my friends. My father grew some vegetables and we kept chickens which roamed freely in a forest of raspberry canes and blackcurrant bushes, the fruits of which my mother bottled or made into jam each summer. The home-grown fruit, vegetables and eggs – and the occasional chicken boiled in a pot for stew, all served to supplement the meagre diet that everyone endured due to rationing, which continued for some years after the war ended. We had a piece of woodland at the back of the garden which made it, in many ways, an idyllic place for a young child to grow up, even though we had few toys and little in the way of material possessions. Only a few people owned motor vehicles so there was virtually no traffic on the road, the avenue being a cul-de-sac, so my friends and I were able to roam safely and we enjoyed a lot of freedom.

Dr Darius could see that, in spite of being born during the war and living through the austerity of the post-war years, my early childhood was happy, secure and stable. Although my father had gone abroad soon after I was born, I remained with my mother, so suffered no maternal deprivation or separation anxiety, a subject of much concern after the work of psychiatrist, John Bowlby, was published during the 1950s. Although many of Bowlby's initial findings proved to be controversial and have since been modified significantly, including by Bowlby himself, his work is still influential and more recent research has supported his original conclusion that maternal deprivation in infancy and early childhood is likely to have an adverse effect on development, both during the period of deprivation and in later life. Loss of a mother by death before the age of five has been found to be more frequent in people suffering from depressive illness and suggests that the effects of early separation can be hidden, only emerging later in life.

Having explored and discounted traumas during my birth or early childhood, Dr Darius then moved on to look at my education. Starting school at the age of four, I was already able to read fluently and I remember being puzzled by the difficulties that other children in my class had in learning to read. I attended a small private school, mainly because, at that time, there was no state school nearby. The curriculum was limited, consisting mainly of the '3 Rs', reading, writing and 'rithmetic; we did no PE, music or art, although in the afternoons I remember we were allowed to play with plasticine or gummed paper shapes, but I loved school, especially the friends I made there. Although a year younger than my classmates, I had no difficulty in keeping up with them and frequently came top in weekly tests for spelling, multiplication tables and mental arithmetic and I suppose it was during these formative years that I learnt to expect high standards and 'perfection' from myself.

Next came success in passing the 11+ examination, followed that autumn by a move to Maidstone Grammar School for Girls. In the summer term before we started at the grammar school, successful pupils all went for an interview and a look around the school, a purpose built building set amidst extensive playing fields. I could scarcely believe my eyes as we were shown the many classrooms with rows of proper wooden desks, science laboratories, a dedicated art room full of easels, paper and paint with colourful pictures on the wall and, best of all, a gymnasium with ropes, bars and other equipment. It seemed like a well-equipped, luxurious heaven to me at age eleven, coming from a school that had none of these, not even a proper classroom. I spent the summer holidays impatiently waiting to attend this wonderful place and wasn't disappointed when I started there, soon making new friends and working hard, eager to learn and to do well.

At this age, I was a well-behaved and responsive pupil and regularly had my name called out in assembly in the 'Red Honours' list. The only subject I found difficult was games, as everyone else had played netball and rounders at their primary schools, so the teacher never bothered to explain the aim of the games or the rules and I floundered for the first few weeks, being too ashamed to admit that I had no idea how to play these games. Gradually, I became more adept at netball, often practising shooting and passing with friends at break-time. At the end of the first year, I was ecstatic when I was awarded my junior gym stripe for reaching a good standard and later my senior gym stripe, only to be a little deflated by my mother's lack of enthusiasm for my success. I realised that my parents were only interested in academic achievement and I never even mentioned the coveted gym stripe to my father. Yet I was not wholly dependent on their praise and encouragement, for I valued my successful performance in subjects like gym, art, craft and my part in a school play, just for myself, without needing their approval. I was learning to be independent and to see my parents as less god-like than I had hitherto viewed them.

At school, I enjoyed most of the lessons and have many happy memories of things I learnt and achieved, especially in the first three or four years. The school rules were very strict and great care was taken to inculcate the school's values, attitudes and standards of behaviour, both in and out of school, as well as the learning of a wide range of subjects. To this day, I am very grateful that I had the benefit of this privileged education which, in many ways, was progressive for its time. We had some remarkable teachers, some of them rather eccentric but passionate about their subjects and, being all female, they provided good role models for the pupils, showing how women could achieve and pursue successful careers through the power of education. We did not all have to become 'housewives' but were encouraged to have ambition and careers in our own right.

Sadly, by the time I reached the fifth form (now year eleven), my eagerness to work hard had diminished and my behaviour deteriorated. My friends had changed, and I became part of a group of seven girls whose main interests lay outside school – pop music, records, clothes, make-up, boys – as well as breaking rules. Most of us had obtained Saturday jobs and were earning money to buy the plethora of goods that were becoming available in the shops and stores as the austerity of the post-war years was forgotten. At the age of fifteen, I started to work in Boots the Chemist on Saturdays and in school holidays. This enabled me to become the proud owner of a Dansette record player and to collect records of the latest pop songs by singers like Elvis, Billy Fury, Marty Wilde, Cliff Richard and many more. It also meant that I could choose and buy my own clothes, without having to rely on my parents and their choices.

I also began to be interested in boys in a different way. Throughout my childhood I had always played with boys as well as girls but now

I was ready for romantic involvement. My first steady boyfriend was introduced to me by a friend's brother and we were instantly attracted to each other. He was a pupil at the Boys' Technical School and was a year older than I was. After several months he left school at sixteen to join the RAF and was posted at a training establishment in Buckinghamshire. Every week he wrote me wonderful love letters using a fountain pen with violet ink and I spent more time writing to him and dreaming about him than I did on my homework. My schoolwork began to suffer but I managed to coast along without too many problems in most subjects.

It was not until our GCE 'O' level results came out that I was devastated to find that I had failed not one but two subjects. This was the first time I'd *failed* at anything. My parents were obviously shocked and disappointed and I was painfully aware that I'd gone down in their estimation, no longer their 'golden girl' who always did well at everything, particularly school work.

I had a further shock on returning to school that autumn to discuss my results with teachers, when I found that I was not being welcomed with open arms to study any subject of my choice at 'A' level. Although I had done very well, particularly in English, French, Latin and Religious Knowledge, the teachers all expressed doubts about my commitment and willingness to work hard and, above all, to behave well. I had never seriously considered leaving school at sixteen, and the fact that I might be denied the chance to study in the sixth form made me desperately want to do so. It was this realisation that made me grow up and become more mature in the matter of a few hours. It was a total mind-shift. I could see how stupid I'd been over the past year, wasting my time and the opportunities offered at this wonderful school which I'd had the privilege to attend. It was hard work to convince the teachers that I was serious about my study and wanted to do well, to gain 'A' level qualifications, so that I could go to university or teacher training college, but my good results in English and French made those two subjects possible. The third subject was more difficult, as I had no wish to study either Latin or Religious Knowledge, and my German results were not good enough. Eventually, I persuaded the History teacher to take me onto her 'A' level course, even though I had not taken History at 'O' level. Miss Parkinson had been my form teacher during the first year at the grammar school and had followed my progress through the school with interest, though she made it abundantly clear that she, too, had been disappointed in me during the past year. As most of my friends from the 'Gang of Seven' had now left school, she decided to give me a chance, which I took gratefully and worked very hard. Interestingly, History finally turned out to be my best and most enjoyed subject; it was this subject that really taught me to question, to think, to consider evidence, to draw conclusions and to make decisions and it was the subject that I was later to study at university.

So, fortunately, my education continued and I never again let my work slide or take a back seat to other interests. I continued to work on Saturdays and school holidays in Boots and later in Marks & Spencer, to have interests outside of school and to have boyfriends but I was always conscientious about my studies and did well. Two years later, it was with mixed feelings that I left the school which had been such an important and pleasurable part of my life for seven years but I was ready to move on into the next phase of my life.

Again, Dr Darius had found no traumatic events, significant failures or relationship difficulties during my school years. In spite of the brief period of difficulty and disappointment over failure with 'O' levels, I had persevered and been successful in completing my school career successfully.

Now we moved on to discuss wider relationships during my teenage years and adult life.

Up until this point, my relationships with my parents and brother were all good but, as I grew older, there were some stormy scenes with my father as I rebelled against some of the strict controls he put in place and I began to question some of his beliefs. These arguments were nearly always short-lived and generally we still had a good relationship. In the main, I accepted my parents' rules and values, even if I did not like or agree with them. I was quite lucky in some ways, as my parents did not try to interfere in my friendships, or in the clothes I wore, or my activities, as long as I came home by their deadline time of 10.30 pm and went to church on Sunday evenings. This wasn't problematic for me as, up to that point, my boyfriends had all been members of the church youth club, so we would go to church and then do whatever we wanted afterwards. Fortunately for me, no one questioned what we did after church and I was careful not to mention the details of some of these after-church activities, including going to a Jazz Club, where I adored the music, the dancing and the whole atmosphere. We heard wonderful jazz musicians like Acker Bilk, whose music, if I hear it today, immediately transports me back to those dark, hot nights in the Star Hotel Ballroom. I didn't drink alcohol there or smoke and it was all very innocent but I knew that my parents would not approve so, to avoid trouble, I kept these activities to myself. Dr Darius did not seem perturbed about the increasingly frequent but short-lived arguments which, I suppose, are common between teenagers and their parents, a normal part of growing up.

A more serious breakdown in the relationship with my parents occurred about a year after I left school. Unable to decide between two careers, I had obtained places both at university to study social science, as preparation for becoming a probation officer, and at a teacher training college. A requirement of the social science course was to have worked for a year before taking up the place and I decided to go along this route, my decision influenced partly because this would mean I could stay closer to my current boyfriend. During the summer in which I left school, I obtained a job as a clerical assistant in the Kent Probation Service head office in Maidstone, enrolled at evening classes for shorthand and typing and spent a very enjoyable and interesting year working and learning there. The relationship with my boyfriend had become serious and we would have married then if my parents had allowed it but, at that time, the age for marriage without parental consent was twenty-one and they were totally opposed to me marrying at nineteen.

After the year passed, my parents were expecting me to take up one of the places in higher education but, by then, the thought of being financially dependent on them for another three years, having to live by their rules when I was at home, as well as living miles away from my boyfriend during term-time, was not an attractive proposition to me. My refusal to go to university caused many heated arguments and a serious rift with my father but I was resolute in my decision. By this time, my boyfriend was working in London, a city that had long been one of fascination to me. So, one afternoon I took the train to Victoria Station, enrolled with an employment agency, went for two interviews that same afternoon and was offered a job at Encyclopaedia Britannica to start as soon as possible. The job was nothing special, another 'clerical assistant' post but the wages were considerably higher at London rates than I'd been earning in Maidstone, and I knew that I'd be able to manage. In the early 1960s, accommodation, like jobs, was easy to find and within a fortnight I'd moved into a flat, sharing with two other young women, and started work in my new job. My parents were upset and angry, no doubt hurt and disappointed at my decisions and my leaving home.

After several months, the atmosphere between us calmed and a relationship was re-established but the closeness that I had enjoyed, particularly with my father, was never the same again. He had been a great father when I was a child, a kind, caring man with whom my brother and I had a lot of fun. It was my father who always organised our annual summer holiday and played for hours with us on the beach, digging in the sand, fishing in rockpools and swimming in the sea, whilst my mother sat in a deckchair, reading. He was the parent who made our lives interesting; he would take us out for drives in the car, arrange days out and build swings and structures for us to play on in the garden. I can see now that my mother had very little say in anything he decided; she could not drive and she had no income of her own, so was reliant on him for money. She did what she could for us in many small ways but he was the one who really controlled everyone in the family and everything in the home. In many ways he was kind and thoughtful but he saw himself as the 'man of the house', the breadwinner, head of the family, and he liked to make all the decisions. He had strong views on what was acceptable behaviour and did not respond well to being challenged or disobeyed. I think my mother had learnt, over the years, to agree with his views and decisions, or at least not to disagree with them, in order to keep the peace. I know that she was upset when I left home but I don't know whether she agreed with him or was more upset because of the angry atmosphere in which it all happened. She didn't express an opinion or support me in any way, about which I was glad, as I would not have wanted my father to turn his wrath on her for disagreeing with him. He was never physically violent but he would lose his temper, shouting and storming, which could be very frightening and upsetting for us all. We were not used to drama, and for years had all lived in a relaxed, peaceful home, where everyone treated each other politely and with respect. Perhaps it was too polite, a place where we did not express ourselves openly, where we hid our irritations, disagreements and disappointments for the sake of 'good manners' or a quiet life and we avoided the possibility of rejection for bad behaviour. I think this is where I learnt to keep my thoughts and feelings to myself, well-hidden and never shared.

Although I didn't dwell on this episode when talking to Dr Darius, I have thought about it a great deal since. The scenes are indelibly imprinted in my mind and I think that I was much more upset by losing my closeness with my father than I realised at the time, or for many years afterwards. But living in London was very exciting; I rejoiced at my new freedoms, being able to be myself and live my own life in the way that I wanted to. I was sorry to have left home in such an unhappy way but had no regrets about my decisions.

It was the start of the 'Swinging Sixties' and I revelled in every aspect of my new life – the exotic foods, the clothes, the music and dance, the clubs, the cinema and theatre, the optimism and fun, the culture and power of young people all around me. It was an exciting time, full of hope, fun, love, promise and celebration. It seemed that life was changing for the better and I loved being a part of it all.

For about eighteen months my boyfriend and I were very happy together. We had money to spend and the freedom to do whatever we wanted in the swinging, cosmopolitan capital. We got engaged on my twentieth birthday but, sadly, our relationship deteriorated soon afterwards. By now I had changed; I no longer dreamt of settling down to a conventional married life in the suburbs. I had no wish to leave my job, to buy a house or to have children. I loved London and our life there. I still wanted to try everything new and to live life to the full but, for my boyfriend, the excitement of London life had gradually worn off. He was older than I was and more conservative. He missed a cosy home life, where his washing was done and his meals cooked for him. While he started to spend more and more weekends going home to Maidstone, I spent the time in London, going out with friends when he wasn't around. It became clear that we wanted different things from life and, some months later, we agreed to part. He returned to Maidstone to live and work there while I stayed in London. After nearly four years together, it was a great wrench. We had enjoyed a very solid, secure relationship that we both valued, being totally loyal and faithful to each other. During those four years we had been good friends as well as lovers and had developed from being teenagers to becoming young adults together, experimenting and learning about many aspects of life – love, trust, values, religion, work, home life. I think we both had regrets but could see that our parting was inevitable, mainly I suppose because I had grown to be a person in my own right, with my own ideas, no longer prepared to follow him everywhere and anywhere, with no thought of how that would affect my life. I had become aware of my own value, my strengths and potential, not just for living a fun life, although that was important to me, but for exploring new ideas and opportunities, having a career.

It was at this point that Dr Darius probed vigorously but he seemed to accept that, although it was hard to part, I had not felt unduly rejected, hurt or abandoned at the end of this important relationship, for I could genuinely see that there was no future in it for either of us, as we had both grown up into different people.

Now that I was alone for the first time in my life, without the daily support and love of parents or a steady boyfriend, I started to think again about a career. I knew that I'd become a valued employee at Encyclopaedia Britannica and had received two small promotions but it was also obvious that women did not progress very far up the career ladder there in the early 1960s. The glass ceiling, or more accurately the reinforced concrete ceiling, was very low.

For several years, I tried various jobs – civil service, police officer, probation officer – enjoying and doing well in all of them but never staying more than a couple of years. Each change of direction was made for very good reasons and I grew up a lot during these years, living in various parts of London and meeting many interesting people. Although I became much more responsible and serious, I still loved life in the city with all its opportunities for work and leisure.

Then I met the man who later became my husband, and life took off in a different direction, especially once my children were born. I was older now, ready to settle down and to become a parent, so did not resent but welcomed a move to Hampshire where my husband had obtained a good job as a design engineer.

Whilst my children were young I stayed at home to care for them. I believed strongly that this was the most important work I could do at this time. I attended an evening course on child development, which inspired me to start and run a pre-school playgroup. I also became a short-term foster parent for children who would not normally be fostered, writing reports for courts and social workers, so I kept myself very busy. These were happy years, but once my children were both at school, I decided it was time to complete my own education and do something more with my life, and so I enrolled on a B. Ed. Degree course as a full-time mature student. As a probation officer, I had studied part-time for a Diploma in Social Studies, as well as undergoing training provided by the Home Office, so studying had become part of my life again but I had to work very hard on the degree course, whilst managing a family as well. It was rewarding work and I loved this period of my life, learning so much, making new friends and satisfying a long-standing, if well-hidden, need to continue my own education.

For the next twenty years or so my family was the important thing in my life but I also managed to progress my career in various jobs involving teaching or training. In 1984 we took a family decision to move from Hampshire to a small-holding in Mid Wales to escape the growing materialism so prevalent in the south of England. Jobs for secondary history teachers were in short supply at that time but I started to work for Powys County Council as a Training and Development Officer, managing a YTS Programme in Montgomeryshire and, after eighteen months, was promoted to Senior Training Officer for the whole of Powys, a large, rural county geographically, comprised of about a quarter of the land mass of Wales, but with a sparse, scattered population.

It was a time of much change and re-organisation but I accepted the challenges and opportunities which presented themselves and enjoyed several more promotions. By now, my children had gone away to university and my husband had retired so I was free to work hard and develop my career. I also studied for an MBA degree with the Open University, having been persuaded by my manager with the promise of a day a week to study at home. A month later, this manager was made redundant in yet another re-organisation and I had to take on a new role. This needed all my time during the working week and beyond and so my OU studies were confined to weekends. The other two female students on the MBA course dropped out after a short time, which made me all the more determined to stay and I was glad that I persevered, gaining much from my studies in terms of knowledge and learning but also in self-confidence. I knew that I was as good as all the men on the course and better than some. I had discovered that my thoughts, ideas and views were well received, that I could discuss, debate, put forward convincing arguments and utilise all that I had learnt to good effect. Gaining this Master's Degree meant a lot to me and gave me the confidence to be successful in a new role as the Chief Executive of a newly formed Careers Guidance Company, under contract to the Welsh Assembly Government. The company flourished and I stayed in this job until I retired about ten years later. It was demanding work and, during that time, we had to cope with much change; there were many challenges to overcome and problems to deal with and, although I had good managers working for me, it was sometimes a lonely position to hold. There were many times when I felt stressed, yet I always managed to work through the difficulties and to support others without breaking down myself. At home, I had the support of my husband and I think that it was our relationship that helped me to survive the pressures.

After taking this extensive personal history, Dr Darius then turned to the circumstances around my depression. At first he challenged me strongly on the issue of losing my memory after the car accident. Could I really not remember or did I just not want to remember? I was quite shocked that he could even think this, but after some discussion, Dr Darius accepted that I had genuinely lost my memory and he concluded that it was an unconscious defence to protect my brain and body. He explained that people react to serious stress in one of two ways; either they consciously keep remembering and re-living the stressful occurrence, which is known as Post Traumatic Stress Disorder or, as in my case, they unconsciously forget it. They may never remember it at all because the short term memory does not transfer the event to the long term memory, so it is never processed and consequently disappears as a memory.

We then moved on to the most disturbing part of the session as Dr Darius began to talk about my personality. He had obviously listened intently to all that I had told him and had come to some conclusions about my personality and the important part that it had played in my breakdown. I was shocked at some of his perceptions about me and I disagreed with him quite strongly in a number of respects. I was also surprised and shocked at how vehemently I disputed them. It was the first time for months that I had felt very strongly about anything in a rational, reasoned way. Until then, I had just been responding emotionally to everything and had been very passive in my thinking. Now I was on fire! He perceived me as a high achiever but also as a worrier who had high anxiety levels and a perfectionist who sets high standards and likes everything to be tidy and in order. He thought I was obsessive about being in control, and inflexible in my attitudes and expectations. I found all this to be an extreme exaggeration of who I was and was most uncomfortable about these labels.

Dr Darius was the only person who really probed in any depth about the potential suicide event – what had led up to it, how I had felt, what I was intending and why I had not gone through with it. I told him that my main reason for walking away from the river at the last moment was because I hadn't left any letters or explanation for my family but he challenged this explanation vigorously, dismissing my explanation as not being the true reason at all. He was convinced that the real reason was that, by the time it came to committing the act, I was no longer feeling completely *hope-less*. The calm of the night and the beauty of the world I could see around me had given me the *glimmer of hope* that saved me from self-destruction. It was *hope* that was needed for me to want to survive and to get better. I have thought a great deal about this since and I, too, am convinced that the bottom of the pit of depression is the complete absence of hope. It is an emotion one has to feel, to experience, not something that can be acquired by reasoned argument or logic. You can know that you ought to have hope but unless you can feel it, it means nothing.

We went on to talk a lot about the months leading up to the incident. Dr Darius stressed that I had been over-involved with my daughter's affairs and problems and this had contributed to my depression. He thought that, after months of intense involvement and hard work, I was unable to say, 'I can't do this any more'. Being a 'perfectionist' and needing to be in control of everything would not allow me to admit that I needed a break, that I couldn't cope with such levels any longer, and that the depression which had caused me to go to my GP was me saying 'I want someone to look after me now'.

He assured me that this is what would happen; he and his team would look after me and he was very sure that, with treatment and time, they could return me to my 'strong, stubborn and involved self' again. The first step would be to increase the dose of Sertraline from 50 to 100mg. immediately, then to 150mg. in a fortnight and possibly to 200mg. later. If necessary, they would add lithium to stabilise my moods. He explained the reason for the big increase was that the dose I was on currently was very low and he went on to stress that I must not, under any circumstances, come off the anti-depressants myself, like I had done with the Citalopram.

The thought of taking these high levels of medication horrified me but I kept my thoughts to myself, feeling that I'd disagreed and challenged him enough and also, by this time, I was feeling quite exhausted, though stimulated at the same time. Finally, Dr Darius told me that he'd been very worried when he received the referral from Dr Alice but now that he'd met me, he was confident that he and his team could help. In spite of my current difficulties, I was still a strong achiever underneath and, as people don't change fundamentally, he was sure that I would achieve recovery.

Dr Darius then told me that Ellie, the CPN who had been present throughout this session, would see me regularly to support me now and that I should cease my counselling sessions with Caden. The thought of immediately ceasing the counselling with Caden was very distressing. I needed to see him again to talk through this interview, what was happening, and could not just end our relationship abruptly. To his credit and my relief, Dr Darius agreed that I should keep my pre-arranged appointment the following week to tie things up positively with Caden. I suppose I could have just gone to see Caden anyway but, after the huge amount of frank and honest exchanges between us during this interview, I was glad to have Dr Darius's agreement and permission.

On the way home, I became very emotional, tearful and deeply upset at some of the aspects he saw in me, which I disputed and saw as an attack on my character. The high achiever part I could cope with but the thought of being perceived as obsessive, stubborn, controlling and rigid was difficult. This picture of an obsessive perfectionist and control freak, who got over-involved in other people's problems and affairs, an anxious worrier with rigid thinking, was greatly at odds with how I saw myself. I knew that I set high standards for myself, that I liked to achieve to the best of my potential; I liked to plan and put all my effort into achieving what I set out to do, but I thought I was tolerant and flexible in what I expected of others around me. I did not always expect perfection and, over the years, had learnt to accept second best in many unimportant things. I wasn't sure where the idea of my being 'stubborn' came from – perhaps my deciding not to take the Citalopram any more. I desperately wanted to talk to Caden and ask him how he perceived my personality to compare it with Dr Darius' perceptions.

My mixed feelings haunted me for the rest of the day. I felt huge relief that someone (Dr Darius) was taking definite action and that he was so positive and optimistic but I was still upset and became quite angry at some of the things he'd said to me. I went to collect the new prescription from Boots, where I encountered some difficulty getting the new anti-depressants, as they couldn't read Dr Darius's writing! Eventually it was sorted out but I decided (stubbornly?) not to take one that evening. I wasn't sure what effect the increased dose might have, especially drowsiness, and I was going to have to drive to the theatre some miles away the following day, as I was taking my friend, Margaret, who had had a minor accident in her car earlier in the week and her car was being repaired. We went to see a satellite viewing of Richard II, which was an excellent production, but I managed to fall asleep briefly during the play, even without taking the higher dose of Sertraline.

Chapter Ten
RECLAMATION

The next evening, I took the first of the new higher dose tablets and felt very sick in the night, though it may not have been those that caused it, as the following day I was very unwell with my deaf ear, sore throat and swollen glands.

On Monday morning, I dosed myself with Paracetamol and went to the U3A Christmas lecture and lunch which I enjoyed and it all went very well, even our recorder playing as part of the entertainment! Over lunch, a few of us became enthusiastic about starting a 'Singing round the Piano' group; this would not be a choir but just a group who would sing for pleasure. Very quickly, we managed to enthuse enough members to start the group, as well as a good pianist who agreed to accompany us and offered his home for a meeting place. It was all very exciting! I was surprised and pleased that I'd had the confidence to volunteer to organise the group for the first meeting in the New Year.

On Tuesday, we had Book Group, which also went very well and I had no difficulty in contributing to the discussion this time. I even recruited another interested member to join the new singing group. The evening was not so good. I was agitated and apprehensive about seeing Caden the following day and very upset that this would be the last session with him. He had been such a source of support and it was he who had given me back some of my old self. I didn't want to lose this relationship now that I had finally opened up to him and trusted him. I wasn't sure that I could manage without him.

Wednesday 11 December

Our session went well. Caden was very encouraging; he thought I looked much better and had regained some of my old self back and he understood about the argument for not seeing two support workers. He knew the CPN, Ellie, and described her as 'lovely'. We discussed some of Dr Darius's perceptions of me and Caden managed to put what I'd perceived as criticisms into a more positive light, which helped. He suggested replacing 'stubborn' with 'determined', which I found much more acceptable and he explained the 'perfectionist' part was what I demanded of myself, not necessarily of others. I knew that I would miss Caden enormously, as I was able to talk to him so easily and he was always very perceptive and quick to understand where I was coming from. But to my delight and relief, he suggested that we meet once more after Christmas, not for an in-depth counselling session but just to see how I was, how I'd got on during the festive period, which he warned me I might find difficult. It meant a lot to me that he wasn't prepared to abandon me to my new support workers overnight.

That afternoon, I met with Margaret. We had arranged to meet at her church to decorate the font with fir branches and a nativity scene, ready for the carol service. Cefn Llys Church is a lovely old church in a beautiful setting at the foot of Cefn Llys Castle, accessed only on foot across several fields. The carol service is held by candlelight as there is no electricity and it is very atmospheric. I have always loved carol services and was pleased to help Margaret with this task as part of preparation for Christmas. After we finished, we had a good walk by the river. By this time I was able to talk about Dr Darius's perceptions of me without getting too upset and Margaret, like Caden, made me see them in a more balanced way. We even ended up laughing together about some of the things he had said. It was so good to have a reliable, trustworthy friend, who knew me well, with whom I could talk things through, as well as the 'professionals'. I was finding that the more I talked about my anxieties and fears, the less awful they felt and this was a deeply important lesson for me, as someone who was used to keeping such feelings well hidden, deep inside myself.

But my troubles were not yet over. That evening, new anxieties and more depression took over. I was due to meet with the CPN, Ellie, the following afternoon for our first session, so maybe it was apprehension but I had a dreadful night and was very trembly and uptight all the next morning, so much so that I couldn't hide it from Don, who was very concerned.

The session turned out to be rather flat and disappointing, which was probably my fault as I found it difficult to talk about anything significant. Even though I'd met Ellie before, during the session with Dr Darius, I just didn't have the energy or motivation to start again with someone new. Unlike Caden, Ellie didn't push me. She was patient, very pleasant and seemed kind, caring, willing to talk and help, but I couldn't respond so I didn't get anything out of the session and came away feeling a sense of failure. She said she would be talking to Dr Darius at their team meeting the following week about increasing the Sertraline to 150 mg. over Christmas and we left it at that.

Over the next few days, however, I began to feel better and better. I was keeping busy and everything seemed to be going well as I went out and about, not overdoing it but enjoying meeting people I knew, getting pleasure out of small achievements and taking part in activities such as decorating the U3A Christmas tree in the local church, in readiness for the Christmas Tree Festival. Several more people showed an interest in joining the proposed Singing for Fun Group and we set a date for the inaugural meeting early in January. My recorder group had been invited to play at an Epiphany Carol Service in a very ancient, small local church in January which was something else to look forward to.

At the weekend, I felt so good that I couldn't believe it, as it had rained most of the day and I hadn't done anything special or nice. In fact, I'd got soaked in the rain when going for a walk to take some leaflets about U3A to put by our Christmas tree in the church. I recorded in my diary, 'Felt really good today and even enjoyed all of the semi-finals of *Strictly Come Dancing*.' This was very significant as, although in previous years, I'd been addicted to *Strictly*, looking forward to every episode, this year I'd found it all very unimportant, irrelevant and boring. I hadn't engaged with it at all, so now it seemed remarkable that not only did I watch it but was capable of enjoying it!

My daughter had phoned and she expressed how much she was looking forward to me going there on Boxing Day. Don had said he wouldn't come but he wouldn't mind if I stayed there two nights. So that was something else to look forward to. Another diary entry for Sunday reads: 'Felt on top of the world all day! If this continues maybe I should not increase Sertraline any more.'

This feeling good lasted over the next few days and I so enjoyed enjoying life again! Every small detail seemed wonderful, the bright winter sunshine which appeared one day out of the gloom, the compliments we received from playing recorders at the Christmas Tree Festival, the receiving of cards from old friends and even my Christmas shopping.

Later that week, I went to see my GP. I told her that everything was going well and I asked her whether I could go back to seeing her on a regular basis instead of the Mental Health team. She was willing but said I should discuss it with Ellie first and wait until after Christmas and New Year before making any decisions. She knew I was seeing Caden once more in January and asked me to come to see her as well.

Filled with energy and optimism, I threw myself into preparing for Christmas – cleaning the house from top to bottom, cooking, delivering cards locally and finishing my shopping online – and enjoying everything I did, as if I'd been given a new lease of life. I know that many people are not lifted out of their depression by anti-depressants and certainly my experience with Citalopram had been awful but this time it was like a miracle and I was full of celebration.

Looking back now, I think it may have been something to do with the timing. I had worked hard with my counsellors over the past two months and given myself time to rest and recover from the initial shock. Perhaps, even more importantly, this time I'd also given the Sertraline time to do its job whereas before I had stopped taking the tablets after only three weeks.

At the end of the week, after a beautiful mild, sunny morning it clouded over and much to everyone's surprise, it started to snow hard and fast that afternoon, so much so that I avoided taking the car out. I had an appointment with Ellie at half past three and walked there, struggling through a blizzard. We had a friendly chat and I was more relaxed with her this time. I managed to put my request to her that I should be transferred back to the care of my GP and she seemed to understand my feelings and to understand why I was making this request. She also agreed with me that, although Dr Darius had intended to increase my dose of Sertraline to 150 mg. over Christmas, as I was feeling so much better, there was no need to do this at present. She offered to talk to Dr Darius the following week and would write to me about his decision, though she thought he may well want to see me again before agreeing to my release.

Having sorted that out, I entered into the spirit of Christmas festivities with relish. Don, who had never been an enthusiast for Christmas, started to join in. Instead of buying a Christmas tree, I had gathered some fir branches which I put into a large pot and which he helped me decorate with shiny baubles, and to sort out the fairy lights. The house was clean and gleaming with vases of holly, ivy and evergreen in all the rooms and Christmas cards all around, making friends and family seem close. I was so pleased that it all seemed to give Don a lot of pleasure too and we both became much more relaxed and positive. Neither of us had any religious beliefs at this time but this didn't stop me from going to every carol service I could find in the locality. I did a lot of singing everywhere, including at home, with Don joining in when he knew the words of those lovely old carols. Everything seemed especially wonderful, particularly joining in the various Christmas activities with all my friends without feeling any anxiety or apprehension.

My downfall came after I went to Carols Around the Tree at our neighbouring village on Sunday evening, a clear but very cold night. I loved the beautiful moon shining down calmly, high above us and the twinkling stars shining so brightly in the crisp, cold air. There seemed to be something special about joining with others to sing together outside on this night so close to Christmas. The experience was so far removed from the gaudy glitter and frantic spending in the shops and the commercial side of the celebration.

Sadly, although I felt good at the time and my mind was having a ball, my body was not so thrilled. I became very chilled and was glad to get home in the warm. By the next morning I had a sore throat and headache and knew I was sickening for something. I tried hard to keep motivated and carried on with the final preparations, making sure that all was ready for a lovely Christmas Eve and Christmas Day.

Ever since our children were very young, we'd always started our celebrations on Christmas Eve. Everything would be ready, so that we could enjoy the Carols from Kings in the late afternoon, followed by a special meal, often joined by friends. I wanted this year to be no exception and, although I'd not felt up to inviting friends this year, we both enjoyed the day together, appreciating the food which I'd prepared and relaxing over a drink, my first alcohol for months.

When I started on the anti-depressants back in September, I'd followed the instructions that accompanied them very seriously and had avoided alcohol ever since. When I saw Ellie the previous week I'd asked her about having a drink or two as it was Christmas and she'd been very clear in warning me that alcohol is a depressant itself so I should be very careful to limit any drinking, especially as this could also lessen the effect of the anti-depressant drugs. Now I took her advice seriously and mixed my cinzano with loads of ice and lemon and, even though I could hear her words in my head, I must admit I enjoyed it enormously. Perhaps there was even an added enjoyment of it being almost a 'forbidden fruit'.

However, with Ellie being present in my head, like a spectre at the feast, I was not so stupid or reckless as to have more than one drink. It made me think of her and I wondered whether she had managed to see Dr Darius and whether he'd agreed to my request. I realised then that I did like Ellie; she had been very kind to me and I thought she would be a good source of support if and when I needed it in the future. I wished that I could continue seeing both Ellie and Caden for, in spite of feeling so much better, I was aware that I was still very vulnerable.

On Christmas Day it snowed again. By this time I wasn't feeling at all well, with my sore throat and a very fuzzy head (not caused by the alcohol!) but I managed to cook a baked gammon with orange glaze and all the trimmings. This was Don's favourite and I had decided to cook this meal for us on Christmas Day, as I would be enjoying a roast turkey dinner with my daughter on Boxing Day. Feeling better after lunch, in the afternoon I packed the car all ready for the morning with presents, food and my overnight bag.

I spoke to my daughter and to my son on the phone and they were both looking forward to us all meeting for a family celebration the following day, so I settled down to watch some of my favourite programmes on television. But soon I was feeling so ill that I had to abandon that and put myself to bed early, hoping I would feel better in the morning.

That was not to be. I felt dreadful. My throat was the worst it had ever been since I had quinsy when I was about twenty, and I was fearful that I was in for a really bad time. I told Don that I wouldn't be going and phoned my daughter to explain, then dozed in a dream-like world all morning and most of the afternoon, just finding the energy to make a gammon sandwich for us both about 3.00 pm. I tried to get up and watch television for a while in the evening but was still feeling too ill to concentrate. At this point, I was relieved that, in spite of the physical illness, I was keeping well mentally. The Sertraline seemed to be doing a good job and I found I was much less angry with Dr Darius now, recognising that in many ways he was probably right in his assessment of me.

The next few days passed somehow. I managed to feed myself and Don but did little else, feeling physically awful all the time and in floods of tears every evening, desperate to get better and longing for 'someone to look after me' but realising this was not going to happen. By New Year's Eve I was physically quite a bit better but my depression had worsened. For some years I had found the New Year a depressing time, though I'd never experienced true depression before. I struggled to do what was needed... shopping, washing, cooking and so on but was exhausted and tearful all the time, so much so that Don even noticed that I looked awful and asked what was the matter. I was totally unable to express to him how I was feeling and he found this very frustrating and hurtful so he became annoyed, which made things much worse. I was also upset and worried about my daughter, as I discovered that she had got up early on Sunday morning and gone off to Kent without telling me.

I was so low that I really could not face starting out on another year but had no energy at all actually to do anything about it. I felt an utterly complete mess once more, and somehow this seemed even worse after thinking and hoping that I may be getting better only a week or so earlier. My exhaustion and depression continued over the next few days but on New Year's Day, Don's niece telephoned to say that her mother, Don's twin sister, had died the previous evening. Don was very shocked and agitated at this news. It really hit him hard, so I was taken out of myself by having to talk to him, to comfort him, to try to get him to calm down and relax, which we eventually managed by the evening. His brother had died a few years earlier and his parents had been dead for some years, so now he was feeling the loneliness of being the only survivor of those generations of his family. We spent many hours talking about his past, especially the times he had spent with his sister, and looking at old family photos, and I managed to get him to talk to his niece again on the phone. I offered to drive us to the funeral in Essex but we decided in the end that it was too long a journey, especially given the dreadful winter weather we were experiencing and that I was still not very well.

It was not until about a week later that things began to improve. Don had recovered from the shock of his sister's death and I began to feel better both physically and mentally. On Sunday 5 January our recorder group played at the Epiphany Carol Service. The tiny church had no electricity, water or toilets and remained very much as it had been when it was built centuries ago but was beautifully decorated with evergreens and holly and lit with candles, which gave a magical feel. The church orchestra took up all the space at the front, so our recorder group all had to squeeze together into a family box-pew, very intimate and cosy! The service was very atmospheric and beautiful and we sang and played some lovely carols on this last day of Christmas. We all joined together afterwards for refreshments and for me this was the highlight of my Christmas, as I'd only just managed to survive through the earlier celebrations.

In spite of dire warnings from leaders of a local choir about the perils of starting our Singing for Fun group as planned, there were enough of us prepared to take the risk and give it a go, so I spent the next few days finding out as much as I could from other U3A singing groups in different parts of the country and preparing for our first meeting on 8 January. It all went very well, with fourteen people attending. After deciding together what sort of a group we wanted it to be, how often we would meet and other practicalities, we sang some old, well-known songs from a community song book, singing around our accompanist's grand piano, and we certainly had great fun! We all came away smiling and in good spirits. I found it difficult to sleep that night, with my brain still reeling, but was very relieved that it had gone well and felt a great sense of achievement, perhaps particularly because we had carried on in spite of the warnings not to go there! I had always been someone who, if told that I couldn't do something, was all the more determined to do it and here was the 'old me' back in action again. No wonder the psychiatrist had labelled me as 'stubborn'!

Becoming the leader of this group gave me a new focus in my life, something very positive and about which I was very enthusiastic. I'd never intended to run the group myself, just to get it off the ground with the hope that a more musical person would agree to act as musical director. I knew that organising was one of my strengths and I was able to use that to ensure we got off to a good start. The singing itself – we continued to sing mainly songs from an old Community Songbook with which we were all familiar from our younger days, even though we hadn't sung them for years – was in itself a mood-enhancing activity but it was the camaraderie and goodwill from everyone to make the group a success that really made it very special. After every session we all came away singing and laughing. I can certainly recommend joining a singing group or choir as a helpful activity to lift depression.

In spite of my dread of the New Year, I think it was a turning point in my depression. It was not just one thing but a number of things combined that made me feel better. First, there was no doubt that the Sertraline tablets were having a beneficial effect. After I recovered from my physical illness, I found that I was sleeping much better and that was a major factor in how I was able to cope with everything on a day to day basis. No more lying awake in the early hours of each morning, with things seeming more and more impossible. If I did wake, I felt strangely warm, comfortable and relaxed and was able to go back to sleep very quickly. I became aware that lack of sleep, good quality sleep, for me is a dangerous situation and one which I learned to recognise as imperative.

Second, Dr Darius had agreed to release me back to my GP for ongoing care, which meant I was able to continue to see my counsellor, Caden, a few more times. I felt pleased that Dr Darius had trusted my judgement enough to agree to my request. This made me feel as if another small piece of my personality had been pulled back through the weeds and currents and fixed back onto the shattered wreck, albeit precariously.

Third, of course, was the successful start of the Singing For Fun Group. As well as the singing itself, which made us all feel good, there was the blossoming friendship, the shared interest and pleasure of all those involved and the feeling of harmony as we all worked and sang together, which somehow produced something much more than just the sum of the individuals' efforts. I knew I was not really fit to be the 'musical director' of the group and had no ability to teach people to sing but somehow this didn't seem to matter very much to the group and therefore not to me. We weren't intending to be a choir or to give performances; the singing was just something we enjoyed doing together and the group recognised and appreciated my organising skills, which made me feel valued again.

And finally, the cherry on the cake was the fact that I could go on seeing my counsellor, Caden, for a while. I kept the appointment on 8 January that we had made before Christmas. He called me into his room about ten minutes early and so we had a long session, which he seemed in no hurry to end early. He hadn't heard that I'd been discharged from the secondary mental health team, so I had to explain how I'd requested it and he was surprised that it had happened so quickly. We went back over everything that had happened and explored how I felt about things now. I told him about my fear now of coming off the Sertraline tablets in the future and also how I might have changed because of my experiences with depression. He pointed out that the experiences may not all prove to be bad; I may feel richer in the future for having had them and come through them positively.

Caden recognised that I was much stronger but was concerned that I might need to talk through my feelings as I was growing and developing into the 'new me' and suggested we continue the counselling sessions for a while but reduce them to once a month. This seemed to me like a good plan. Although my wreck was rebuilding itself rapidly, Caden was still acting as my anchor, to prevent any further damage if further storms should arise.

Life continued as usual but without major mishap over the next few weeks. The Singing Group proved extremely popular and continued to grow in numbers, with everyone enjoying the sessions. I continued to meet with my friend Margaret every week for a walk and a sharing of confidences, which she seemed to appreciate as much as I did. I'd come to realise that if you open up to people they don't see you as weak and pathetic but as human, fallible like themselves. They will share their fears, anxieties and troubles with you and this makes you feel as if you are helping them, by listening, as they have helped you.

I found that I was now enjoying reading fiction again and was able to join in discussions at Book Group with enthusiasm and interest. Recorder Group was hard work but I was keeping up and persevering to overcome the challenge of new and difficult (for me) pieces. The group had a lovely evening out for a meal together at a Greek Evening in a local bistro. I was managing social contact, not just with individuals now but in groups of twelve or more people, so this was very encouraging progress.

During these weeks in January, I spent a lot of time with Don, talking about his sister, Mavis. We had decided that he was not up to travelling all across England to the funeral, but it seemed to help him come to terms with her death just remembering and thinking about all the years they spent together. He worked through a lot of feelings – those that I came to know later as a normal pattern of feelings in someone who is grieving. He wasn't happy but we were communicating well and not arguing, so all was peaceful and stress free.

By now, I knew the value of exercise and, particularly, of walking, so I was conscientious about getting out for a walk on most days and also, with some reluctance, returned to swimming after a five week break. Margaret and I continued our weekly afternoon walks in spite of getting drenched and muddy on occasion, and I'm convinced that both the walking and the talking were crucial in my continued recovery at this time. I shall always be grateful to her for her company on these occasions.

There were a few minor dips in mood, when things didn't go well, and I was very conscious of these, always fearing the worst and realising how vulnerable I still was. Usually, they didn't last long and I could overcome or prevent them by making sure I got a good night's sleep and a walk in the fresh air and rain.

In spite of these actions, I can see now, looking back, that my anxiety levels were creeping up and this was having an insidious effect. One of my major concerns was about Don's state of mind, precipitated by an incident with a dish of apple and blackberry that he had noticed in the fridge. It happened on a Sunday morning as I was preparing the weekly roast for lunch. He came into the kitchen and asked me what we were having and I told him it was roast pork. He then went on and on asking the same question, 'But what are those black things?' and I had no idea what he meant. Even showing him the joint of pork, ready for roasting in the oven, didn't help to dispel his obvious anxiety. He couldn't explain or show me what he meant. Then, when I looked in the fridge, it all became clear, as I saw the dish of apple and blackberry defrosting with which I was going to make a crumble. The black things were the blackberries, in amongst the apple, and they were in a dish that I often used to roast a joint, which is why Don was so confused. We cleared the matter up then but it made me realise that his mental capacity was significantly deteriorating and that the dementia had moved on from just being difficulties with remembering names, places, words, to a more serious cognitive dysfunction.

Another event that had made me anxious and then feel low was a visit to a singing group in a nearby town, run by a very accomplished musician, who both played the piano and was a confident singer and teacher. What she achieved with her group was impressive and inspiring and she agreed to come to visit our group to share some of her experience and expertise. Whilst I was delighted at this opportunity, it wasn't long before I began to worry about inviting her. I knew that I did not have her talents, so would never be able to follow in her footsteps and was worried that, after a session with her, our members might become dissatisfied and leave our group. This was, of course, the 'perfectionist' part of me rearing its head and wanting to achieve greater things than were possible.

In fact, I needn't have worried and agonised over this, as the visit never actually transpired due to the winter weather and, even if it had, I know now that, whilst our members would have enjoyed a session with this musician, they were quite content to continue as we had started and didn't share my perfectionist ambitions and ideals. I didn't see this at the time and experienced several broken sleeps at night, which didn't help my state of mind.

The final worry was that I had become aware of my legs becoming very jumpy and shaky. This was very different from the jumpiness and starting at sudden noises that I'd experienced during the early weeks of my illness. It affected both legs but mainly the left one and was confined to the bottom half of my leg and my foot, which would start shaking uncontrollably at intervals. Any minor stressful thought or feeling could set it off, or sometimes it would also start for no obvious reason.

I made an appointment to see Dr Alice about this and asked her if it might be a side effect of the Sertraline, now that I was on a higher dose. She agreed and suggested reducing the dose from 100 to 75 mg. I was reluctant to do this and risk losing all the benefits that I'd enjoyed, so we agreed that I would see her again in a month, or sooner if it became worse. I struggled on with the symptoms for a month, becoming very frustrated at times when my leg refused to be still and I became very jumpy altogether at any sort of stress. By now, though, I could tell the difference between feeling fed up or miserable and being 'depressed', a very different state, so I was thankful for that.

My counselling sessions with Caden continued to be positive and helpful and I learnt from him the importance of not expecting to feel good all the time. He was his usual patient, understanding and kind self but he more or less told me to 'get real'. Like everyone else, there would be times when I would feel sad, fed up, angry, hurt – and this is a normal part of life. It does not mean you are becoming depressed. It is important to let yourself feel these emotions, not to block them off, but just accept them. To expect to live without such feelings was not real life and it is necessary to accept that you will feel these unpleasant emotions from time to time, knowing that they will not last and do not presage a major breakdown.

Although I tried hard, it was still difficult to cope with my emotions, which sometimes overwhelmed me. I wasn't particularly happy or sad or angry, just full of emotion, which made me tearful but I tried to let it all wash over me and not to worry that I was heading for another breakdown. This fear of going back into depression was so strong that it was very hard to overcome it.

I was no longer looking for ways of committing suicide but was interested in finding out more about suicide and suicidal intentions, so that I could gain some understanding of what had happened to me. It was around this time that I discovered a report by the organisation *Sane,* which had carried out some interesting research into suicide, funded by the Lottery and the James Wentworth-Stanley Memorial Fund. I was truly amazed at how closely my experiences seemed to fit with the findings described in the report and it helped me greatly to understand more about why and how I had succumbed to depression. It took away a lot of the mystery; I felt less strange, weird and less alone, knowing that many other people had been along a very similar path. The study used a qualitative method called 'grounded theory' believing that 'quantifiable risk factors are never sufficient as reasons for suicide; focusing on them renders suicide impossible to understand.' The findings identified three contributing factors to the process of suicide; lack of worth, lack of trust and suicidal exhaustion. The report explains each of these in detail and is well worth reading in its own right. Here, I will simply pull out some of the ways in which I identified with these three factors.

People who are suicidal have difficulty in maintaining feelings of worth which is fundamental to satisfaction and joy in who we are and what we do. In my case, after the car accident, I was unable to continue in my role of helping my daughter and her family. I felt I had failed her and also found it difficult, sometimes impossible, to carry on in other roles. I could just about care for my husband but everything was a great effort; nothing was done to my usual standard. I had been unable to drive for a while and I could not participate in the activities that I normally valued and which gave me pleasure – things like reading, playing the recorder, socialising. I felt a failure, ashamed and guilty.

Lack of trust – for many years my husband had been the person whom I trusted, with whom I would share my feelings, worries, anxieties and together we would solve problems but, over the past year or more, I had gradually lost that trust, as his health had deteriorated. He was no longer the person he had been, often in pain or discomfort from various physical ailments and more recently had shown significant cognitive decline. I realised that I had gradually ceased sharing my thoughts and concerns with him and would often go to considerable lengths to hide them from him, not wanting to burden him with more issues. Also, he had become more emotionally volatile and I could no longer be sure how he would cope with problems or difficulties; if he became upset, angry or despondent about them, I would have the additional task of coping with his reactions and states of mind, as well as dealing with the problem itself. So, for his protection and for my own, I had shared less and less with him. As far as trusting other people, I had never been someone who talked very much with friends or family about my feelings or problems, preferring to be independent, in control and to deal with them myself. I was used to listening, helping and supporting other people, not needing them to support me. All of a sudden everything changed. I was clearly unable to cope any longer; I had lost my confidence and motivation and felt that the person I'd always been was now a wreck. Suicide seemed a good way out for me to find peace and to relieve others of any possible burden of caring for me.

Suicidal exhaustion – the previous six months of trying to care for two families and two homes, travelling up and down, had been physically and mentally demanding. I rushed from one place to the next, working hard to maintain high standards in each, with never any time to think of my own needs. Then, being involved in the car accident was the final straw that brought me down. The lack of worth and the lack of trust that had been building up and had taken over in my life had contributed to my exhaustion. Now everything required great effort. I had only continued to carry out everyday tasks and activities by forcing myself to do them and had used up emotional energy in trying to hide my difficulties, trying to give the impression that everything was alright, that I was still in control. My sleep had become disrupted and poor in quality, contributing further to mental exhaustion. The suicidal exhaustion had robbed me of hope. I could not see a brighter future or commit to further effort. I no longer trusted myself and felt my inner-self had been shattered. I was no use to anyone any more and my family would be better off without this damaged wreck who had no value and would just become a burden on them. So suicide seemed something beneficial for everyone.

This research had a great impact on me and helped me to understand how I had been brought so low on this occasion. I was still mystified at why I had suddenly chosen to go out in the middle of the night with the intention of drowning myself, with no thought of putting into action my carefully prepared plan, but at least it had given me an insight into the process of how and why suicidal intentions develop and an awareness of danger signs for the future.

A few weeks later, I was shocked to learn that one of my managers in a previous job had committed suicide by drowning in a lake. I had known him well and this disturbing news affected me profoundly. He had always seemed such a confident, able person and I knew also that he, like me, was a good swimmer. The fact that he, too, had chosen drowning as his method of suicide, so like my own circumstance of a few months back, hit me like a sledge hammer. It was very much a feeling of 'There, but for the grace of God, go I.' Knowing the state of mind he must have been in to take this desperate action made me very sad and sorry that he had found no-one to help him.

It also made me realise how far I had come in recovery. Even though I was still jumpy, easily made anxious, very emotional and sometimes lacking in confidence, I knew that I was no longer badly depressed and I was getting my life back to normal, engaging in activities and gaining enjoyment from them.

Chapter Eleven
GETTING STRONGER?

Life continued much as normal for the next couple of weeks. I was still very jumpy at sudden noises, particularly noticeable when I went to the theatre, and I had some up and down mood swings, becoming very emotional at times. I tried to remember what Caden had said, 'Don't try to block your emotions and you will feel richer for experiencing them,' but I wasn't too impressed with this idea as a solution, as it continued to make life difficult and painful.

Several incidents with Don had been difficult and it was obvious that he was deteriorating but he still refused to see a doctor or do anything about his memory problems. This was a continual worry to me but there seemed little I could do without his agreement. I was very upset on one occasion, shaking uncontrollably again and in tears.

February came and I went for my counselling session with Caden, where I was so glad to be able to unload my worries and concerns. He was his usual kind, patient and reassuring self, listening carefully to everything I told him, and making me see that it was quite reasonable for me to have been upset and hurt by Don, even though I knew it was not deliberate but an effect of his deteriorating mental state. I found that I was even able to tell Caden about seeing a black cloud coming to descend on me from the right. We talked for a long while about perceiving things that aren't physically there and I was reassured that what I'd experienced was different from hallucinations in psychosis.

Once again, we talked about emotions and the importance of

accepting them for what they are and not expecting to be 'happy' all the time, however nice that might seem, because it's not reality. I was in tune with what he was saying and accepted the importance of living with them, that it is legitimate and normal to be upset at times and does not herald the return of depression.

In view of my 'wobble', Caden asked to see me again in three weeks' time. As usual, I left the session feeling much lighter, very relieved and that I was really beginning to come to terms with everything now. With Caden's help my structure was holding fast, in spite of the winds and waves, and I felt very positive about the future, even though I recognised that Don and I were going to face some difficult times.

The Singing Group was going well, building from strength to strength; my recorder playing was back to normal and we were practising for a concert towards the end of March. I was also feeling confident enough to make some enquiries about volunteering in a local primary school to help children with their reading. I was keen to do something for others in gratitude for all the help I had received during my difficult time and so, having been a teacher at one time, I thought this would be something I could do well.

The other important thing Caden had told me about at this stage was 'Mindfulness' and how it could be useful. I was very interested and went away to look up more about it on the internet. Having found a good website, I listened to some online sessions which were very relaxing, almost hypnotic, and seemed to make a difference to my jumpiness. I was totally hooked and sent off for an eight-week course in the form of a CD and a book by Dr Mark Williams of Oxford University, and was not disappointed when they arrived. I started to work through the sessions each week, finding them of great interest and help. Dr Williams has the most wonderful voice, calm and thoughtful, which relaxed me and made listening to and participating in the sessions such a pleasure. It seemed as if he was there in the room with me and he seemed to have all the qualities that I'd found so helpful in Caden. I was ecstatic at having discovered this new way of looking at myself and the world and from this time on, over the following months and years, practising Mindfulness helped me to cope and proved to be a very important tool in my recovery.

Throughout February we endured rain, floods, gales, snow, hail and numerous power cuts. I kept walking whenever the weather eased a little and was very mindful when we actually had a beautiful day with blue sky and sunshine. Don was suffering a lot of physical pain with arthritis but was fit enough to have a visit from my son, daughter and grandchildren. Everyone noticed how bad his memory was when we played charades and he couldn't remember the names of anything but we had a good time and Don enjoyed their visit and seemed much more cheerful.

At the end of February, I went again to see Caden and as usual had a good session, talking about emotions again. I told him how sometimes I felt so full of emotion – not necessarily sad or angry or happy, just so emotional that I wanted to scream or shout, and felt as if I would burst. He asked how I coped with it and I told him that I sometimes would bite my arms. Doing this had made me understand, for the first time ever, why people cut themselves. I assured him that I hadn't cut myself, or even wanted to, but I could understand the release it might bring. Fortunately, due to the Mindfulness programme, I was now coping by breathing exercises and thanked him for introducing me to that.

All went well during the session but, at the end, Caden told me that these sessions were due to come to an end in March. This was devastating news and I felt myself sinking to the bottom of the sea, though I managed to hide it from Caden. In spite of learning to be more honest and open about my feelings, I couldn't bring myself to admit during the session how much I would miss his support. Even when he asked me how I felt about this, I muttered something about realising the sessions couldn't go on for ever, hiding my true feelings away, instead of admitting them in front of him. I can see now that I had reverted to behaviour that I'd always employed to hide my hurt or rejection; no tears, no expressions of feeling bereft or hurt in front of anyone else. I had always been secretive whenever I was hurt, only releasing feelings when I was alone in private, so in some ways this wasn't surprising but, considering all the honest talking and sharing we had done over the past few months, it was strange that I couldn't have been honest with Caden but there it was, the old patterns were still lurking even in the 'new me'.

The tears and emotions came soon enough once I left the surgery and they kept returning at times throughout the rest of the day and evening. I knew I was going to find it extremely hard. Caden had been my anchor for the past six months and sometimes it was only his support that had kept me going – the knowledge that I would be able to discuss any problems with him for an uninterrupted hour on a regular basis. My friends were wonderful at listening to me and I'm sure my family would have helped if I had told them more about what I was going through but it was the professional relationship with Caden that gave me licence to talk freely about anything, in complete confidence and without emotional ties, that enabled me to learn to unload my anxieties and, very often, my guilt.

For the rest of the day I tried to keep busy; walking with Margaret in the afternoon and going to my recorder group in the evening, keeping my emotional state well-hidden, packed away, at the back of my mind.

The next day, I had an appointment to see Dr Frances, a physician specialising in the care of older people, at a health centre in a neighbouring town. As I was worried about what she would find and have to tell me, I'd asked Margaret to accompany me and we set off apprehensively in the morning. Dr Frances was delightful. She had an amazing capacity for establishing a caring but very professional relationship within minutes and carried out a very thorough physical examination which, with anyone else might have been embarrassing, but with her it was relaxed, dignified and just 'what it was – a physical examination'. At the end of all the tests and assessments, Dr Frances told me that I definitely did not have Parkinson's Disease but that she would arrange an MRI scan to rule out any other neurological cause. She thought that the tremors, jumpiness and shaking legs were probably a side effect of the increased dose of Sertraline and she recommended reducing the dose gradually back down to the original 50 mg. and coming back to see her in two weeks, with the proviso that if I experienced major difficulties I could increase it again. This time I agreed to her suggestion of reducing the Sertraline and left feeling greatly relieved and much more positive.

As instructed, I reduced the Sertraline to 75 mg. over the next week but the jumpiness continued to be very bad, especially in the evenings and in bed at night before going to sleep. My legs would jump and jerk quite violently and sometimes my arms and body as well. It seemed as if my whole body had hiccups. During the second week, I reduced the Sertraline on alternate days to 50 mg. and by the end of the week it did seem as if there was, perhaps, a slight improvement. By the time I went back to see Dr Frances, I was still jerking and jumping but not quite so frequently and much less severely.

She had written to the psychiatrist, Dr Darius, who had prescribed the increased dose of Sertraline, to ask whether he could prescribe a different antidepressant but as yet had received no reply. My GP had told her that, when she spoke to Dr Darius about reducing the dose, he had given a warning to go ahead with great caution, as I had suffered a very serious depression. However, Dr Frances recommended that I continue on the Sertraline at 50 mg. but that I should go back to the previous dose if I felt any symptoms of depression. She felt that I was aware enough to recognise the signs and increase the dose or seek help if necessary and she still wanted me to go ahead with the MRI scan, when the appointment came through. I thought this was a good plan of action and was happy to continue for the time being.

Reducing the Sertraline to 50 mg. had no detrimental effects during March and the jumpiness and jerking in my legs gradually reduced, with an improvement also in other bodily functions. As the weather dried up, I started to work out in the garden again for short periods and it was encouraging to see the crocuses and daffodils come into bloom, along with signs of growth on many plants and shrubs, a sure sign of spring approaching. Don and I celebrated our wedding anniversary and had a pleasant day together. We didn't do anything very special but, for once, Don wasn't in pain with all his physical ailments and, after a particularly busy week, I was pleased to have a day at home. I cooked a lovely meal with some good food and he found he had some winnings on his Premium Bonds, which always cheered him up!

Knowing that my counselling sessions with Caden would shortly be coming to an end, I was trying hard to keep busy and my mind occupied during this period and to be confident in managing myself. I was quite shocked, even appalled, at how dependent I had become on Caden and tried to convince myself that ending the sessions would be a good thing. I had no idea at that time how other people, who often pay for therapy, go for months or even years, without feeling guilty at their need for such support. I had been having counselling for six months and to me that seemed like eternity. I now know that people suffering from depression often experience a change in their perception of time. Certainly time had gone very slowly for me during the past months, with every day seeming like a week and every week like a month. I had often asked how long it would take for me to recover but never received an answer, other than the need to be patient. I began to realise that ' a short time' in psychological terms means something very different from usual. Thinking about the final session with Caden, I was determined that I would not cry or be pathetic but leave on a grateful but confident note. I found that I cared now about how Caden saw me; I wanted him to see me as someone strong and capable, someone who had recovered with his help. I did not want to let him down after all his patience and help. I thought that he needed to see me as being worth all his efforts, though I can see now how stupid this was and what a relatively short time I'd received his help.

On the evening before the last session, I was invited to go with friends to see the film *The Book Thief* and I went along to the cinema, hoping that I would be engrossed and would have no time to worry and fret about the approaching session with Caden. The film certainly held my attention all the way through, with brilliant photography and excellent acting but, from halfway through to the end, I was in floods of tears, identifying with the characters in the film and their 'goodbyes'. First, there was the heart-rending scene when Max, a young Jewish man, that Lisle's family have been hiding in their basement, has to flee when there is a basement check in their area. Lisle has become so close to Max, talking and reading to him for hours, to bring him through a serious illness. She is still only a young girl but has kept the secret of the fugitive for months and she is heartbroken that he now has to leave to keep her and her family safe. Then her adopted 'Papa' is conscripted and has to go away to war and Lisle goes to see him off on the train. Now, all the people to whom she is close have left her. She is abandoned and bereft.

These were highly emotional scenes but it wasn't just the sadness of the story in the film but my identification with these characters in saying 'Goodbye' to someone very special that really broke me down and left me in such a state. I couldn't explain the reason for this to my friends but nevertheless felt wrapped in kindness by them, even though they were gently laughing at me, thinking it was just the effect of the film and assuring me that it wasn't real. When I went to bed that night, I practised a Mindfulness session on 'turning towards difficult feelings', for the second night running. Again, I was in tears but this did help me to find some release and I was able to feel that I was letting some difficult feelings just drift away out of me.

The next morning I got up early, feeling dreadful, tired and worn out with all the crying of the previous evening, but I pushed myself to get organised and get to my counselling session. I'd written Caden a card thanking him for everything he'd done for me and I went to the supermarket en route to buy a plant. The shop was stacked out with plants all wrapped up appropriately for Mothers' Day but I managed to find a pretty cream rose in a pot, without too much sentimental wrapping and no mention of a mother.

When I arrived, clutching the card and the rose, the first thing Caden said to me was that he had discovered I was entitled to one further session, according to NHS rules, so I would be able to have another one next month. We had an excellent session, covering a wide range of subjects including my interest (even obsession) with Mindfulness and how useful I had found it. He was very pleased with how well I seemed to be, and how much enjoyment I was getting out of my various activities. It struck me again how in tune we were with each other and how easy I found it to talk to him about all sorts of things, both good and bad, and to share my worries and anxieties with him – except, of course, my feelings about the sessions coming to an end. This was still a taboo subject as far as I was concerned and I managed to maintain a cheerful, positive attitude. As the session progressed, I knew that I couldn't face going through the hell of parting yet again, so made the decision that I would not come for another session but would leave that day as planned, sounding positive and confident. Needless to say, I didn't tell Caden my reason and he assumed that I felt no need for further counselling. We shook hands, said our Goodbyes and thanks and I walked bravely away down the long corridor that had become so familiar over the months, without looking back. I was determined to be strong, or at least to appear so. It wasn't too difficult because the session had gone so well, and Caden had seemed to appreciate his present and card and had told me how much he'd enjoyed working with me. I was still on a high when I left and later wrote in my diary that I was sure the timing was right and I was glad that we'd agreed not to have another session. How wrong I was!

Chapter Twelve
ANOTHER STORM

Initially, my high mood and confidence in myself continued. I knew that Caden had been my 'Someone to Watch Over Me' – the title of a Gershwin piece that we'd been playing in our recorder group and which had seemed particularly poignant and relevant to my needs in previous months – but now I thought that I didn't need him any more, feeling that I was again independent, strong, healed and at peace with myself. Mindfulness was beginning to help me. During April and May I completed the 8-week Mindfulness programme by Mark Williams and Danny Penman, from their book *Mindfulness: A Practical Guide to Finding Peace in a Frantic World* and was profoundly grateful for all that I learnt, even though I had a long way to go to becoming skilled at meditation and living more of my life in 'Being' mode rather than 'Doing' mode. Professor Mark Williams was the founder of the Oxford Mindfulness Centre and, before that, the Centre for Mindfulness Research and Practice at Bangor University, as well as being co-founder of Mindfulness Based Cognitive Therapy (MBCT) which studies have shown to be effective in preventing a relapse into serious depression.

Whilst mindfulness has become a buzz word in recent years, it seems to me that it is often over-simplified and commercialised, with things like 'mindfulness colouring books for adults' becoming popular. But mindfulness is about much more than this. It requires practice and commitment to achieve a way of being which, when achieved has been shown to exert a powerful influence on one's health, well-being and happiness.

This book and the accompanying CD engage the reader/ listener in a series of practices that are based on MBCT to teach a simple form of meditation. It uses breathing as a focus, to enable understanding that thoughts will come and go without conscious thinking and that the essential 'you' is separate from your thoughts. You learn to observe your thoughts, to accept them without criticism or guilt for what they are – just thoughts that are transient; they will come and go of their own accord – and become more compassionate with yourself.

Scientific research has shown many benefits of mindfulness meditation which are detailed fully in the book, together with references to the research studies. It is an impressive list that not only includes a decrease in anxiety and depression but also other important benefits, such as a reduction in the impact of serious conditions such as chronic pain, cancer, drug and alcohol dependence and hypertension, along with a bolstering of the immune system.

Whilst the practices are simple and straightforward and involve nothing mystical or religious, they do require patience and commitment. It was with some difficulty, given my impatient nature, that I managed to follow the sessions in the right order, keeping to the recommended timetable and to resist the temptation to skip ahead to something that looked more interesting. I found session five, *Turning Towards Difficulties,* a profound emotional experience and afterwards felt as if I was a new person, who would never again require any sort of help. Of course, that was not the case but it was an important lesson that has helped me gain a different kind of strength that I could draw on for support through some of the difficult times ahead.

In fact, that spring I felt as if I'd been reborn, not in a religious sense but in a physical and spiritual sense. Emerging from both the winter and the darkest days of depression, I was so conscious of the beauty all around, the lambs in the fields, the flowers, leaves and catkins, the sunshine, sky and clouds and even the wind and rain. Never before had I appreciated the world in which I live so much as that year. It must have been a particularly warm, sunny March, as I spent a lot of time outside, walking and gardening. I was sometimes using gardening as a therapeutic activity. If I felt upset or overwhelmed, I found that working in the garden helped me to calm down and think more clearly. One particularly bad day I went out and was busy clearing an excess of weed in our pond, when I came across several frogs and even more newts. Somehow, these pond creatures gave me such delight that I was able to see things differently and think more clearly. On other occasions I was surprised to find various bulbs and plants coming into leaf and flower; I must have bought them the previous summer and planted them somehow during the dark days of my illness in the autumn, though I had no memory of doing so. I must have been on 'automatic pilot' mode when I did it. Now, that whole time when I was seriously depressed seemed hazy and almost as if it had happened to someone else. The memories I did have were like looking through thick glass, blurred and distorted. I was also still very conscious and aware of how important my friends had been in my recovery, never giving up on me, always there if I needed them, patient, caring, kind and willing me to get better but without putting pressure on me. I felt very grateful and lucky with all the care I had received from everyone.

At the beginning of April, I went for the MRI scan organised by Dr Frances and a week or two later had the results which were reassuring. Dr Frances had now retired but I saw a locum, Dr George, another specialist in the care of older people. He explained that the scan showed several 'unidentified bright spots' but these are often are found on older people's MRI scans and, as the spots were old, they were nothing to worry about. He assured me that whatever they were, they were not related to the TGA or to depression or to the jumpiness and tremors that I was experiencing. He was sure the jumpiness and tremors were simply side effects of the Sertraline and that they would disappear but, as Sertraline had been so effective at lifting the depression, he suggested sticking with a reduced dose for the time being. He gave me a programme of reducing this medication very gradually over the next few months but stressed that if I felt the depression returning, I should see my GP immediately and she would prescribe a different anti-depressant. Whilst I was very pleased to have this positive meeting with Dr George, there was unfortunately very bad news to come. Another storm was on its way.

My friend, Catherine, confided in me that she had recently had some more tests for cancer and the results were not looking good. She was suffering with bad back ache and was afraid the cancer had spread to her spine. This was not a definite diagnosis yet and she had not told anyone else at this stage. Catherine and I had been through so much together and supported each other for many months. She had been diagnosed with breast cancer about eighteen months previously but, after a mastectomy and course of chemotherapy – all of which I lived through with her week by week – she thought she had recovered. All the signs were looking good and she had started to pick up her life again. We had fun choosing a wig, which she then wore proudly as she re-joined her usual activities and, when feeling strong enough, she took over again as leader of our Book Group which I had been leading temporarily while she was receiving treatment. By now, her hair had regrown, she had gained the confidence and motivation to look to the future again and she had finally made the decision to go for breast reconstruction. It was when she went to see the consultant to discuss this treatment that she had been given the worrying news that all might not be well after all. It seemed such a cruel blow after all that she had suffered and overcome to find, just weeks later, that it might all have been in vain.

The next couple of months were difficult ones for Catherine and her husband, both good friends, as it became clear that not only was the cancer back, but it had metastasised to her lungs, her spine and her brain. She deteriorated very quickly and once again was unable to participate in all the things she loved doing. Once more I took over as temporary leader of our Book Group, as her illness became known to others. Everyone was very sad and shocked.

As she became weaker, Catherine could no longer cope with visitors but we kept in touch frequently by email and telephone. She stayed remarkably cheerful and was interested to know everything that was happening. When contacting her, I tried to be cheerful, interesting and to give her some good news about the activities we had previously gained so much enjoyment from together but, after every conversation, I was in pieces, stricken with grief. She was so brave in her time of adversity.

On one occasion, I met her husband by chance in the town car park, after he had just been shopping. He looked dreadful, worn and exhausted, and was unloading a trolley full of medications, incontinence pads and a food supplement into his car. He explained that Catherine could no longer tolerate ordinary food and it was then that the full awfulness of her condition hit me. She was unable to walk and he was carrying her up and down stairs. We stood there talking for some time; I had tears streaming down my face as he described the pitiful state to which Catherine was reduced. He must have told Catherine about how upset I was when he got home because she rang, concerned about me. This was how kind and caring she was.

Although physically very weak, her mental functions were not yet impaired and Catherine kept herself busy, sorting out all her affairs and, unknown to me then, she also planned her funeral in some detail. Before long, Catherine was talking about going into a hospice when her illness reached a certain stage but it happened much more quickly than her husband or any of us expected. At the end of May, she made the decision that the time had come, having been told that she probably had no more than six months to live. Her husband thought it was still too early but Catherine was adamant and he respected her wishes.

Only a week later, on 7 June, I returned home in the evening from a family day out. It was my son's birthday and Don and I had travelled down to see him where, joined by my daughter, her husband and the grandchildren, we all enjoyed a lovely meal in the garden of a local pub. The weather was warm and sunny and we all had a good day. As we opened the door and walked into our house in the evening, the phone was ringing. It was Catherine's husband, David, with the sad news that she had died that morning. I shall always remember that day.

A very emotional time followed. As I have come to learn, bereavement and grief are strange and powerful emotions, which take many different forms as people struggle to come to accept what has happened. I was torn between being thankful that Catherine's suffering was now at an end but still stricken at what she had been through over the past year or more and what her husband was going through now. I missed her dreadfully and had to face up to the fact that we would never again share the things we'd loved doing together.

I became angry at the way other people who had known her expressed sympathy and sorrow but then just got on with their lives, when I couldn't do that. I knew this was unreasonable, as other people who knew her hadn't been as close to her as I had been, but that didn't stop me feeling hurt and incensed. Of course, Catherine's husband had been even closer to her and he was totally lost, not knowing how he could face the future without her. I knew no words of comfort for him and his desolation haunted me.

The funeral was a small, private one at a Green Burial Ground in a beautiful rural spot, on a lovely sunny, summer's day. The burial field was a meadow, full of long grasses and wild flowers, surrounded by trees. It was a peaceful, natural place, with just the sound of birdsong, bees and butterflies busy on the flowers in the warm summer sunshine. Those of us there were glad she had chosen this place and thought the occasion reflected Catherine's personality, feeling her calmness and presence in our minds. Catherine had worked out what she wanted and who should be asked to attend. It was a simple, informal occasion but which had great meaning. Friends and relatives were invited to speak about what Catherine had meant to them. Some had known her for many years; others, like myself, for a much shorter time but we all had something unique to say and it became very clear what a special person Catherine had been to us all. I was still very sad at losing her but leaving her body in that meadow, surrounded by peace and beauty, seemed a right and fitting end to her life and I gained some comfort from that thought. Her husband held up well and, during the refreshments later at the hotel in which they had been married, he shared some thoughts of his own about their treasured time together.

Catherine's suffering and death had affected me deeply and my anger about the unfairness of it all lasted over the next few months. This was not really a good time for me to be reducing my anti-depressants. Over the weeks that followed, I tried reducing from 50 mg. to 25 mg. on alternate days but I never made any consistent progress, always reverting, in mild panic, to the 50 mg. as I would become unreasonably tearful and upset at any minor mishap or any emotional film, TV programme or book. I was still angry about the unfairness of Catherine's suffering and death, just as she was about to enjoy her long awaited retirement with her husband, only to be cut down so cruelly. Theirs had been a second marriage for both of them and they were looking forward to the future together.

I had suffered bereavement before with the deaths of my parents and grandparents but they had been much older, in their eighties, and my mother ninety-two. Naturally, I had been very sad when they died; I grieved for them and missed them but they had continued to live on in my memory and somehow their deaths, at the end of a long life, had seemed more natural, something that we know will happen to all of us. Catherine's death was different. She had suddenly been plucked from us, from everything she loved, in a painful and shocking way, long before she was ready.

Whether my heightened emotional state at this time was due to the natural process of grieving or a return of depression, I don't know but, at the time, it seemed to me that I would never manage to stay well and be free from depression. My anxiety had also increased again, not least because I'd been informed that the driver of the car that had caused the accident was being prosecuted and I may have to attend court and give evidence. I had some very dark and shaky days trying to cope with everything.

I went back to see my GP who was very sympathetic and encouraging. She took pains to explain that, in fact, I'd done very well in a relatively short period of time, as most people stay on anti-depressants for at least six months after they feel well, before starting to reduce, whereas I'd been on an accelerated programme of reduction after only four months altogether. Still having little faith or belief in myself, I needed to hear that I was doing well and I was grateful for the time and effort she put in to reassure me. Dr Alice encouraged me to keep at 50 mg. for another few months and then we would review what was happening, both with the jumpiness and the depression.

So the summer continued. There were some good times and achievements. Our Singing Group had been asked to provide some entertainment at a fête organised by the Friends of our local hospital. It was a successful afternoon, with lovely weather and lots of singing to an appreciative audience, whilst they enjoyed refreshments on the lawn. Our group also ran a plant stall which did well, and overall the fête made a good profit so all our hard work seemed very worthwhile. I was proud of our achievements.

At the beginning of the summer term, I had started voluntary work at a local primary school, just a couple of hours, one afternoon a week. This was progressing well and I was enjoying it, as were the children, who were so enthusiastic and eager to read to me. It made a very pleasant change to spend time with these young children and with their teachers, who were all so full of life, energy and happiness and I was sorry when the end of term came in July.

Yet, in spite of so much going well, there were many times when I would still easily become tearful and low. Often this would hit me suddenly and unexpectedly, triggered by some small thing or difficulty, certainly nothing that warranted a response of that degree. My reaction to these events always shocked me; it seemed as if, in spite of all the progress and the fact that my life was mainly good, that I was still weak and vulnerable at the slightest sign of stress. Would I ever get back to being a normal person again?

By this time, I knew from experience that I should try to keep busy with a variety of activities as this would help me keep on track with my recovery. The weather was good that summer, so I spent a lot of time outside, gardening and regularly walking and talking with my friend, Margaret. I also started to walk with the U3A walking group and this introduced me to some lovely new walks in places to which I would not have ventured on my own and with people whom I hadn't met before. I found it easy to talk as we walked and it was good to share the lovely views and places that we explored.

Sometimes I had to make a big effort to be sociable and to mix with people, especially in larger groups, but I found I could do it, even though it caused me some anxiety beforehand. I was careful to pace myself and not to overdo things, to get plenty of sleep and to accept without worrying about it that, on some days, I was just too tired to do anything very much.

If I stopped for a minute to think about Catherine, which seemed to happen frequently, I would still be overwhelmed with grief and would feel upset and angry that no-one else seemed to be feeling this too. Everyone was living their lives as if her death hadn't happened or as if it were of no importance. The saying 'Life goes on' took on a new meaning – it was happening to everyone all around me but, to me, life had changed and I was missing this dear friend.

I had become very interested in mental health in general and depression in particular and, now that I was sufficiently recovered to be able to read books again, rather than the odd article on the internet, I started to look around for new reading matter. The first book I came across was *Depressive Illness: the Curse of the Strong* by Dr Tim Cantopher, whose theories impressed me greatly and I could not understand why no-one had explained the cause of depression to me in this way before. I now know that psychiatrists hold different views on the causes of depression and on the most effective ways of treating it. Some think that there is a biological or genetic cause or a chemical imbalance in the brain; others think that psychological or sociological factors are the root. Even when treatments prove to be effective, no-one really appears to know why this is so, what makes them effective, and there is no one effective remedy for everyone. People respond differently to different drugs and treatments. Medical professionals cannot tell you how long a depressive illness will last or whether it will recur because they do not know. Every sufferer is different.

In this book, Dr Cantopher puts forward a confident and compelling argument that depression is a physical illness (rather than a mental illness) in which the limbic system – a structure within the brain that controls a lot of the body's processes, including mood – is damaged and it needs time to repair itself and heal. He explains that there are a number of factors that can cause this damage, including things like illness, drugs, alcohol, but that the most common cause is stress. He goes on to claim that the type of depressive illness caused by stress nearly always happens to one type of person – a person with strong moral values who is reliable and diligent, with a strong conscience and sense of responsibility. Such a person will tend to focus on the needs of others before her or his own needs and will be particularly vulnerable to criticism, with self-esteem dependent on the evaluation of others.

I recognised these traits; they all fitted my personality without exception. I was astounded to realise that I was such a good fit to a personality type and could see now how Dr Darius had been able to categorise me so quickly. His questions, apparently innocuous at the time, were designed to probe into these well-known traits and, once he had some evidence, he was confident in describing my personality to me.

The most important message in Dr Cantopher's book, though, was how he goes on to develop his theory to show that, when faced with stress, a weak person will give up before becoming ill but a strong person will try to overcome the challenges as s/he has always managed to do so in the past and will keep on trying in spite of the pressures building up. This person cannot stop as s/he cannot bear to think of others being disappointed and will continue to keep going until the body and mind breaks down. This seemed to describe so exactly what had happened to me. Suddenly, it all made real sense and relieved me of some of the guilt I'd felt about giving way under all the stress.

There is much, much more in Dr Cantopher's book that is not only interesting but also very useful to anyone suffering from this type of depressive illness. The first time I read the book, I don't think I absorbed more than a small percentage of the valuable information and advice he gives but I have read and re-read the book many times, each time gleaning a little more or strengthening and building on what I'd already learnt. The trouble is, when you're suffering from depression, your memory and your cognitive functions are often not firing on all cylinders and even important things that you read and understand at the time are forgotten, or not brought to mind when the next difficulty occurs and you are in most need of them. In spite of this, his book brought light into the darkness and mists and I began to believe that I may find a way through this difficult journey. Dr Cantopher re-iterated things that Dr Alice, Dr Darius and Caden had all told me – you will get better. It will be a treacherous journey, with many pitfalls, but don't give up. I was beginning to believe them and to have some faith in my capacity to recover. If I had read the book earlier, I may have heeded some of Dr Cantopher's helpful advice, instead of struggling on clueless and trying to find my own way, particularly with regard to trying to rush recovery in the middle stage. I may then have recovered without so many false hopes and disappointments.

That summer, Don and I had decided not to go away on holiday. He was not in good health physically, with many aches, pains and ailments, and preferred the comfort of his home. I had also noticed that he was increasingly agitated by change, which was another reason for staying at home. This became very apparent when we had builders in for a couple of weeks to replace the guttering for, although the work was entirely outside the house and was not particularly disruptive, Don found it difficult to cope with the noise and with people being around in the garden, disturbing his peace. He was very agitated by change of any sort and I was increasingly worried about him as the decline in his social and mental capacity was steadily getting worse. He would still not consider seeking help, even though he was aware of his deterioration, and it obviously caused him frustration, not being able to solve problems or do things that he'd always been able to do. I think he often tried to hide his difficulties, maybe even to himself. There was one occasion when I came home in the evening and found him sitting in the dark, completely confounded because all the lights had gone off downstairs. He had not thought to find a torch, to use a lamp or to check the lights upstairs and, when I asked him if he had checked the trip-switch in the garage, he seemed to have no idea what I was talking about. When I explained that a light bulb must have gone, this meant nothing to him; he didn't even seem to know how to change a light bulb. This was a real lesson to me in understanding how his mental abilities were deteriorating. It was no longer a case of forgetting words or names or not being able to recall people, places or events until prompted by photos or visits when the memories would return, but a significant decline in cognition, even though this was not apparent every day. Some days he would seem almost normal but on others it was very different.

Fortunately, he had by this time largely overcome his fear of going out in the car and we managed some enjoyable day trips and drives in the countryside. We didn't have to drive far as we are lucky enough to live in a beautiful area with wonderful scenery and it wasn't hard to find a parking place with a good view to enjoy. When we arrived at our destination, he was very happy to sit in the car listening to music, whilst I took a walk to explore and get some exercise. I would take some CDs to play or set the radio to Radio 3 if there was some suitable music and check that it was all working before I left him, as it became obvious that he was unable to carry out these tasks himself.

Sometimes, I would take a flask of coffee and a snack or, occasionally a picnic lunch, so that we could travel further afield or stay out longer. We both enjoyed these excursions and the changes of scene gave us new topics of conversation. On the Bank Holiday Monday at the end of August, however, the anniversary of our car accident, we stayed firmly put at home.

Chapter Thirteen
DOG DAYS

Don and I had talked on several occasions about getting a dog. We thought this would be good company for Don, especially when I was out, and good company for me when going on walks. During my counselling sessions, Caden had talked once about the therapeutic value of dogs but, at the time, I had no energy, either physical or emotional, to spare for a dog and all that would entail. I was just struggling to cope with everyday life.

Towards the end of that summer, I was feeling very much better and I was prepared to think again. At the end of August, we went to see a chocolate Labrador that a friend had told me about as he needed a new home. He lived on a small farm, owned by a fantastic woman, Claire, who had a truly amazing way with all her animals – horses, goats, sheep, geese, chickens, ducks, cats and dogs, including two litters of energetic, playful Labrador puppies, some golden and some black. All her animals were beautiful, well cared for, so friendly and happy, but Claire had broken her neck and was encased in plaster. She was finding it difficult to cope, so she had decided to re-home her chocolate Labrador, Ivor. He was a good looking dog, one year old, well trained, very obedient and well behaved.

We spent a long while looking around her farm, as Claire introduced us proudly to all her animals and explained how she had come to collect such a menagerie. We met the parents of the puppies who followed us around and played exuberantly at our feet. I picked up one of the puppies who seemed a bit left out of the general puppy antics and he snuggled into my neck very affectionately, sniffing and snuffling with contentment as he breathed in my scent. He was round, soft, cuddly and had that wonderful, fresh, clean puppy smell. We seemed to bond instantly and I couldn't put him down. Don seemed equally impressed by this beautiful puppy and I'm afraid poor Ivor didn't stand a chance with us from that moment onwards. We agreed there and then to buy the puppy and to return to collect him the following day, after we had got organised and bought all the necessary items to care for him.

The following morning, we went to the local pet shop to get kitted out. The owner of the shop was very helpful, insisting that we buy a cage and bedding in large sizes, which seemed ridiculously enormous for a small puppy but which she assured us he would be needing before very long – and she was right! We were so excited and couldn't wait to get back to the farm to see our gorgeous puppy. On the way, we had a long conversation about a name for him, eventually deciding that he would be called Prince Llewellyn but Llewi for short. Claire gave us instructions about when and how to feed him, four times a day, and she packed us an initial supply of the food he was used to. She fed all her dogs on raw meat and fish and we took the frozen salmon and tripe home with us. Llewi cuddled up to me immediately I picked him up and then travelled home in the car on Don's lap without a problem.

The weather was fine and dry, so it was easy to put him out in the garden every hour to avoid any accidents indoors and he soon enjoyed exploring his new surroundings. He was such a loving and lovable little dog and had such a joy of life – playing, exploring, eating and sleeping. The neighbours all came round to see him that afternoon as we sat outside in the sun and proudly showed him off. The next day we took him to the vet for his vaccinations. He behaved beautifully and didn't even flinch at the injections. Everyone was very impressed!

For the next few weeks I didn't get very much done, other than look after and play with Llewi. My friends all loved him and he found many things to play with, as he 'helped' me with tasks in the garden and clearing out the shed. Plastic flower pots were a particularly favourite plaything. He learnt very quickly, responding to his name and how to retrieve a ball in just a couple of days. He loved to play and was such a bundle of fun that you couldn't help but laugh and love him for his antics. He thrived on the food we had brought back and grew visibly day by day.

When term started again in September, I managed to keep going to my recorder group and I went back to the primary school on one afternoon a week, during which times Don was very happy to look after Llewi who was completely house-trained by now and would curl up on a chair with him, happy to sleep for an hour or two, after an active playtime and a meal.

My daughter came to visit us with the baby, now fourteen months, for a day in September, and both Don and I were captivated by him, such a friendly, happy child and he loved Llewi! They enjoyed playing together in the garden.

For the first two months of having Llewi, I found it I difficult to keep up with all the chores in the house and garden, as well as looking after this little dog, but things were getting easier as Llewi started to wake a bit later in the mornings as he got older and, rather to my relief, I no longer had to play with him at 6.00 am which I must admit I had found tiring. I am not an early morning person at the best of times! We enrolled at puppy training classes to start at the beginning of October and attended the first session successfully. Unfortunately, there was then a problem with the hall in which the training was held and, although the trainer found a new venue, she had to change the day to Wednesday, the one evening in the week that I couldn't attend. However, Llewi's recall was already excellent and I managed to teach him some basic commands very quickly at home.

By now, I had even managed to come off the Sertraline anti-depressant tablets completely but, in spite of the happiness Llewi had brought into our home, I was easily tearful if things went wrong and still missed talking to Caden. I thought of going for counselling at the local Mind organisation but didn't really have the time, being so busy with Llewi. Margaret and I had become very close and saw each other regularly, supporting each other when one or other of us felt down, and this was a great help. Llewi was able to go out on short walks now, though we had to avoid steep hills, as these are not good for a puppy's joints and could lead to problems in later life, but he enjoyed the local park and had got used to going in the car, with the reward of a walk at the end, and he was getting used to meeting other dogs. Soon I started to take him on my walks with Margaret and with the Walking for Health Group, provided we were not going too far.

I was managing well until, at the end of October, I became unwell with a sore throat and a bad cough. I struggled on for a few days, just doing what was essential and sleeping the rest of the time, but after ten days went to the surgery, where I was told I had a chest infection in one lung, and was prescribed antibiotics. These soon made me feel much better and the coughing eased enough to enable me to attend the annual recorder workshop. Although I found it exhausting, the day went well and we made some wonderful music! It made me think back to the previous year and realise how much progress I had made, not only with the recorder but, more importantly, with my mental health.

But over the next couple of weeks, things took a downward turn and I started to slide visibly backwards. The chest infection had taken its toll; I was still tired, drained of energy and worn out, even though the coughing had eased. The weather was colder and wetter, the days shorter and darker and my mood seemed to be sinking down and down. The thought of sliding back into depression horrified and terrified me. By mid-November, my sleep was poor and I was waking frequently in the early hours, anxious and miserable. I could feel that despair was not far away and I was again beleaguered by dark thoughts. Should I give up and end it all? I still had my plan and the means to carry it out.

In the early hours of one morning, I was again filled with a restless energy, needing to do something to alleviate my condition. This time I didn't feel as if I had been 'taken over' by some malevolent force, driving me towards death as a means of finding release, but the urge to do something active was overwhelming. I got out of bed and dressed, intending to go out in the cold, dark morning and curl up on the steps of the mental health centre, to wait there for someone to come and open up. I was desperate for someone to care for me.

The thing that stopped me in my tracks was seeing my lovely puppy, curled up asleep, so loving and trusting, that my heart took over from my head and the urge for immediate drastic action lessened. How would he fare without me if anything happened to me? I could see how irresponsible and pointless it was to go out this early, to wait outside in the cold, probably making myself even more ill. So, I managed to go back to bed for a while, to keep warm and safe, knowing that I could go to the mental health centre later when it was open and ask for help.

When I was discharged from the secondary mental health team at the beginning of the year, I had received a letter notifying me that I could return to the team directly if I needed to, without referral from my GP, so I went along later that morning, hoping to prevent things from getting to a critical point. The centre was very busy but I was seen by the duty CPN who listened to my feelings and fears and gave me assurance that I'd done the right thing in coming to seek help so quickly. She was confident that they could help me and prevent the depression becoming very serious again. She told me that it was quite common for people to go downhill at this time of year, with the approach of winter, and that was partly why they were so busy. We talked about the type of help I was seeking. I explained that I was not looking for more medication but rather some talking therapy so she asked me to come back again, after the weekend, when she would be able to give me more time. This was rather a rushed interview; the CPN was under pressure to complete it before the time of her next appointment and knowing this also put me under pressure, feeling guilty at taking up her time when she was already so busy but, as I left the centre, I felt relieved, reassured, so much better having talked to her, as if a pressure-valve had been released. Things seemed more manageable and I felt fairly confident I could get through the weekend, knowing that I would be given more help and support the following week.

This was to prove to be the case. Over the weekend I was more relaxed and felt more energetic. My tiredness and lethargy diminished; I slept better and even found some energy and enthusiasm by Sunday to attend a friend's seventieth birthday party. I had been looking forward to this party for weeks but, in recent days, was doubtful whether I would be well enough to attend. All went well; it was a lovely party and I was so pleased to be able to enjoy it, with many other friends there, although once again I felt as if I were outside my body watching myself eat and socialise, as if that was a separate person acting automatically, so I knew that all was not entirely right and normal.

On Monday afternoon, I kept my assessment appointment at the mental health centre. The CPN had been busy before my visit, talking to a psychiatrist, Dr Helen, who had agreed to see me and would be in touch shortly. She explained that Dr Darius, whom I saw previously, had now left the county but that Dr Helen was also a specialist in the mental health of older people. Although I had not requested any medication, on the psychiatrist's advice the CPN had obtained a prescription for anti-depressants and also for Zopiclone, a drug to help me sleep for the next few nights, as a temporary measure. She was also arranging for another CPN, a specialist from the older people's team, to support me on an ongoing basis with talking therapy as I had requested. Much encouraged by this session and the promise of more support from the team, I took the prescription to Boots and collected the tablets, even though I was not enthused at the thought of taking them.

Later, I decided not to take either of them for the time being. The antidepressants were Sertraline, the drug that had previously caused the problems with my shaking, trembling legs and which I had spent months trying to wean myself off, so I was reluctant to go down that road again. I was tempted to take the Zopiclone but worried that, if I took these sleeping tablets, I might not wake if there was an emergency, or if Don needed me during the night. Strangely, I had a wonderful night's sleep and awoke in the morning feeling very rested and relaxed. If I'd taken the prescribed tablets, I would have thought it was those having such a beneficial effect but I think it was more the fact that I had taken control of the situation and had talked about and put my fears and concerns into words with someone who would help.

The following day, another CPN phoned on my mobile while I was out walking the dog and offered to see me that afternoon or later in the week. The call took me by surprise as I was not expecting to hear from him so quickly but, as I was feeling fine and more positive that day, I declined his offer, agreeing instead to an appointment for the following week. I don't know why I delayed seeing him, as I knew I was very vulnerable in spite of feeling better. I think I was trying desperately not to be ill again.

When I talked to my friend, Margaret, later that week, she told me that she, too, often gets depressed in November. I suppose it has something to do with the season changing and the darkness increasing as the days get shorter. Everything is dying and it is colder and wetter with frequent gloomy, grey skies. For many years I had always dreaded autumn, with the decay and dying it brought, and the absence of warm, sunny days for months to come, but I'd never been depressed before. My feelings this year were on a different scale. This was something new.

Feeling fine didn't last long. I managed to do everything I needed to but without any real motivation, enthusiasm or satisfaction. I had retreated into acting like an automaton, with no feelings except tiredness and exhaustion. I managed to cook meals and keep up some of my usual activities half-heartedly but, all the time, it felt as if I were floating above my body, just watching it carry out these tasks, unfeeling and emotionless. By the end of the week, I was feeling very tired and exhausted, with a slightly sore throat which threw me into a mild panic, as I couldn't face being physically ill again but, fortunately, it didn't develop into anything serious.

Tired and jaded, I kept the appointment with the CPN but it didn't go well and I came away feeling very disappointed. It was not his fault; he was obviously unwell himself, suffering from the same sort of cough and infection from which I'd just recovered. I felt sorry for him and felt like telling him to go home and go to bed, as he looked as if he had a temperature. In these circumstances, I found it hard to relate to him and became very despondent, as I realised once again how lucky I'd been to have Caden as my counsellor. Unfortunately, no-one else could come up to the standards I now longed for and I knew that I was unlikely to find that sort of relationship again. Not at all hopeful, I returned home to await my appointment with the new psychiatrist in a few days' time, wondering what she would be like.

I struggled through the next couple of days, trying to cope and to ward off the 'black dog' of depression, such a different dog from my lovely Llewi. Two days later, I had an appointment to see Dr Helen. She was lovely, very different from Dr Darius, whom I had seen the previous year, and I found it easy to talk to her, once we finally managed to get started. Our meeting was taking place in an annexe to the local hospital where she'd been working in the morning. She arrived in the waiting room and introduced herself to me but then found that she had left all her paperwork over in the main hospital, so had to excuse herself while she went to fetch it, and I waited for her to return. Then, when she came back, she discovered that she'd locked herself out of the room in the annexe where we were due to meet! She had left her keys inside, so we then had to wait for a caretaker to come with a spare key to open the door. Interestingly, I found all this quite inspirational! I knew that, if I had done something like this, I would have been mortified and embarrassed but she remained calm, pleasant and friendly and it really helped me to know that even a professional psychiatrist was human and could make mistakes. Although she was sincerely apologetic for her mistakes, she remained self-assured and just matter of fact. This experience has stayed with me and was perhaps the most important aspect of our meeting on that occasion! I learnt so much about how to deal with whatever problems arise, without becoming over-anxious or racked with guilt.

When we eventually started the session, I found Dr Helen easy to talk to and opened up at once, telling her about my problems, my progress and my new fears of depression striking again. She told me that the symptoms I described were those of classic clinical depression and pointed out that this new low corresponded almost exactly with my stopping taking the Sertraline six weeks previously. She explained that it takes that length of time for the medication to clear from the brain completely.

Although I was at first resistant to the thought of re-starting on anti-depressants, Dr Helen recommended strongly that I try a different type, Mirtazapine, which she had found to be particularly effective with older people. She assured me that it was not addictive but had a sedative effect which would help me to sleep at night, and it was known to have very few side effects, other than weight gain in some people but she thought this would be unlikely in my case. I agreed to try taking Mirtazapine for a month, at which time she would see me again to find out if it helped. She warned me that it would take at least two weeks to have an effect but I could try talking therapy with a CPN in the meantime and telephone her if I experienced any problems.

That evening, I felt great relief that someone, Dr Helen, actually seemed to understand and that I could talk to her and admit things that were difficult to say. I thought over the things we had talked about. She had stressed the importance of taking antidepressants, along with talking therapy, to allow the brain time to heal. With older people, she said healing can take much longer, up to seven years, if left to itself without medication, and that timescale assumes that nothing else happens in the meantime to make it worse or to cause self-harm.

Another important issue we had discussed was Don's mental deterioration. She was the psychiatrist who dealt with older adults suffering from dementia and fully understood my dilemma. She stressed the need to get him diagnosed, both for his own good, as medication could delay or prevent the condition from worsening, and for me to get some support before things became too critical. As Don was still refusing to see his GP, she suggested that I make an appointment to see her and tell her of my concerns, so that she would be aware of the situation and could perhaps raise his memory problems with him when she next saw him. I felt that this could be a useful way forward and was very encouraged by having this plan to work with.

Having agreed to try the medication, I had collected the Mirtazapine tablets that Dr Helen had prescribed and decided to take the first one that night. Unfortunately, the sedative effect didn't seem to work and I tossed and turned for several hours with my brain very active, going over and over the discussion with Dr Helen. After finally drifting off, I woke early, about 5.00 am having experienced some very vivid dreams. I couldn't recall any of them but felt exhausted by them.

By the time I got up out of bed I felt dreadful, very tired, with a headache and my limbs felt very heavy, like lead weights. I tried to eat breakfast but felt too nauseous. My mouth was dry and I had a foul, metallic taste in it. My head felt full of cotton wool and spaced out. I was completely lethargic and had no energy at all.

Forcing myself to get ready and go out, I hoped that being in the fresh air might make me feel better but it didn't. I struggled with pilates and gave up completely on one new exercise and just sat there until everyone had finished. Back at home, I struggled to climb the stairs, my legs still feeling heavy and cumbersome and, as I tried to read, my eyes grew heavy and closed. I gave in to sleep for a while and then somehow managed to cope for the rest of the day, falling asleep again twice in the evening but, in spite of this, still feeling tired. At bedtime, I decided not to take another tablet that night, as the side effects were so unpleasant and debilitating. I fell into bed at 10.15 pm and slept heavily all night until 7.45 am

Much to my relief, the following morning, I felt much better after all the sleeping and able to face the day. I had none of the symptoms from the previous day, just some slight stiffness from pilates, and I felt very good and stable mentally. I was able to take Llewi out for a good walk in the park where I enjoyed meeting several people with dogs and chatting to them. In the evening, I watched TV without falling asleep, so I decided it would be worthwhile trying another Mirtazapine tablet that night, particularly as the following day was Sunday, when I didn't have very much to do. I took the tablet and went to bed shortly afterwards, this time falling asleep quite quickly.

After a very good sleep, just waking briefly twice during the night, but falling back to sleep very quickly on both occasions, I awoke in the morning at 7.45 am again feeling good. In spite of it being November, it was a beautiful sunny day, very mild with no wind. Don and I decided to make the most of this lovely weather, so I made some sandwiches and a flask of coffee and we drove to the coast, where we sat on some rocks on the beach and had a picnic. Llewi was mad with excitement, running in and out of the sea, not at all afraid, even when the waves broke right over him. He made us laugh and his joyfulness was catching. After lunch, Don sat in the car listening to some music on the radio, while I walked with Llewi along the promenade to dry him off before coming home. Although we were only out for a few hours, it was a wonderful day which made us both feel glad to be alive. I was very conscious of feeling so good, both mentally and physically, and decided to take another tablet that night to see what happened.

I had no more unpleasant physical symptoms after that but, as life went on and difficulties arose, for a week or two I still was very tearful every time anything, big or small, went wrong and I found it hard to cope with everyday problems. As we moved into December, Don admitted that he was aware of the problems with his memory and we made an appointment to see his GP but, a few days later, he cancelled it, saying there was no point, so we were back to our old position. I knew that he would need to see his GP in March for an annual review of his medication, so I decided that I would take Dr Helen's advice and go to see her myself in February. At least this gave me something to hold onto and made me feel more positive and in control.

It was now that I discovered the first of many moving books, written as memoirs of depression by people who have suffered this bleak, debilitating illness. The first book I came across was *Black Rainbow* by Rachel Kelly, a journalist on *The Times* for many years, who writes poignantly of her shocking journey into perhaps the very worst depression. She writes beautifully to tell of how words, in the form of poetry, helped to heal her, quoting from a vast variety of poems ranging from an extract from the 'Song of Solomon' in the King James Bible, through history to 'You'll Never Walk Alone' by Oscar Hammerstein. I was aghast when I read of her suffering, as I had no idea that depression could cause such physical pain and suffering as she experienced, as well as the mental anguish. Completely bed-ridden for periods, sometimes unable to sit up, stand, walk or eat, this amazing woman somehow found the strength to survive and then to work at recovery from two major episodes of depression. She was fortunate to have wonderful support from her husband, her mother and her psychiatrist but it was her own brave acceptance of the illness and her perseverance and determination to get better that I admired and which gave me hope. I have read this book many times, on each occasion gleaning something new, perhaps a shared emotion, a piece of useful information or an appreciation of a different poem. Some people have questioned me about whether it is morbid to immerse myself in books about depression and this is a sad story but it is also a story of courage, kindness and comfort. Poetry was not the thing that helped me most – I needed something more active – but that does not mean that I couldn't empathise with this author or appreciate the poems she loved and which brought her solace and hope. I found her book inspirational. It transformed my thinking and helped me to cope with the mundane tasks of everyday life.

The weeks before Christmas were busy and I managed well. I wasn't high but neither was I low. I seemed to be fairly stable and was able to undertake all the pre-Christmas events and tasks without anxiety or stress. Don and I enjoyed a quiet Christmas Day together and I drank my first alcohol for months, just a small aperitif before lunch, a glass of red wine with lunch and a glass of dessert wine with the pudding. The alcohol had no ill effects and I continued to take the Mirtazapine tablets as usual. This was our first Christmas with Llewi and he enjoyed himself greatly with some new toys, quickly developing a taste for the festive fare of roast turkey and gammon. On Christmas Eve, I cooked a gammon joint as usual and left it on a work surface in the kitchen to cool. A little later, I heard a deafening crash, rushed to the kitchen where I found the plate smashed into pieces and the joint on the floor, with Llewi just about to devour it. I hadn't realised that he had grown so much that, when standing on his hind legs, he could now reach food on the kitchen units, if they smelled sufficiently enticing. I cleared up the broken crockery, carefully removing shards from the joint and washed it under the tap, then left it well out of reach of my dear dog and closed the kitchen door firmly. Our supper had been rescued and it later made an amusing anecdote to share with other dog-owning friends, all of whom seemed to have tales of their dogs' food thefts. We had joined the club!

On Boxing Day we had planned to go to my daughter's but snow was forecast and we decided it would not be wise to risk the journey. As I'd been rushing around right up to Christmas Day, it was rather nice to have another quiet and relaxing day at home. We had plenty of cold turkey and gammon, so little cooking was required and I enjoyed taking Llewi for a walk. At lunchtime I had another drink but this time it slayed me and I fell asleep in the afternoon and all the evening. After that, I avoided alcohol completely and rarely drank again whilst on anti-depressants.

The snow didn't materialise, just heavy showers of sleet and rain and, over the next few days, it turned very cold with heavy frosts and ice. We stayed at home in the warm, just taking Llewi who wasn't at all put off by the cold weather, out for walks.

Chapter Fourteen
YEAR OF DEPRESSION AND DEMENTIA
(January to December 2015)

By the time the new year 2015 came in, I seemed to have stabilised
and was keeping depression at bay. After the Christmas break, I
resumed all my usual activities as they started again and made sure
that I walked every day with Llewi whatever the weather, which
was now cold, frosty with bitter winds, full of sleety showers. But
we went out every day, being mindful of the feel of the weather on
our faces, the sounds as we scrunched along frosty paths or broke
the ice on puddles, the smells of damp and cold, of wood-smoke
from fires and sometimes the taste of rain or sleet on our lips. Llewi
loved to go out whatever the weather and, as long as I dressed up
warm and kept dry inside, I no longer worried about getting wet
or windswept. It was often exhilarating and made me appreciate
the warmth and comfort of home on our return.

I still walked regularly with Margaret, although she was finding
it increasingly difficult to walk on any terrain other than firm, level
ground, as she had begun to experience problems with her balance.
I also started to walk quite often with Ann and her dog, Cari. We
lived on the same side of town and often met first thing in the
morning. Our dogs got on well together and we started to explore
some new walks, as well as going once a month with the U3A
Walking Group.

In early January, I attended another appointment with my
psychiatrist, Dr Helen, who was pleased that the Mirtazapine was
working well. She decided to keep me on the low dose of 15 mg. as

I'd been very sensitive to the Sertraline in the past, but she gave me reassurance that this dose could be increased up to 45 mg. so there was plenty of leeway if we needed to increase the dose. She stressed that it would be important to stay on these antidepressants for at least a year and probably for up to two years, explaining that each time a person comes off the drugs and has a relapse, it becomes more difficult and takes longer to get the depression under control again. I took her warning seriously and was happy to continue with this treatment. All my previous concerns and anxieties about being on anti-depressants had evaporated and I no longer had any false hopes of a very quick recovery. The most important thing now was to feel well enough to cope and to get some enjoyment out of life, whatever that took.

We had a long discussion, initiated by Dr Helen, about Don and she suggested again that I go to see his GP, in confidence, to prepare her for when he went for his annual medication review, due in March. She told me that there was a lot of help available for people suffering from dementia, including financial help, but it was essential to get a formal diagnosis first in order to be eligible. When I left Dr Helen, I felt very positive, pleased to have a plan of action and I thought her practical advice to be very useful. It made me feel that I could begin to take control of the situation which, up until now, had made me powerless. By this time I knew how, for me, being in control is very important for my mental health.

Over the next few weeks, life went on much as usual, with ups and downs but, even when things went wrong, I coped without having a major panic or feeling ominous black clouds pressing down on me. I was both surprised and pleased at how well I was managing. By the beginning of February, I was feeling very well mentally and it made me realise how ill I had been and also to appreciate the depths of my unhappiness for a long period when struggling to get better. I realised that I no longer had to set myself one task each day as I was now coping with many tasks without giving them much thought. They were just a normal part of everyday life; in fact, I was quite glad to have a day when I had nothing particular to do and could just take it easy, take my time instead of rushing to fit everything in. I didn't know whether I would be the same if I came off the Mirtazapine but this didn't seem important and I had a strong sense that I was healing properly. Dr Helen had been adamant about giving the brain time to heal and now I was willing to give it this time.

It was during February that I decided to start to write this book. Finding the time was difficult but I managed an hour here and there and made a start, only to discover that my memory was very misleading. Looking back in my diary, which I'd written at the time, was very revealing and I had to rewrite some of what I'd started to write earlier. Also, reading my diary, I was forcibly struck by the fact that I was much more seriously ill than I thought at the time, when the depression was at its worst. My perceptions of what was happening to me had often been unrealistic in spite of everything that my GP and my counsellors told me. I could see it all much more clearly now, especially when I thought back to the very first days when the depression first hit me. I particularly remembered the incident during a concert when our recorder playing had sounded piercingly shrill and shrieking, like the screech of a car braking violently and my reaction to this. Although this happened months previously, I had never, up until then, been able to face watching a video clip which had been recorded live at the concert by a friend in the audience. I couldn't bear the thought of hearing and reliving those awful moments but now, over a year later, I plucked up the courage to look at the video on my camera. To my astonishment there was no ghastly noise, no shrieking or screeching to be heard and I doubt whether anyone in the audience would have even noticed that we had gone wrong. I was astounded. I had been convinced that I had heard these noises at the time and could still hear these sounds in my head when I thought about that event but it was now clear to me that my auditory perception of this episode was totally skewed and I could see how I had also mis-perceived other issues during my illness. These were sobering realisations and it was not until then that I fully recognised the depth and intensity of my depressive illness at its worst time.

I was glad that I had made notes of what happened and how I felt at the time, as these notes were now very useful. Although I had not intended to write this book for my own benefit, I found that by starting to write about my experiences more coherently than in my diary, now that they were distanced in time, was very cathartic. I felt that this process would help me finally to put that phase of my life behind me and enable me to move on positively with confidence. After each writing session I felt very good, which was an added bonus.

Everything was going along well until the end of February, when one major setback occurred that later made me realise I was not fully recovered, in spite of all the progress I'd made. It was not, in reality, a big or serious event but it managed to take on a huge importance in my mind and cause me serious distress. It hardly seems worth writing about now, as the precipitating event was so insignificant, but I think it illustrates how fragile my new found mental health was and how easy it is sometimes to assume that you are better when, in fact, the depression is still lurking, waiting for an opportunity to pounce and rob you of all the progress you have made. It also shows how my perceptions were still faulty and dangerous.

The Recorder Group and Singing Group had decided to go out together for a meal at a local Italian restaurant. Being a member of both groups, I offered to organise it and made all the arrangements. The owner of the restaurant was intrigued by the nature of our groups and asked if we would perform some of our music after the meal, to which everyone agreed, albeit with the usual moans and groans, but no serious objections.

On the evening, everyone turned up with their music and recorders and we all enjoyed a delicious meal. Then, one of the members called me over and said that she was acting as spokesperson for the people on her table and they had decided they did not want to perform. At the time, I made light of it, put on a brave face and, with good grace, cancelled the arrangements to perform. Beneath this cheerful exterior I was feeling gutted, as if someone had ripped my body open and slashed at my heart. To my relief, the evening finished soon afterwards, so I did not have to keep up the pretence that everything was good for very long but was able to go home and there let my feelings out.

I felt so hurt and humiliated that this had happened in front of everyone present. My confidence was totally undermined, for I saw the objection to performing as a vote of no confidence in me as leader of the singing group. I felt that I had made a decision that no-one agreed with and they were now in revolt. A sleepless night followed, with thoughts and feelings swirling around in my head, tormenting me. Everything seemed magnified, black and white, in the darkness and I came to the decision that I would be unable to continue as leader of the singing group. I could feel that I was going into complete withdrawal and shutdown and, although I had some vague knowledge drifting in the mists at the back of my mind that all this was an overreaction, this somehow made it all worse, rather than better. It made me feel so hopeless, to know that I couldn't cope.

The next morning I felt and looked dreadful, still very tearful and upset. I went out early to walk the dog, before anyone would be around to see me, and then spent the rest of the day at home, hiding away, feeling totally drained, without the energy to do anything. I still felt the same the next day and was unable to face going to pilates, or to a previously arranged DVD viewing organised by the book group. I gave the excuse of not feeling well and I hid away, subdued and quiet at home, with no contact with anyone outside. My husband just thought I was having a 'tired' day and I didn't try to explain to him what had happened. No-one phoned me that day, not even my two best friends, so I then began to wonder if they were avoiding me, which made me feel even worse. My feelings of total worthlessness were rapidly taking over and beginning to envelop me once more.

Fortunately, over the weekend, my two friends did contact me. Margaret had heard from others in the book group that I wasn't well and she telephoned to ask how I was and whether I needed any shopping. It was clear from her demeanour that she was just concerned that I was unwell and hadn't made it to pilates or the book group meeting. She made no mention of what had occurred at the meal and I didn't bring up the issue, as she seemed perfectly normal. The next day, Sunday morning, when out walking the dog I heard my name being called from a lane across the road and, to my surprise, it was Ann, walking her dog. She could easily have avoided me, as I would never have noticed her had she not called out, so I concluded that she must have wanted to see me. We joined up and she did mention what had happened at the meal, suspecting I may have been upset by it. Her kindness and sympathy made me break down in tears and I told her how it had affected me and how bad I was feeling. Although she was sympathetic and understood how I felt, she was horrified when I told her of my decision to give up as leader and leave the Singing Group. In spite of her protestations, I was still determined that this was my only course of action.

That afternoon, I drafted a long email to the singing group

members, explaining my decision. Instead of just sending it, I phoned Margaret to ask if she would read it first and we arranged to meet the following day. So, the next afternoon we met in a café where we had a long talk. Like Ann, Margaret was horrified that I was taking what had happened so seriously. Up until then she hadn't even given it a second thought. Eventually, she made me see that I was over-reacting and it was all just a storm in a teacup. She told me that all the members of the singing group loved having me as the group leader and it had been their spontaneous suggestion that they should pay for my meal, as a token of appreciation. It was this that finally convinced me that, maybe, my feelings were irrational. It was as if a switch went in my head and my feelings of self-worth and self-confidence trickled back in. Once again, I was so grateful that I had such good friends who had, on this occasion, kept me sane and prevented me from acting and behaving in unhelpful, negative ways.

Two days later, I braved the singing group with some trepidation but all went well and we had a hilarious evening practising for a performance the following week. I was so pleased that I had been made to see sense and not to ruin one of the good things in my life. I would be in much need of these good things in the months to come.

Towards the end of February, I made an appointment to see Don's GP when I explained my concerns about his memory and general mental deterioration and asked her to bear this in mind when he came for his next appointment. Initially, she was taken aback and seemed uncomfortable that I'd taken this step of coming to see her but, after I assured her that I appreciated that she could not discuss Don's condition with me and I just wanted her to be aware of the situation when he came for his next appointment, she listened to what I had to tell her. I could see that my visit put her in a difficult position and I was glad that I could back up my action by telling her that this was something my psychiatrist had suggested. Without this, I may not have had the confidence to pursue the matter. Don's doctor encouraged me to tell him that I'd taken the step of going to see her which would make it easier for everyone. I said I would try to do this over the next month but I did not commit myself, knowing how resistant he'd been in the past to consulting her about these problems.

As it turned out, Don's next appointment happened sooner than anticipated, when I took him to see his GP as he had a bad cough. He always wanted me to accompany him in to see the doctor, as he would not always understand what was said or remember instructions afterwards. Although he'd been complaining for several days about the cough and that was the reason we had made the appointment, when his doctor asked him how he was, he immediately started to talk about his difficulties with memory, seeming oblivious to the reason for the visit! Once I recovered from the shock of his revealing these difficulties, I was relieved but had to intervene and explain about his cough which was then diagnosed as a chest infection and for which the doctor prescribed antibiotics. As usual she was very good at communicating with Don, managing to convey sympathy, care and encouragement and Don then agreed to do a short memory test, which left everyone in no doubt that there was a significant problem. The doctor also managed to get his agreement to be referred to the memory clinic. In spite of all his previous reluctance and refusal to consult anyone, Don now seemed quite happy to talk to her about his difficulties and to participate in the tests. I was extremely relieved that, at last, some action was being taken.

Over the next few days, whilst Don was taking the antibiotics prescribed for his chest infection, I realised that he had become incapable of managing his own medication. He couldn't work out which pills to take when, and had no idea afterwards what he had taken or even whether he had taken them at all. He had a number of other pills to take each day, at different times, so it was quite complicated and I offered to organise his medication in the future, so that I could be assured that he took everything as required. Rather to my surprise, Don did not resent this. Instead, he accepted the offer and seemed relieved not to have to deal with it himself any longer.

Another event, soon after that, also highlighted how his cognitive functions were deteriorating. The clocks changed to summertime that weekend but Don seemed completely unaware of what was happening. Changing the time on all the clocks in the house had always been his job. Usually, he would go around carrying out this task but, on this occasion, he didn't appear to understand either the concept or the practicalities of the time change. Explaining that we were moving to summertime meant nothing to him. He seemed to have no recollection that this happened every year. Although he was able to change the time manually on most of the clocks, he was completely blank about how to adjust the digital clock on the oven, even though this was something he had done many times in the past. I had to find the instruction manual and read the instructions to him on how to do it. All this signified another step-change in his mental deterioration.

Most of the time, Don still enjoyed life, especially going out for drives in the car and taking an interest in the garden, watching the birds on the bird table and feeders and appreciating the flowers as they bloomed; first the snowdrops, then crocuses, daffodils and tulips, their bright colours heralding spring. On one exceptionally warm sunny day in early April, we drove to the coast with a picnic, where he loved to watch our dog play in the sea. It was a lovely day and we were fortunate that we could make the most of the good weather.

At this time Don was still able to engage in long conversations on the telephone with our son, mainly about football and politics. He also enjoyed seeing our daughter and grandchildren on their visits but they had all begun to express concern and had noticed his mental deterioration by now.

During May, Don attended the Memory Clinic for an assessment, when the extent of his memory loss and the impairment of his cognitive function became even more evident. I was very shocked. It was very obvious to me what was happening but we then had to wait several months for an MRI scan of his brain and referral to a consultant, before a formal diagnosis of dementia could be made.

Meanwhile, Don enjoyed his eighty-fifth birthday and other family celebrations during the summer. I kept busy with my various activities but had cut these down so that I did not leave him alone unattended for any longer than an hour or so at a time. Sometimes I would take him with me, if he was willing and fit enough. An appointment for his MRI scan came through in July but we heard nothing of the results until September.

At the end of August, Don surprised me by agreeing to come with me to a performance by our Singing Group, at a local event during the town's Victorian Week. He amazed me by joining in the singing and thoroughly enjoying the afternoon. Up until now, for months or even years, he'd always refused to come to events like these with me but this was the start of a new phase in his life, which proved very positive for both of us. He seemed finally to let go of his resistance, to admit his difficulties and to be willing to talk to people about them. It made life a lot easier and more pleasant for both of us. Looking back now, I think that he had been aware of his mental deterioration for many months, which was why he was reluctant to meet people or join activities, where he would not be able to hide it from others or from himself. He had become more and more socially isolated, apart from seeing members of the family, and this, along with his poor physical health, may have caused him to suffer from mild depression. I was aware that he had become more and more miserable, irritable and lethargic but there was little I could do until he was willing to accept help and support. Now, it seemed that the gates had opened and he was no longer a prisoner behind them.

We finally met with a consultant psychiatrist in mid-September and received the formal diagnosis of dementia; it was identified as a mixture of vascular dementia and Alzheimer's Disease. The consultant prescribed some medication which would help delay the progress of the disease and gave us some practical advice about actions we needed to take, which was very helpful. We were told that we would be able to apply for Attendance Allowance and the consultant suggested that I start to look into getting some help with caring for Don, as this could take some time to get in place. He advised that there was no doubt that I would eventually need help as the illness progressed. The consultant's words and diagnosis didn't appear to impact on Don at all. I think they just went over his head. I wasn't shocked or upset at the diagnosis because I had known for months what was happening. I had some previous experience of caring for Don's mother, who developed dementia in her old age back in the seventies. She came to live with us for some months, before the illness became too much to cope with. We had two young children and two foster-children at the time and, night after night, our sleep was disturbed by her rambling around the house or going outside to roam the streets. She became increasingly aggressive and unpredictable and, after she nearly set the house on fire one night, we found her a place in a care home, where the staff were better able to protect her and those around her from danger. Maybe it was a long forgotten or hidden memory of this that made Don so fearful that I would have him 'put away'.

Now that we finally had an official diagnosis for Don, it was just a relief to be able to think about getting some help and planning for the future. The next few months were surprisingly happy ones for both of us. Don wasn't upset or distressed about the diagnosis and, in spite of some physical aches and pains, he continued to come out with me to various events. In October, he joined U3A and started coming to the monthly meetings, where he didn't always understand the lectures but nevertheless enjoyed meeting people who were always friendly and kind. It did him so much good to get out of the house for an hour or two and he seemed much more cheerful, sociable and amenable.

Unfortunately, I became unwell again that autumn with a very bad cough, which left me feeling exhausted for a number of weeks, but I managed to keep going and to deal with all the tasks that now had to be undertaken. Filling in various forms, applying for Attendance Allowance and Power of Attorney, as advised by the psychiatrist, was time consuming but at least I felt we were getting things organised for the future. The medication seemed to be helping as, not only was Don seeming less confused, but he was actively taking pleasure in all sorts of things: buying a new pair of shoes; having new floor covering put down in the kitchen; going for drives in the car and to the garden centre to choose some autumn plants. He started to come shopping with me once a week and took great pleasure in wandering round the supermarket. It took a long while to do the shopping but was worth the extra time to see him become more positive and cheerful.

Once more, physical illness was taking its toll on me and it was difficult to shake off my chest infection yet, in spite of some days when I felt dreadful physically and very low emotionally, knowing that my patience and tolerance were at a very low ebb, I used what I'd learnt in Mindfulness to stave off real depression and suicidal feelings. I managed to accept the bad feelings, recognise them for what they were and to avoid panic or guilt at being weak or depressed. I knew that all these feelings would pass in time. The main difference was that all I wanted this time was to recover and feel better again; I certainly had no wish to die.

Just as I was getting better at the end of October, there was another minor drama when Don became ill, complaining of chest pains. I took him to the surgery where the duty doctor diagnosed another chest infection. She also arranged for an ECG and blood tests, to determine whether the pains were caused by the heart or the lungs. When the results came back, she then called us back to the surgery in the evening. The blood tests were inconclusive and so she offered immediate hospital admission for further definitive tests but we decided to decline, as the ECG had shown no sign of a heart attack and we went home with some strong pain killers and antibiotics, with instruction to go back or ring 999 if the pains became worse. After this initial panic, things settled down; Don responded well to the antibiotics and life returned to normal.

In early November, our local 'Mind' started up a Memory Café once a week where people with dementia and their carers could go for a couple of hours to chat and join in various activities. Don and I went along to the initial meeting, where we met several other married couples. All the men had been diagnosed with dementia and had been brought along by their wives. The idea was to create a café atmosphere where we could meet for a coffee or tea, talk together and engage in other activities if we wished. We all became great friends and this café became a regular activity once a week, which both Don and I enjoyed together. There was a very relaxed atmosphere in comfortable, pleasant surroundings, with interesting people to talk to and a programme of regular speakers for an hour once a month. The speakers were mainly aimed at the carers and they provided us all with lots of useful information. The most useful and important benefit though was gained from talking to each other about how we coped, what we found useful and how we had solved problems. There was a variety of craft activities on offer as well as games, reminiscences and sometimes singing or armchair exercises. We started to make 'Memory Boxes' and this activity provided hours of interest, both at the café and as we continued with it at home. One of the best things about the café was being able to talk to other carers, to share our problems and solutions.

I was glad that I had reorganised my life, given up my book group and the voluntary work in school, to make more time for us to do things together. We both continued to go to U3A and, around this time, I had become involved in producing a pantomime. It was to be a joint effort involving several U3A interest groups: the Creative Writing group was writing the words; the Singing Group and the Recorder Group would be performing songs and music and the Art Group later became involved in painting the scenery. We were due to perform at the U3A Christmas Lunch in early December, so the next weeks were very busy with finalising the story line, learning songs, sorting out costumes and rehearsals. Everyone worked together very well and we all had a great deal of fun. Don was not involved in the performance itself but he came along to some of the rehearsals, including the final rehearsal of the singers which took place at our home on the Sunday afternoon before the great day. Our performance on that occasion left a lot to be desired but we practised well and, with no time to forget what we had learnt at the rehearsal, all went very smoothly on the day itself! Don sat in the front row and loved every minute of it, particularly as he had got to know the people involved in acting and singing. He knew the words to the songs and was able to appreciate the humour. The audience was appreciative and it was well worth all the effort.

November and December had both been busy months, with the start-up of the memory café, preparing for the pantomime and other pre-Christmas events; we made Christmas shopping trips, attended several concerts and were invited to several celebratory lunches. One evening, we drove to our granddaughter's school concert where she played a solo on the euphonium. We were very proud of her. Much to my delight, Don was keen to go out and he enjoyed all these activities with me, telling several friends that, in spite of his memory problems, he was very happy and enjoying life. He had never been very interested in Christmas but this year he took great pleasure in all the preparations, even buying Christmas presents for the family and for the dog. His obvious enjoyment and happiness made me very happy too and I felt very well both physically and mentally. I wrote in my diary at this time: 'I feel that all my shattered pieces are not only back in place but also are well-fitted and glued solidly together.' It had been a long, hard road with many ups, downs and hold-ups but I had persevered and come through it all.

Our Christmas and New Year were fine, in spite of some cancelled plans due to illness, and both Don and I enjoyed the festivities, caught up with some old friends and had a successful visit to the New Year Sales, in which Don bought himself a new reclining leather armchair. It seemed as if our lives were on track and going well, in spite of all the potential difficulties of coping with depression and dementia.

Chapter Fifteen
TURBULENT WATERS
(January to March 2016)

This happy life, however, was soon to come crashing down when, all of a sudden, Don's mood changed dramatically. First, he became miserable and silent, refusing to talk or to eat or to go out anywhere for a few days, then this mood changed to one of anger and aggression, with him shouting, swearing at me, threatening to hit me and calling me a liar. He even brought up the car accident of more than two years ago, accusing me of trying to kill him by crashing the car. I was at a loss to understand what had happened, what triggered all this abuse and the complete change of personality, so different from the last two or three months, when he'd been so happy, content, loving and pleased with our life together.

These few days were very difficult and came to a head one afternoon, when he came into the bedroom as I was getting ready to go out. He became extremely threatening, bringing his clenched fist up to my face, threatening to hit me and ranting on and on. He wouldn't let me get by him to leave the room, grabbed hold of my car keys, shut the bedroom door and refused to let me out. The phone rang but he grabbed it and wouldn't let me answer it. Trying to reason with him just seemed to make him worse. Somehow, I remained very calm and just let him rage on and on, until at last the tirade petered out. He suddenly threw the keys at me, left the room and went downstairs. I just sat down in shock, feeling sick and faint, unable to move, to think or to believe what had just happened. Not only had he come very close to physical violence, but I felt I had been taken prisoner in my own home, which I found very shocking. Even as I write this now, several years later, it makes me feel physically ill. People have since asked me why, given his physical frailty, I didn't push him out of the way or knock him to the ground, and I suppose this may well have been possible. The answer is I don't know but the thought of being violent with him never occurred to me, especially as I was in such a state of shock and fear at his anger and rage.

I just seemed numb. I stayed in the bedroom for several hours, wondering what to do. I wanted to escape from my home, which now seemed like a prison but I didn't see how I could leave Don without any preparation or making any arrangements for his care, and also I couldn't stop crying so didn't want to see anyone. The evening passed in silence, with Don downstairs and me upstairs, too afraid to make a phone call in case he heard and this would start his anger up again. Exhausted, I finally went to bed early and slept until 5.00 am

When I woke, it all hit me again. I was still numb with shock, horror and fear; at a complete loss to know what to do. Feeling very tearful and with my legs trembling, I went downstairs and crept out with the dog for his usual morning walk. When I returned home, I found Don in the kitchen, calm and quiet. I suggested we had a talk, during which he told me that he didn't want me to leave but wanted us to return to how we'd been before. It was mystifying but we sorted out some practical issues that he was concerned about and it was very apparent that he was completely unable to manage on his own. Things were calm now but the day passed with us both being emotionally exhausted and unable to do very much, before we went to bed quite early.

On Sunday morning, when I got up, I found Don asleep in an armchair downstairs and it was obvious that he'd been drinking whisky. I let him sleep whilst I busied myself with the usual Sunday morning tasks, taking the dog out, preparing and cooking lunch. I roused him at eleven o'clock but he just groaned, grunted and refused to have a shower. He seemed quite drunk by then. I hoped that the smell of roast beef cooking would make him hungry, as this was one of his favourite meals, and that then he would feel better, but he refused to eat anything and it became clear that he was working up to an angry state again. I forced my meal down somehow, cleared up and took Llewi out for a long walk in the afternoon, just leaving Don alone.

When I got back about 4.00 pm all was quiet and I thought Don must have gone upstairs to bed but then I heard Llewi scuffling around in the sitting room and went to see what he was doing. Don was lying on the floor, conscious, but his speech was very slow and slurred. He refused my help to get up off the floor, shaking me off aggressively. I was concerned that he'd fallen and knocked his head or injured himself, so I phoned the out-of-hours doctor service and was told that a doctor would visit within four to six hours. By now, I was very distressed but managed to help Don up from the floor. He then threw me off violently, obviously very angry again, and I left him to slump down into an armchair, incapable of moving on his own. He was in no mood to talk and I didn't want to risk inflaming the situation by trying to reason with him, so I went upstairs and stayed there until the doctor arrived at about 7.00 pm.

Still very drunk and angry, Don was shouting at me and blaming me for all sorts of things. He seemed convinced that the doctor was a policeman and refused any help from him, including any tablets to calm him down. After some considerable time, it became clear that Don was not going to respond to talking, or to accept any help from the doctor. I was very fearful of being left with him in this state and my body was visibly trembling all over, so the doctor suggested that, being a Sunday when it would take hours to get anything else organised, I should leave the home for the night and contact the mental health service in the morning. I decided to take up this suggestion while I had the chance with the doctor still in attendance and so hastily put together an overnight bag, put the dog in the car and drove off while the doctor was still there.

I was fortunate to find a reasonable bed and breakfast place quite easily and booked into a nice warm room, where I finally managed to stop shaking and to relax over a hot chocolate. Llewi settled down without any trouble and I managed to sleep from about 10.00 pm until 4.00 am when I woke, worrying that Don would have locked me out of the house and I would be unable to get in.

Just after 9.00 am I put in a phone call to the mental health team but was unable to speak to the duty officer immediately and then missed a call from her when she phoned back. I went back to the house, where Don was in the kitchen. Our kitchen is at the front so he saw me arrive and let me in but he was still in a very angry mood. Later that morning, I managed to get him to agree to sit down and talk sensibly. However, he just repeated all his grievances, some real, some imagined, and, some of the time, he was clearly mixing me up with his first wife. Very little of it made sense. He seemed in a terrible state physically, with his hands shaking, very unsteady on his feet and complaining of a headache and a bump on his head. I thought these symptoms were probably a result of the alcohol the previous day as, although he denied drinking very much, I knew from the state of him that was not the case.

Don was sitting in the dining room when I went into the kitchen to make some lunch and he was convinced that there were people in the kitchen with me; he said he could hear them talking and see their reflections in the hall door. Whatever I said could not convince him that there was no-one else there but, in spite of being agitated by these hallucinations and my denial of them, he didn't become angry again, much to my relief. After he'd eaten, I helped him from the dining room to the sitting room, as he couldn't stand or walk unaided, and left him to have a sleep on the sofa.

One of the GPs from our local surgery and the mental health duty officer both phoned. I told them all was quiet now but, later that afternoon, the mental health duty officer and her colleague appeared at the, door wanting to check out the situation for themselves. Fortunately, we all managed to avoid winding Don up again and they left, satisfied that all was calm at the moment.

Our uneasy truce continued the following day but I could feel the tension gradually building again and I was concerned that Don would try to prevent me from going out to an appointment previously arranged with my psychiatrist the following afternoon. I felt in desperate need of going to that appointment to talk through what was happening and, as a precaution, I packed a bag and put it in the car in case I needed to leave again. My fears were well founded, as Don erupted again that evening. He again threatened physical violence and the depth of his rage was extremely frightening. I could see that he was only just controlling himself not to hit me. I lay in bed that night frozen, unable to move or make a sound, a feeling I'd experienced as a child, when I thought burglars were under my bed. Knowing that I couldn't continue to live in a state of fear like this, I worked out a plan of action for the next morning.

I escaped from the house by saying that I was taking the dog for his usual walk but I took my car keys with me. When I returned, I left the dog quietly in the side porch and made a quick getaway in my car, before Don could realise what was happening. Once again, I was trembling and shaking all over, relieved to have got away but not knowing what to do next. I was sitting in the car by the side of the road, completely numb, when my friend, Ann, came along, walking her dog. She knew nothing of what had been going on for the past few days but she could see the state of me and took me home to her house. I was feeling terrible, shivering with cold, and feeling faint but improved a little after a cup of tea and a seat in Ann's warm kitchen. I told her the story of what had happened and she immediately offered me the chance to stay with her for the time being, for which I was very grateful. Ann then phoned our GP surgery to explain the developments and to express my concerns over leaving Don alone. After some time, we received a call to say that my psychiatrist, Dr Helen, and a CPN would visit Don and that I should keep my appointment with Dr Helen at the Health Centre that afternoon.

So later I drove there with some trepidation and saw Dr Helen, who also had two medical students with her. I was in floods of tears and upset with myself at being so fearful, as well as being shocked and emotional because of what had actually happened. Dr Helen was very sympathetic and told me about her visit to Don, who was still very angry but she thought his aggression may be a result of the medication for dementia. As far as my fears were concerned, she explained that fear is a very powerful emotion and no-one knows how they will react until faced with something they find frightening. She prescribed diazepam to calm me down and suggested that I stay away from home for a week, to allow myself time to feel stronger again, assuring me that she and her team would be responsible for Don's care. She advised me not to go home on my own during this time. If I had to go there for any reason, I must be accompanied.

I left feeling a little relieved, especially that I did not have to make decisions for the time being. I went back to Ann's and, as I was concerned about Llewi, we both went to the house to ask Don if I could take him. The side door was locked so I had to ring the front door bell and Don appeared, looking very aggressive. When I asked to take Llewi, he just pushed him out of the door and slammed it shut. I was just thankful to have Llewi with me, knowing that Don would be incapable of walking him or looking after him properly. We gave him a short walk, then went back to Ann's house. She was very kind and caring but I was in no state to respond very much, just extremely thankful to get into bed that evening with a hot water bottle. I took one of the diazepam tablets and fell asleep quite quickly although I had some distressing dreams.

The days immediately following this trauma are difficult to remember. I did not keep a diary and I think I was still numb with shock most of the time. The thing I remember most was feeling cold, shivering much of the time, as I seemed unable to get or keep warm. It was just a bleak, cold time when I hadn't even the energy to think for myself. The CPN phoned me each day and told me that I was still suffering from shock and not to worry about the state I was in mentally as it was only temporary and would pass. Ann looked after me well and I appreciated just doing as I was told for a few days. I didn't have to think or plan or make any decisions. After a few days, I managed eventually to summon the energy to phone my daughter to tell her where I was and to give her brief details of what had happened.

That weekend, my daughter drove up to collect me and take me to her house. I had arranged with the CPN to meet her at my own home so that I could collect some clothes and some things for the dog but, as the time approached, I was feeling so physically ill, sick, faint and on edge that my daughter went instead to collect what I needed.

Time seemed to stop over the next week and it seemed to me like a much longer period. Everything was cold and dark, even though I was with my family. I suppose the diazepam kept me calm and I must have made some effort to appear normal to my grandchildren but that time is like a black hole, about which I remember very little, just feeling crushed and somehow violated. I knew that I couldn't stay at my daughter's indefinitely, there just not being the room, and I tried to find accommodation in a women's refuge but nowhere would let me bring the dog. Llewi was the one constant thing in my life at that time, such a good friend and totally dependent on me. If it hadn't been for him, I'm sure I would have just given up completely. As it was, I had to keep going, to make an effort for him and for my family who were being so supportive.

My daughter had spoken to Don on the telephone several times. Although he seemed to have calmed down, she was concerned that he wasn't coping well and seemed very confused. She had previously contacted our doctor, who had visited but was unable to do anything as Don had refused any help.

When Menna, my daughter, had spoken to Don on the phone, he had told her that he wanted me to come back so, after a few days when I was feeling a little stronger, I decided to face up to things and to go on a visit to my home. My son agreed to accompany me and we travelled there one morning, taking a meal that I'd prepared the previous day. The atmosphere was strained but we all ate lunch and I successfully cleared all the out of date food from the fridge but things then started to deteriorate. Talking soon broke down into angry recriminations by Don, so my son and I left for a while to go shopping and then returned with some supplies of food. The atmosphere was no better and it was clear that there was no point in staying any longer.

A few days later, I returned home again. It was one afternoon when the CPN was due to visit Don. Things went slightly better this time and Don agreed to try some new medication which the CPN told me would also help to calm him, as well as helping with the dementia. She had brought a social worker with her to discuss a care package that would be needed if he was to remain on his own but, as there seemed to be some improvement, I agreed to stay and see how things progressed.

Over the next few weeks, our relationship generally improved, although there were still some difficult occasions from time to time. On some days he was very quiet and confused, seeming not even to know who he was or what had happened; on other days he was irritable and argumentative but there were also some positive days when he started to enjoy life again. The CPN visited us regularly but sometimes these visits made Don suspicious and anxious and, on one occasion, he accused me of trying to collect evidence to get a divorce. On another occasion, he blew up saying he wanted to make his own decisions and objected violently to people trying to help him or take over his life but, fortunately, these episodes didn't last long and by the next day he had forgotten all about them. One thing he did enjoy was attending physiotherapy sessions at the Falls Clinic at our local hospital. These not only helped to improve his balance but also gave him a sense of achievement and they seemed to boost his self-confidence.

It was a difficult time for both of us but I was coping from day to day until, early in February, I became unwell with a sore throat and cold, when I became very depressed with serious suicidal thoughts once more. The CPN was still visiting us once a week and she told us that the psychiatrist had suggested Don might benefit from Advocacy. He wasn't at all keen on the idea and the suggestion made me very angry, upset and hurt. I didn't know why they felt it necessary for him to have an advocate, now that I was home and we were coping. I felt they didn't trust me and I had a strong feeling of betrayal as, originally, Dr Helen had been my psychiatrist but now she seemed to be more interested in protecting Don. This seemed unfair when I was the one who'd been threatened and forced to leave my own home. Don, however, wasn't at all interested in the suggestion of advocacy so nothing more became of that. I went to bed early and cried a lot before going to sleep.

The following morning, I was still tearful: I really did not want to get up and face the day, and suicidal thoughts entered my mind once more. With great willpower, I did get up and dress but I felt so awful with a headache, nausea and a cough that I had to go back to bed for a while before I was able to take Llewi for his walk. We did very little else that day and I was worried about my daughter who was ill with flu. I felt very guilty that I was not helping to care for her when she had been so good to me.

The next few days followed a similar pattern. I had great difficulty in getting up each morning but managed to force myself to cook meals and walk the dog, even though I was feeling dreadful, both physically and mentally. When I slept, I was having terrifying dreams, which left me feeling exhausted and low. Even though I was sleeping, it wasn't restful sleep and it didn't provide me with any respite. I was aware that I was fighting hard to stave off depression once more and this was a terrifying thought.

The following week, I was feeling better physically but Don erupted once again with no apparent cause. We'd had quite a good day together and I took him out for a drive in the car during the afternoon which he enjoyed but, in the evening, he became very angry again, shouting and saying that he wanted to hit me but he managed to control himself. When he'd fallen asleep, I packed a suitcase and put it in the car, in case I need to make a quick escape. The thought made me anxious, distressed and tearful and I felt awful about being prepared to leave him alone during the last years of his life. But, also, I knew that I was not prepared to live in fear in my own home and that it was difficult to trust him.

I decided not to leave again, unless he became violent, but was prepared to flee at short notice, keeping my car keys on me at all times and my suitcase in my car. The next day, I just felt numb and suspended from reality in a bubble. Whilst out walking the dog, I thought of walking in front of a van on the road but was saved from doing so because of my concern for Llewi. Totally lethargic, I had no motivation to do anything positive and all I could think of was how soon I could go to bed to block everything out with sleep.

The eruptions of anger and rage continued over the next week or so but there were no further threats of violence and then Don became preoccupied with his physical ailments for a while. I had taken him to have a steroid injection in his shoulder, arranged by his GP, but a large swelling had come up on his ribs and the physiotherapist decided to send him for an X-ray and wait for the report on this before doing the injection. We managed to get an appointment to see a GP that evening who did a ten-minute blood test to eliminate a clot in the lungs and this proved negative. The GP also arranged some further blood tests to be done the following day but he thought the cause was probably muscular, so we went home after an hour, with painkillers and ibuprofen gel to relieve the pain.

The swelling gradually decreased over the next week, by the time we went back to see the GP, who told us that the X-ray was clear, so it was definitely muscular and he prescribed some stronger gel, which seemed to help. Don was able to go to his physiotherapy sessions which he enjoyed and he responded well to the attention and praise from the physiotherapist.

We then entered a period of intense mood swings for a few weeks. One minute Don would appear happy, joking, sometimes a bit childish, but this could change rapidly and he would suddenly become irritable, negative and angry. The good thing was that the anger was no longer directed at me, personally. Most of the time and with patience and time, I could talk him through what had happened and calm him down. I came to realise that these eruptions usually occurred when he couldn't understand something and this made him frustrated and angry. On one occasion, when I was out walking the dog, a letter had arrived in the post about his premium bonds. He couldn't work out what it was about and he became convinced that National Savings were swindling him out of his money. By the time I came home he was fuming. He was also receiving invoices from the London Mint, in respect of coins he'd ordered by phone (without my knowledge), and became very agitated about these demands for money. It took me weeks to work out the complicated details but, after numerous conversations with people at the London Mint and several letters, we were able to sort everything out and return some of the coins. It was clear that Don didn't like being so dependent on me and was sometimes suspicious that I was defrauding him but, by writing things down very simply and explaining in clear steps what was happening, I could usually calm him down and get him to understand, at least in that moment. He would have forgotten again an hour later.

Was I suffering from depression again during this time? I don't know the answer to that. It was a difficult time with our relationship smashed to pieces. The trust in each other, built up over more than forty years together, was no longer there. Many of my previous symptoms of depression were present or there, just under the surface. I was nervous, twitchy, easily given to trembling and shaking, and tearful whenever things became difficult. I no longer took part in my usual activities and avoided social contact with everyone I could. It was just a matter of keeping going, doing what was essential and taking each day at a time. I had no real interest in anything but kept myself busy within the home, doing fairly mundane tasks. On the positive side, my cognitive functions were working properly and I was very aware of my survival instincts being back on track. I wasn't happy but I certainly had no wish to be a victim of violence or to die. I felt some guilt at having left Don on his own but was now working hard to try to make our lives work together again.

Looking back now, I think that my leaving had a huge effect on Don. In spite of his difficulties, he realised that I would not put up with his threats of violence and he managed to control his temper to some extent, although he found it very difficult. He expressed some remorse over his actions and we spent much time talking with the CPN about the effect that coming from a home where his father was physically abusive to his mother had on him. I think, had I not taken the chance to escape from my home on that dreadful weekend, his threats would have escalated into physical blows before long.

Slowly, with each day feeling like a week and each week like a month, we struggled through February. It was my daughter's birthday but she and her children were all unwell with coughs and colds, so we didn't see them for some weeks. In spite of the cold weather, I took Don out in the car for a few drives. He would sit in the car, listening to music on Radio 3, while I walked the dog. This was about all I could manage, apart from the essential tasks of shopping and cooking meals. I always seemed tired and it took enormous effort just to keep going. I was unable to read or to concentrate on television or films. Life was grey, sometimes black, and always joyless, just a matter of survival and avoiding too many eruptions or dramas.

Our weekly meetings with the CPN gradually became less fraught and, by the end of the month, Don seemed to respond to the new medication, which had built up gradually during that time. He was no longer losing his temper or being aggressive and gradually I started to allow myself to relax a little, too. Sensing that our relationship was less fragile, the CPN ceased her visits during March but advised me to contact her again if matters deteriorated.

Over the next couple of months, I gradually started to engage with one or two close friends, very tentatively at first, and although still often feeling exhausted, I managed to return to pilates, thinking that it was something I should be doing. I didn't enjoy it and avoided social contact with members of the group, just attending the session and leaving straight afterwards. I had made progress but was far from being fully recovered from the trauma.

Chapter Sixteen
AN EVEN KEEL

Over the next few months, Don was becoming more and more confused as the weeks passed, with some days much worse than others, but his mood was mellow and usually cheerful, which made life manageable. His physiotherapy programme came to an end during March but we both enrolled at a 'Round the World Cookery' course for six weeks at our local Mind and, surprisingly, this was a great success! There were only six of us on the course and we had an excellent tutor, who kept us busy working together at preparing and cooking a meal, which we then all sat down to enjoy at lunchtime.

The food we produced looked amazing and was so delicious! In that first session, we cooked Italian meatballs in tomato sauce, with tomato and mascarpone salad and grilled peppers. We couldn't believe what we'd all achieved together and these sessions soon became the highlight of our week. The relaxed, friendly atmosphere of the class, yet with a sense of purpose and co-operation, made it a pleasant social occasion and the course did wonders for my self-confidence, especially as I was able to help others, as well as learning new skills myself. I noticed that Don was very happy chopping up vegetables and herbs; it gave him a sense of purpose and achievement, so I started to encourage him to do the same at home sometimes. This meant I had to start preparing lunch quite early in the morning, as it took him a long while, and continual supervision was needed but, once we got organised, it helped both of us.

Realising this made me reflect about other aspects of our lives. I saw that I would need to change some of my activities and spend more time on things that we could do together. The other members at the memory café had invited us to join them at a 'Singing for the Brain' session they went to twice a month in a neighbouring town so, in spite of some reluctance on Don's part to join in at first, we persevered and, later, he came to enjoy going to sing with this group twice a month. It was run by a brilliant tutor, specially trained by the Alzheimer's Society, who somehow achieved the impossible and got us all singing, often in four parts! Don remembered most of the old songs and found that he could still sing well when he tried. Receiving compliments from the other singers and helpers about how well he could sing really boosted his confidence and enjoyment. We always started the session with tea and biscuits and got to know the others in the group, so it was a nice social occasion as well and we now had another regular enjoyable afternoon together.

Unfortunately, I had to give up swimming to attend these sessions, as both were on a Monday afternoon. I'd long since given up Book Group and had also stopped going to the local primary school to hear children read, as I just couldn't find the time any more. Looking after Don and helping him with personal care was time consuming. Just getting him up, showered, dressed and breakfasted in the morning took a huge chunk of time and couldn't be rushed. Any sort of pressure would soon result in him becoming very agitated and upset. Everything had to be done at his pace, which I found difficult at first but soon learnt that it was the only sensible way to manage.

Since the upheaval at the beginning of the year, I hadn't attended the recorder group and had passed the Singing for Fun Group over to another member to run while my life was in chaos.

I was again finding it difficult to attend anything which involved large groups of people but was beginning to be able to talk to individuals and found everyone I spoke to very sympathetic and supportive. I surprised myself by being open about what had happened, rather than buttoning it all tight inside me, having learnt about the value of sharing from my previous experience of depression. I still found it hard to share difficult feelings and events but was particularly touched when two friends, quite independently, responded to my 'confession' by offering me sanctuary in their homes, should I ever need to escape from threats or from violence in the future. This made such an impression on me; I began to feel valued, less angry about how I'd been treated, and it brought about an improvement in my self-esteem. I was able to let go of some of the resentment that I'd been harbouring.

Walking each day was still important to me and I somehow made time to take the dog out twice a day, whatever the weather, always taking the time to notice and reflect on everything around me. My diary entries during the month of March read rather like a nature diary but they are a good illustration of how I had taken mindfulness on board and how my close observation of what was surrounding me in the present moment was playing an important part in enhancing my awareness during my daily walks:

Friday 8 March

A blustery day with frequent showers. Twigs and branches litter the path, blown down by the gales overnight. The wind ruffles the water of the lake but the birds are not deterred today; swans, ducks and geese cluster and crowd together at one end, pushing and shoving, shaking their wings, the geese calling stridently to each other in strange mating rituals. Moorhens move furtively in and out of the reeds. The puddles are bright with reflections and, when the rain falls on them, the drops make lovely patterns, hundreds of concentric circles, ever moving and changing. Another shower falls. This time it is hail, the stones biting and stinging my face as they fall, bouncing and dancing on the ground before they melt and disappear.

Saturday 9 March

Another windy March day, the clouds scudding across the sky; low clouds, dark and heavy; light grey clouds higher up, shining silver, back-lit by the sun; highest of all, fluffy white clouds among patches of blue sky, through which the sun suddenly makes a brilliant entrance for a few minutes, before the clouds move on to cover it again. There has been heavy rain, and water still streams on the road along the gutters, tinkling as it trickles into a drain half-blocked with leaves and debris.

We walk through the cemetery and listen to the wind in the trees; the deciduous trees bare silhouettes against the sky but the coniferous trees green and vibrant – cypress, yew, tall Scots Pine and a group of majestic cedars, spreading their horizontal branches like wings. I have grown to love the cemetery; it holds no horrors for me but is a place of calm, peace and timelessness. There are several seats donated in memory of loved ones and sometimes I sit here with the sun on my face and I think of all those people who have been laid to rest here, some of them for many years, and I wonder what life was like for them, when they lived here in a different era.

The hedges have all been cut now; some have been pleached, their layers looking neat and cared for, whilst others have been massacred by the hedge cutters and look like unkempt hedgehogs with their tops all shorn and bristly. Sheltered in the hedgerow are one or two celandines in bud and a cluster of primroses, their lovely flowers looking rather pale and bedraggled after the wet, windy weather, perhaps feeling sorry that they have bloomed so early. The hawthorn bushes have tightly furled green buds, just waiting for some warmth to break into leaf, whilst the blackthorn twigs are covered in minute pink buds, looking as if they have been sprinkled with hundreds and thousands. These are one of the few shrubs whose flowers appear before their leaves and the buds will shortly become a cloud of frothy white blossom. Spring is definitely waiting just around the corner.

We stop for a brief rest on a bench at the top of the hill, from where we have a good view of the town in the valley below. The wet slate roofs gleam brightly in the sunlight, while the hills surrounding the town stand proudly against the sky. There are daffodils planted by the bench, nodding their yellow heads and somehow staying upright in spite of the wind. As we come to the village there are more signs of spring in the gardens, yellow forsythia about to burst into flower and clouds of pink blossom on the trees. On the way back home, we skirt around the outside of the cemetery where the moss on the walls is growing vigorously and feels spongy with all the water it has absorbed. The wind is still strong but the sun is out and between them they are drying everywhere out.

15 March

After heavy rain overnight, the river is full and flowing fast but, surprisingly, hasn't burst its banks. The water swirls and eddies as it travels over submerged rocks, with branches, twigs and other debris propelled along in the rapids. The streams that feed the river are rushing torrents, pouring down the hillsides, splashing and crashing over the stony base.

The wind is strong but the sheep are still in the field, up to their ankles in mud but still feeding with heads to the ground. The field is like a miniature battlefield from the First World War, pockmarked with tiny craters made by the sheep's feet, the holes full of water which glints in the brief bursts of sunshine.

One or two celandines have buds showing but these are firmly closed against the weather. High up on the top of a group of oak trees, crows stand, silent and motionless like sentries guarding their nests, apparently unperturbed by the swaying branches in the fierce wind.

It seems that spring is on hold today.

16 March

This morning the sheep in the field are up to their knees in wet mud but most are managing to persevere in the foraging for food. A small group is gathered in one corner of the field, lying down in the shelter of the hedge. They look as if they've given up the search for food but maybe they're just replete.

The wind is still blustery but the sun is shining and the crows are flying frantically around over the tree tops, their raucous cries piercing the air. Two red kites are high in the sky, swooping and gliding on the thermals. The celandines have suddenly burst open, their brilliant yellow petals shining like miniature suns amidst the thick carpet of heart-shaped green leaves.

Primroses are standing straight and strong today, their faces turned towards the sun, luxuriating in its light and warmth.

20 March

The spring equinox and a glorious sunny afternoon. The wind has dropped, the sun feels warm on my face. Everything is bursting into life – pale green leaves unfurling on the brambles, brighter green ones on the hawthorn, and clouds of white frothy blossom on the sloe bushes. It's still wet and muddy underfoot and pools of water lie in the fields. The dog gallops joyfully through deep ditches, splashing everywhere, then rolling in the dead bracken to dry off. He seems full of life in the spring sunshine. Flocks of birds crowd the lake, their different cries competing for attention, swans, geese, ducks and a huge number of gulls, whose white bodies shine and shimmer as if they are made of silver foil as they circle and dive above the glistening water of the lake. A willow tree is transformed from its winter nakedness by a cloak of misty, delicate green.

During March, our wedding anniversary, my birthday and Easter all passed by quietly, although we did manage a visit to my daughter on Easter Sunday, where we had an enjoyable day with the family whom we hadn't seen for a couple of months. Things were gradually returning to something approaching normality, but a new normality.

In April, we seemed to have a spate of people calling on us: the Occupational Therapist came to do an assessment of Don's needs and put arrangements in place to have a seat and handrails fitted in the shower, and a trolley to help him move around the house so that he did not have to carry things; then two District Nurses came to see us; and also a lovely person from the Carers' Organisation, who suggested that I obtain a Carer's Card to keep in my wallet, so that if anything happened to me, people would know that Don would be in need of care. We followed up all their suggestions and also arranged for Don to have an emergency call-button to wear, so that he could press this if he had a fall or felt ill when I was out. He had an appointment with the physiotherapist for steroid injections in his shoulder and a respiratory review with the nurse at the GP surgery. It was a busy time but it was a relief to get things organised, which would make life easier for both of us, and having to focus on all these practical arrangements helped me to avoid ruminating on the events of the past few months.

I started taking Don out with me almost wherever I went and mostly he accompanied me without complaint. Occasionally, if he really didn't want to go, we would stay at home and, when Don was snoozing or watching a programme on television, I used the time to write more of this book. He could no longer follow a drama or a film but still enjoyed watching sport and the various antiques programmes, which seem plentiful on daytime television. Most of the time when we were at home, though, he would follow me around the house, watching whatever I was doing and, again, I started to find small tasks with which he could help.

During May, I received an appointment to go to see my psychiatrist,

Dr Helen. I was worried that Don would want to come with me, as I really wanted to be able to talk to her without him being present. Fortunately, on the day of the appointment, Don fell asleep in the armchair after lunch so I left him a note and went alone. I was still very angry about the way I'd been treated, which made me approach the appointment with some trepidation but Dr Helen was so caring and kind that it didn't seem important any more. She made it clear from the outset that this time was about me but, at the same time, she needed to know how Don was, as he was a major influence on my mental health.

We had a long talk about what had happened, how things were progressing and we identified my danger points which might trigger depression. I knew by now that the main ones were getting overtired or being unwell. She was particularly concerned when I told her that Don now followed me around the house like a puppy, watching everything I did. She explained that continual 'shadowing' like this is very exhausting and that I needed to take care to look after myself as well as Don. She stressed the need for me to get some help and advised me to apply for Attendance Allowance and use that money to pay for a 'Personal Assistant' for Don, in order to give me respite for several hours a week.

We also talked about Don's medication and Dr Helen's opinion that his aggressive episode had probably been caused by the drug, Aricept. The new medication, Nemdatine, would have a calming effect and, although it was not as effective as preventing memory/cognition deterioration, she thought it was more important to keep him on an even keel emotionally, to avoid anger and paranoid feelings which made him unmanageable. I was able to talk to her in detail about my feelings of fear, of guilt and of anger, which helped to release them and to relieve me of the worst of them. Dr Helen strongly advised that I stay on the antidepressants for at least another year as, although I had made good progress, I would still be in significant danger of suffering depression again, with all the stress of Don's dementia to cope with. She would see me again in about six months but stressed that if I felt in need of support at any point before then, I should pick up the phone and ask for help.

I found this meeting immeasurably helpful, including all the practical advice, and left with a new confidence, very motivated to get things moving.

It was now that I decided the time had come to re-join the U3A Singing for Fun Group and I took Don along with me. I was very apprehensive about going to the first session but Don had got to know several of the people there from the pantomime and everyone was very friendly and supportive to both of us. At first, I stayed in the background, just easing myself back into the group but, later in the summer, I took over as leader again when we started to plan and rehearse for a performance at the Victorian Festival, which is held in the town every year during the last week of August. There is always an exhibition in the church and this year the theme was children's literature from Victorian times to the present day. The singing group had been asked to perform and we decided to dress up as characters from famous children's stories and sing some songs related to the titles of those books. There was a lot to think about and organise but the group was full of enthusiasm and we had great fun over the following weeks preparing for the festival. We chose one book from each decade, starting with *The Wizard of Oz* and going through *The Secret Garden*, *The Railway Children*, Winnie the Pooh and so on. Don joined in happily and even agreed to dress up as Dick from the Famous Five!

The rest of May proved to be a very positive month. Don's eighty-sixth birthday dawned as a beautiful, warm, sunny day, so we packed up a picnic lunch and drove to the coast. We enjoyed the sunshine, sitting on the beach and watching Llewi play excitedly, swimming for sticks in the sea. Later we bought ice creams and sat on the promenade, watching the world go by, before driving home across the mountain road with spectacular views.

The good weather continued and we enjoyed going out together. We started going to the U3A Church Visiting Group and this led to some very interesting visits to churches, followed by excellent pub lunches. Don was able to appreciate looking around the churches and finding out a little about their architecture and history. Then one Sunday evening, a friend asked us if we would like to go with her to *Songs of Praise* in a nearby village. This was not the BBC version but a local annual event, always very well attended at a small village church at the top of a steep hill. We had to park at the bottom and were ferried up the hill to the church by kindly parishioners in a convoy system. So we went along and sang our hearts out for two hours, staying on afterwards for some very welcome refreshments. It was a great evening!

Don loved this occasion so much that he announced that he would like to go to church every week because he believed in God. He seemed to have completely forgotten that he had been a self-confessed atheist for most of the time that I had known him, nearly fifty years. So, the next Sunday evening, we attended Evensong at our local Parish Church. This was a very different service from Songs of Praise but we were made to feel welcome by everyone there and the Vicar took pains to ensure that we knew how to find and follow the Church in Wales service in the Prayer Book. Although I had not been very keen to go and only went because it was something Don wanted to do, I found it a very calming, pleasant experience as the evening sunlight streamed through and lit up a beautiful stained glass window. As I was reflecting on this, a phrase came floating into my memory, 'the peace that passeth all understanding' and I knew that this was what I was feeling so strongly, sitting there in this quiet place of worship. When I got home, I looked this up in the Bible and found it is a quotation from Philippians 4:7 (KJV) when Paul wrote, 'And the peace of God, which passeth all understanding, shall keep your hearts and minds through Christ Jesus.'

It was exactly what I was feeling. I was at a loss to understand why I found this service so peaceful and yet I did. I'd only gone on that occasion because Don had asked, so I wasn't expecting to believe or to feel anything. I was not very familiar with Anglican worship but had found the experience of this service so very moving and it made me realise the importance of peacefulness in my life. After that I was happy to take Don along regularly to services in the future.

As a child, I'd been brought up by Christian parents, attending a Baptist church and Sunday School from the age of about four. The services in the Baptist church are very different from the set Anglican services laid out in the Prayer Book. I had been a member of the Girls' Life Brigade attached to the church, from the age of eight, and later I had joined the church youth club as a teenager. All this time I considered myself a Christian and I retained these religious beliefs up until my late teens when I began to question many aspects of Christianity. I could no longer believe or accept literally many aspects of the Bible, so I lost my faith and hadn't been to church for years, apart from the occasional wedding or funeral.

A few weeks later, we attended church as usual in the evening, only to come across a very different service. On the second Sunday of each month we found that the beautiful, peaceful service of Evensong, which I had come to love, was replaced by 'Contemporary Worship'. We didn't know what to make of this! The prayer book and hymn books were abandoned; modern songs were projected from a computer onto a screen at the front and, instead of the organ, the singing was accompanied by a small band playing on a keyboard and guitars. Some of the congregation waved flags or expressed their praise by dramatic gestures. There were jokes and sketches to illustrate key messages from the Bible. It certainly wasn't a peaceful service, though the passion and sincerity of their praise shone through. It took us a while to get used to this type of worship but, as we gradually learnt the songs and it all became more familiar, we began to enjoy these services in a different way.

Everything seemed to be going so well that summer that we made plans to go away for a short holiday to Devon in June. We chose an area to which we'd never been before and my friend, Margaret, came round one afternoon to tell us about all the places we should visit in the South Hams area where she grew up. Armed with a long list of suitable places that would accommodate both a dog and a wheelchair, we set off to a caravan park at Challaborough Bay. The weather was warm and sunny and we had a good journey there, arriving in the afternoon, with plenty of time to sort ourselves out before sitting down to a meal, as we watched a dramatic sunset over the sea.

Our first day there was glorious, the weather warm and sunny, and we drove to Salcombe, a place we particularly wanted to visit, as one of Don's ancestors had originated from there in the 1800s. I think the Salcombe of today, packed with tourists, bears little resemblance to the fishing village of the nineteenth century but we had a splendid day there, including a delicious seafood meal at a local pub, sitting in the garden in the sun. The holiday seemed full of delights and promise.

Unfortunately, the following morning, Don woke feeling violently sick and ill and spent the day in bed, very feverish and vomiting at frequent intervals. He was unable to stand unaided and it was difficult getting us both into the tiny bathroom in the caravan, for me to hold him over the toilet bowl. By the afternoon, I was extremely concerned about him, as the sickness didn't seem to be easing, so I left him with a bucket by the bedside, while I walked down to the Reception office, there being no mobile phone signal on the site. Eventually, I managed to contact a doctor who talked me through what I should do, including ringing 999 if he became worse.

We spent the next few days confined to the caravan, keeping Don in bed and drinking plenty of water to keep him hydrated. Although the sickness ceased, he was very weak, unable to walk or to eat.

By Friday, we decided to try to come home, so I packed the car and managed somehow to get Don carefully out of the caravan and into the car. The journey home was horrendous, with several major traffic hold-ups on the M5, but Don survived and we arrived home in the late afternoon, much to everyone's relief. He was pleased to be able to sleep in his own bed and it was much easier to cope at home than in the confined space of the caravan.

The next day, Don was still very weak whenever he tried to get out of bed and I called the out of hours medical service. A GP came to visit him that afternoon and gave Don an injection to prevent sickness and giddiness and some new tablets. Although these didn't work immediately, by Monday he was able to manage to come downstairs, to have a shower with help from me, and from then he made a gradual improvement over the next few days.

The following Friday, we had another drama, when Don woke with bad pains in his chest and I had to phone 999. The service was excellent and the ambulance arrived within minutes.

After an ECG and other initial tests, the paramedics were fairly sure that it wasn't a heart attack but, in view of Don's age and the other difficulties of the past week, they decided to take him to hospital, where he spent the rest of the day having many tests, none of which showed up anything of immediate concern. The hospital doctor expressed concern about his anaemia and weight loss and recommended that I take him to see his GP to refer him for scopes in his stomach and colon.

We then went home and, although the pains had ceased, the whole experience left Don feeling very confused and agitated for the next few days. I was extremely concerned about the mental and physical deterioration that had occurred over the past two weeks, particularly as he was still very unsteady on his feet and needed help with everything. He had started to confuse dreams with reality and to say some very strange things that I did not understand at all; for example, one morning he kept asking 'When are the children coming here to be blessed?' I was also worried about the hospital doctor saying he could have 'lesions in the gut' which, when I looked this up on the internet, turned out to be a possible range of various cancers. He had certainly lost a great deal of weight in the past few months, which I didn't think could entirely be explained by either muscle loss or the recent sickness episode.

Our GP, when we visited her, was also concerned and made a priority referral for an endoscopy but she thought he was too frail to stand a colonoscopy at the same time. This took place within a fortnight but showed up nothing sinister, just a hiatus hernia of which we were already aware. A few days later, Don's GP phoned to say she'd had the report from the hospital and was concerned that the blood tests had shown a further drop in haemoglobin. She was now going to do an urgent referral for a colonoscopy.

By this time, we were well into August, with the Victorian Festival fast approaching. We'd managed to get to the Singing for Fun Group a few times for rehearsals and to sort out the programme and costumes. We also kept up with one or two other activities when Don was feeling well enough. He seemed to be very tired much of the time and would often fall asleep during the day. The days when his confusion was bad increased in frequency but, in between the bad days, he was still able to enjoy life. We went on an interesting church visit, had a wonderful day at the coast and engaged in some new activities such as glass painting at the Memory Café. It was a matter of taking each day as it came, and making the most of opportunities when they arose, whenever Don was well enough.

At the end of August, we received an appointment for Don's colonoscopy and he coped with this procedure surprisingly well. When we got the results, it didn't show any major problems but his blood tests were still of concern, the haemoglobin being persistently low and the white blood cell count had dropped significantly. His GP decided next to send him for a CT scan of the whole chest and abdomen.

In spite of this being a worrying and difficult time in many ways, I was well both physically and mentally. Although life was up and down, I had no feelings of depression or concerns that this dreadful illness was about to envelop me again. I was quite surprised by how quickly and easily I adapted my role to being very much a physical carer, attending to Don's new needs. I had never been attracted to nursing or caring as a career but looking after Don was something I took to easily and I found a lot of satisfaction in doing it well, to keep him comfortable and happy.

We had sailed through some choppy waters over the summer but at least it felt as if we were now on an even keel.

Chapter Seventeen
NEW BEGINNINGS
(September to December 2016)

The autumn seemed to bring a new phase to our lives, like the start of a new school year when everything is fresh and full of promise. After the disastrous holiday in June, Don made a good recovery and now seemed to be in relatively good physical health, so we decided to try another short break before the winter set in. This time, I booked a comfortable cottage in the Sussex countryside during the first week of October. This would give us the freedom to come and go as we pleased and it had all the comforts of home. From there, we would be able to visit relatives and friends in Kent and re-visit the Sussex coast, which held many pleasant memories for us both. It was something to look forward to, as the days started to shorten and cool down after the summer.

Then, early in September, I heard that our application for care support had been successful, with the six hours a week that I had requested approved by the local authority. With everything that had happened over the summer, I'd almost given up hearing about this application, made in May, but now I was delighted that I could go ahead and look for someone suitable to come in twice a week to provide Don with some social support and stimulation. I had chosen to go down the 'direct payment' route, which meant that I would recruit and employ a 'personal assistant' for Don and we would receive money from the council for this purpose. So, using the expertise of the organisation appointed by the council to manage some of the recruitment and payroll issues, I advertised for a personal assistant.

The recruitment process took a couple of months, as there were many formalities to be observed. We weren't overwhelmed with applications but I shortlisted two candidates who had suitable qualifications and experience and arranged to interview them. That was the easy part. Then, I had to tackle the difficult task of explaining to Don what I was doing and why. He didn't really understand either what was happening or the need for any new arrangements but, rather to my surprise, he made no objection and seemed quite happy to go along with it. By involving him in the interview process, he was able to meet the applicants and I was able to observe how he responded and related to them and they to him. This worked well and he enjoyed chatting to the two potential carers, telling them about the sorts of things he liked to do. We finally decided to appoint Malissa, a personable young woman, to start work towards the end of November, as first I had to take up references and arrange the various checks that were necessary. Although young, Malissa had a qualification in Social Care and some previous experience of working with elderly people in a care home. She was very enthusiastic and committed to working in a care environment.

In the meantime, our trip to Sussex took place. The cottage where we stayed was spacious, warm and comfortable and the weather was mild, with plenty of autumn sunshine, but it was whilst we were away that I was struck afresh by how much Don had deteriorated mentally. He was totally disoriented in the lovely old cottage, unable to find his way around from room to room. He had great difficulty in remembering where the different rooms were, where things were kept or how to get in and out from the garden. One day I left Don eating his breakfast while I took the dog out for his morning walk across the fields behind the cottage, only to find on my return that he was very agitated, not knowing where he was or where I was. The layout of the cottage was unusual and he couldn't find the toilet or the way to get upstairs to his bedroom.

Even by the end of the week, it was still a mystery to him and it was a relief for him to get back home to familiar surroundings.

We had planned to visit relatives and friends in the area but it became apparent that Don had no recollection of who any of these people were, until we actually arrived at their homes. Then he would begin to remember places and faces, which pleased him enormously and he enjoyed seeing these people again.

In spite of his confusion, Don was happy and enthusiastic about travelling around in the car, seeing both old and new places in the pleasant autumn sunshine, as long as I stayed close to him all the time. I found that when driving around he was only conscious of his immediate surroundings inside the car and wouldn't notice anything outside. He seemed to be unaware of the views, the buildings, animals or what was happening outside, though he would always be interested and appreciative when I pointed things out to him. I found that I had to keep up a running commentary to ensure that he made the most of the journey. Not only was he now living just in the moment but also just in the space immediately around him. His perception of both time and space had changed.

By the time we arrived back home, we were both exhausted. The travelling, the visiting and the strangeness of it all had worn Don out and I had found the experience difficult too, looking after Don 24/7, never having a few minutes to myself. Taking him out and about had become rather like looking after a toddler, getting him ready, making sure he had suitable clothes, explaining everything, making sure he'd gone to the toilet before getting in the car and never letting him out of my sight. I thought this would probably be the last holiday we took away from home but I was glad we had made the effort whilst he could still get some pleasure from it, and it was another holiday we could remember together.

Once we were back home, another train of events began, this time related to Don's physical health. Following the scare in the summer, when he was taken to hospital suffering from severe pains in his chest, his GP had referred Don for a CT scan of his chest and abdomen. The appointment for this scan came through and, at the end of October, we saw a lung specialist who explained the results, which showed some soft tissue nodules in the lungs. The consultant thought that this indicated an early stage of lung cancer, as well as damage to the lungs caused by COPD but, in view of Don's age and general frailty, he advised that further investigation or treatment would not be appropriate. He recommended that the best thing to do was for Don to go home and enjoy life for the present. A week later, however, the hospital phoned to say that, after a team meeting at which they had discussed Don's condition, they had decided to offer a bronchoscopy, which was not too invasive a process, and this took place about a fortnight later.

When the results of this came through, we had another long discussion with the consultant about possible treatments and were faced with a difficult decision as to the way forward. The hospital team was offering a lung reduction operation in both lungs. This would involve cutting away the top part of the lungs, which were very badly affected with emphysema, and they would, at the same time, cut out the nodules to do a biopsy. This would be a major operation, which would have to be undertaken in Birmingham and would require a stay in hospital there for about a week.

This news was shattering and I was very concerned about the effects that this surgery might have on Don, due to his frailty, both physical and mental. I knew of other people with dementia who had been severely adversely affected by having a general anaesthetic, and the whole experience of being in a strange place with strange people. Also, I had been warned that there were very strict limits on visiting in the ward in which he would be at Birmingham, so I wouldn't be able to stay with him or to spend much time with him.

Knowing how difficult he found strange places and people, particularly if I was not there with him for reassurance, I was extremely doubtful about the benefits of this course of action.

Although we tried to involve Don in the discussion, it was clear that he had great difficulty in understanding the issues and couldn't cope with having to make a decision. I discussed the matter with my daughter and son and with Don's GP, who was in agreement with my reluctance to go ahead with surgery. She stressed that it was important to look at the whole person and consider all the implications and not just see the issue from a respiratory point of view. After much thought and discussion, we decided that the best way forward, at that point in time, would be for Don to have another scan in December, to see if there was any change, and then decide on further action. We all agreed that a major operation would not be in his best interests but, if cancer was confirmed, we would take the option of spot radiography which would be much less invasive and traumatic. Don's GP was still investigating the cause of his weight loss and also the low haemoglobin and low white blood cell levels, as the lung problem did not explain those issues.

By this time, the appointment of Don's personal assistant had been finalised and Malissa started to come to our home on one morning and one afternoon a week for three hours at a time. She was a delightful young woman, always cheerful, pleasant and friendly. She and Don got on so well that it was like having a ray of sunshine coming into our lives every week. At first I stayed at home, in the background, while she and Don got to know each other and established a pattern of activities. Malissa quickly gained my confidence, as it became clear that she was very competent, and Don enjoyed the time they spent together, always looking forward to her visits.

So, after the first few sessions, I was able to go out while Malissa was there, to go to pilates, to my recorder group or just to walk the dog without worrying what was happening to Don at home, or feeling that I must rush back. It was only a few hours a week but this made such a difference to my state of mind. It was time I treasured as I was able to relax and feel that I could be a person again, not just a carer. I had friends at the memory café whose husbands also had dementia and I suspect they thought I was rather selfish to want some time away from the caring role but Don loved these visits from Malissa and thoroughly enjoyed her company. I knew that he was safe and well cared for, so I could afford to relax for a few hours. I always returned home about fifteen minutes before Malissa was due to leave, during which time she and Don would tell me enthusiastically about what they had been doing and they would often have something to show me proudly, that they had made or done together.

I always left suggestions of activities they could do, splitting the time up, so that nothing went on for too long or became too demanding or boring. They would usually do some sort of practical art or craft activity for the first hour; then do a jigsaw puzzle together or play a board game for the next hour, and for the last hour, when Don was tiring, watch a film or listen to music. I bought some DVDs of old musicals – *Oklahoma*, *South Pacific*, *The King and I*, *Oliver*, *Annie*, and so on – all of which Don knew well and could sing along with the songs. Most of these were new to Malissa but she seemed to enjoy the films and she took pleasure in Don's obvious enjoyment, too. They both became addicted to jigsaw puzzles and had fun with the art and craft activities. Malissa would often take one of the craft activities home with her to do again with her young brother, a seven-year-old, and she enjoyed sharing the ideas with him. At first I was careful not to make the activities seem too childish for Don but this seemed to matter less and less as time went on. He seemed willing to try anything. His mind was clearly working in a different way now and some of the patterns and designs he came up with were unique and interesting, though I don't pretend to understand the significance of them.

This structure seemed to work well for both of them. Sometimes I would leave them a recipe and ingredients to cook something simple. They started out with baked tuna treats for the dog, which were very successful, and they soon progressed on to biscuits, cakes and sweets which lent themselves to being decorated creatively. Making fruit salad was another great favourite and we tried all sorts of combinations of fruit in as many different colours as possible. Don was always very proud of what he produced, and loved to show me what they had achieved together when I came home. He also enjoyed eating the products!

Malissa was very patient with him and she was also very good at motivating Don, getting him to participate in whatever activity they were doing. Her enthusiasm seemed to inspire him and she took on board the principle that it was not the *result* that was important but the *participation* in these activities, which would help to keep Don's brain as active as possible. Together they made a book, *All About Me*, in which they stuck pictures that they cut out of magazines, of all things Don liked to eat and drink; photos of the clothes he liked to wear; pictures of characters from TV programmes and films that he liked to watch; and other things like sport that he liked to watch or had enjoyed doing in the past. Doing all this provided lots of opportunity and stimulation for Don to talk about himself, his interests and his memories. The book became a big scrapbook that he liked to look through sometimes on his own, or to show to friends who called to see him. It was a great conversation piece and we thought it might be useful if ever I was ill or unable to care for him so that other people could find out about what he liked.

Another activity that we worked on was the creation of a Memory Box. As well as photographs, this contained a wide variety of small objects that had been important to Don at different times during his life. There was a pair of bootees that he had knitted when our son had been born; a letter that he had written to his mother when he had been evacuated; the tie that I had made for him to wear at our wedding and which matched my wedding dress; the band off one of his sailor's hats when he was in the Fleet Air Arm; a photo of a special purpose machine he had designed; some headed notepaper from the business that he started. All of these objects would trigger special memories and were a great aid to conversation. He loved this box and everything it held. As time went on, I had to label the objects but, once he was reminded of what they represented, he could remember stories and events from different phases of his life.

Photos were another great aid to triggering memories and we sorted out and labelled many pictures from which Don, with Malissa's help, could create a new photo album specifically about him. It is interesting that, with dementia, it is the most recent memories that disappear first. Whilst Don could not remember what he had done the previous day, he could, with prompting, remember people and events from his childhood and younger days, sixty or seventy years ago. His past, going back to life from the 1930s onwards, seemed like a different world from today, and Malissa was intrigued by some of the things she saw and heard about.

She was also fascinated by the travels that Don and I had undertaken when we were young, particularly working our way across France and Spain in a Land Rover, then crossing over to Africa and our journey into Morocco, Algeria and across the Sahara Desert. At that time, I was only a few years older than she was now and I think it gave her a new perspective on us, that we too had been young, energetic and adventurous once!

Malissa became like a member of our family; we all got to know each other very well and both Don and I really enjoyed her company. She would tell us about her life, her family, her other part-time jobs and what she had been doing in her leisure time which kept us up to date with the lives of young people in our town. It was refreshing to have a young person in the house, especially as Malissa was always so cheerful and positive. Knowing that Don would enjoy himself while she was with him and having these few hours a week to myself, made such a difference to the quality of both our lives. I had coped well enough over the summer and autumn months but, if I had not had this respite during the winter, when it was too cold for Don to go out very much, I fear that the strain and stress would have slowly built up again, as Don's health, both physical and mental, continued to worsen.

By this time, our application for Attendance Allowance had also been approved and I decided to use some of it to employ a cleaner for a few hours a week. I knew of a friend, Nic, who had just started up her own business, doing cleaning and other jobs, and she was pleased to come in once a week to clean the house. I don't dislike most cleaning tasks but the advantage of this arrangement was that it gave me more time to spend with Don, planning and preparing the activities that he would do with Malissa, and doing things together. Time was the thing I was still short of and this seemed like a good solution. Don and Nic already knew each other, as she had been involved in the early days of starting the memory café, and he was pleased to welcome another cheerful, friendly person into our home once a week. Somehow, Nic managed to keep up lengthy conversations with Don whilst she carried out her cleaning duties and sometimes they would play music and both sing along at the tops of their voices while she worked! Nic was an excellent worker and good company for Don while I got on with other tasks, and her contribution was also very valuable to the quality of our lives.

The other important thing that helped to make our lives easier was obtaining a Blue Badge, which enabled us to park in Disabled

Parking bays, much closer to the shops or other venues than we might otherwise obtain. It was Don's physical disabilities that made this possible, as he was unable to walk very far due to arthritis and COPD, but it had the added advantage of my not having to drop him off by the door of the shop and then going to find a parking place, all the time worried that he would wander off, or forget where I was, due to the dementia. I am pleased to see that dementia has recently been added to eligibility for Blue Badges. Although, earlier in the autumn, I seemed to spend a lot of time filling in lengthy application forms, the effort had now paid off and had been well worthwhile. The new care arrangements, the Blue Badge and the Attendance Allowance payments all contributed to making our new lifestyle work well.

Unfortunately, Don suffered from another bad chest infection in December, which made it impossible to go out very much in the pre-Christmas period that year. He responded well to yet another course of antibiotics but was weak and tired and unable to go out in the cold. We had to concentrate on finding activities at home that he would enjoy, and he was soon busy making Christmas cards for our grandchildren and his friends at the Memory Café, making an Advent Calendar and all sorts of decorations, gifts and treats. When our children were young, Don was always at work so had missed all the preparations of this kind. This year it seemed like a wonderful revelation to him and he wasn't even bothered about the mess of glitter, pine needles and tiny bits of tinsel on the floor, that are an inevitable result of decorating the house and preparing for a festive time! Together we chose some pictures on old Christmas cards and cut them out carefully, one for each day of December until Christmas Day, and every day he took great pleasure in opening a door on his advent calendar, seeing a picture of a cheery robin, snowbound sheep or Christmas bells and so on. I thought, again, how dementia seems to make a person regress right back to childhood, both in what they can do and how they perceive their life. They live very much in the present moment and appreciate the small details around them to which, as we get older, we tend to pay scant attention. Although it was sad in some ways to see him reduced to such a childlike state, he was so content and happy that it was good and, if I just accepted that, it didn't distress me so much. I had no false hopes that he would improve and I knew that things would get progressively worse, so all I could do was try to ensure that his life was as pleasant and enjoyable as possible, whatever that meant.

In spite of the cold, icy weather, we managed to go out for one pre-Christmas lunch, with everyone from the Memory Cafe, and we enjoyed a lovely couple of hours with our friends. It was a fine meal and a happy social occasion. We had all become very close, sharing so much of our lives and the problems and difficulties common to all of us. The friendships that we made in these circumstances proved to be very supportive and have lasted, even though all of the four original dementia sufferers have since died.

Our daughter had invited all the family for Christmas Day, so that morning we packed up the presents and food that I'd prepared and set off to join everyone at my daughter's home. It turned out to be the best Christmas Day for many years. Everyone was in good health, the meal cooked beautifully and everyone appreciated their cards, gifts and treats. Don coped well with all the festivities, then had a sleep after lunch, whilst we took all the dogs for a walk in the woods. Later, when we were all refreshed, everyone joined in some games, with much laughter and enjoyment. We were all conscious, in view of Don's deteriorating health, that this might be the last Christmas we would have all together but were satisfied that we'd all played a part in making it an enjoyable time to remember. It seemed particularly important to ensure that his life was as happy as it could be in the circumstances and all the family made an effort to make that Christmas Day a wonderful, memorable time.

Chapter Eighteen
ENDINGS

On New Year's Day 2017, I overslept, not waking until just after 9.00 am When I went downstairs I found that Don was up already, sitting very still like a statue in the kitchen and extremely confused. He said he'd been there since eight o'clock but he hadn't even made himself a cup of tea, a task which he could still do himself and the first thing that he would think of every morning. He told me he'd already been to work but there was no-one there and he couldn't understand why there were no neighbours around. The street was quiet and everyone's curtains still drawn. This was a new stage in confusion and, although he recovered as the day went on, it was a worrying development. It took several hours to get him back to 'normal' and I think, if I had not been there to talk to him and look after him, he might well have stayed there all day, just sitting still and silent, not eating or drinking or getting dressed. It was as if his mind was completely blank about the present.

Similar episodes started to occur every two or three weeks. He would sit, or even stand, completely still, as if in a trance, unaware of his surroundings or the present time but often reverted to the past, usually thinking I was his mother. Sometimes he would wake in the morning, not knowing who he was himself, or who I was, or where he was. He would ask me questions like how long I'd lived there and whether we were married. On some occasions he would be very unsteady on his feet, unable to walk without his stick or with help from me. His speech would be very slow and he would seem completely 'vacant'. There were no signs that these symptoms were a TIA or a mild stroke but they seemed rather a progression of dementia. I learnt that the best way to cope with these states was to suggest that he had a sleep, either in bed or tucked up with a blanket on the sofa and, after a couple of hours of rest, I would then be able to coax him back into the present and everyday life.

In spite of these strange episodes, Don still looked forward to Malissa's visits twice a week and getting back to a normal pattern after the Christmas/New Year break, seemed to help ground him. It was too cold and sometimes snowy to go out very much but friends called in and he enjoyed chatting to them. In mid-January, we went to see the chest specialist at the hospital, who told us that he couldn't believe his eyes when he'd looked at the latest scan. He showed us the images on his computer, where we saw that one of the nodules had disappeared and the other had reduced in size, and so he had concluded that it wasn't cancer at all, but an infection. We were all extremely relieved and very glad that we hadn't gone ahead with the major operation. It was clear that Don's lungs had been damaged by emphysema, which explained the frequent chest infections, but the consultant recommended no further action, other than monitoring, and we agreed to see him again in six months' time.

We were still visiting Don's GP regularly with chest infections and for blood tests. She had been liaising with a consultant haematologist at the hospital and told us that they had concluded Don was suffering from MDS (myelodysplasia), a rare type of blood cancer, in which the body fails to make enough healthy blood cells. This was the reason for his anaemia and for the low red and white blood cell counts. The only way of being one hundred percent certain of this diagnosis would be a bone marrow biopsy but this course of action had already been rejected, as it was too invasive a procedure, given Don's frailty and other medical problems. She explained that, although the MDS would inevitably get worse, the anaemia could be regulated by blood transfusions when necessary. Once again, we all agreed the best way forward was monitoring, and to let Don continue to enjoy his life while he could. In spite of frequent complaints of fatigue and breathlessness, it was possible for Don to engage in the activities he had come to know and love, so Malissa continued with her work. We still went to the Memory Café once a week and to singing groups two or three times a month. Don still wanted to go to Church regularly on a Sunday evening, when feeling well enough, and the Evensong service seemed to bring him great comfort and peace.

Towards the end of February, we had another scare. One morning I left Don at home, eating breakfast while I took the dog for a walk. Don had seemed particularly active and alert that morning and I was not at all worried about leaving him for a short time on his own, so I was very shocked when I returned to find him still sitting in his chair in the kitchen, slumped over, with his head on the table. At first, I thought he had fallen asleep but soon realised he was completely unresponsive and had collapsed. I called for an ambulance, which arrived within minutes, and the paramedics were concerned that he had suffered a stroke, so they blue lighted him to hospital at Hereford, forty miles away. By the time he arrived there, Don had regained consciousness but was kept in hospital for several hours for a multitude of tests and X-rays. Later that day, he was discharged but an appointment was made for him to return to see the haematologist the following week, as the blood test results were of great concern. So, after a quiet weekend at home, we returned to the hospital where we saw a very caring consultant, who confirmed the extremely low level of red and white cells and platelets. He thought the collapse was unlikely to have been caused by the MDS, so it remained a mystery. Everyone agreed once more that regular monitoring was the best and only way forward.

From this time on, I decided on a new routine in the mornings to avoid a repeat occurrence. I would give Don his breakfast in bed, get him washed and toileted and then he would stay in bed and snooze, with strict instructions to remain there, out of harm's way, while I took the dog out for a quick walk. I was reluctant to leave Don on his own after this episode and I organised our lives differently, so that I would only leave him at home when someone else was present. As well as Malissa coming in twice a week, Nic was still helping with the housework, as I was spending more and more time caring for Don, with his ever increasing need for help and assistance with personal care. While she was there working, Nic was happy for me to go out shopping or to do other tasks, which meant that I rarely had to leave Don alone and this saved me a great deal of worry and anxiety. On other occasions I would take him with me to wherever I was going.

As the weather improved and spring approached, we were able to go out for drives in the countryside and even to take short walks, with Don in his wheelchair. I managed to find some flat walks, not easy where we live with hills surrounding us, where I could manage to push the wheelchair without too much effort. It is surprisingly difficult to push a person in a wheelchair, even with someone as light as Don, now that he had lost so much weight, particularly on hilly or uneven ground. The end of March brought some warm, sunny days and it did us both good to get out of the house, to enjoy the joys of spring, everything coming back to life, the birds singing and the lambs skipping and gambolling in the fields.

As Easter approached, Don was kept busy making Easter cards and gifts for the family. As at Christmas, he loved doing this and was very happy preparing for a visit to our family on Easter Sunday, looking forward to seeing our children and grandchildren and to giving them the things he had made. The days immediately before Easter were very special. Little did we anticipate how special they were to become.

On Maundy Thursday, we went to the Memory Café, where we had a visit from a beauty and wellbeing practitioner who set us all up with footbaths containing soothing, fragrant oils. This was a very pleasant and relaxing activity as we sat there, first with our feet immersed, then wrapped in warm towels while we chatted and had refreshments. Don had made chocolate cornflake Easter Nests with tiny chocolate eggs and these were much appreciated by the other members. He was very proud of these and of the Easter cards he had made for everyone, with pressed spring flowers. He handed them out to the other members and it was lovely to see him participate and enjoy these activities so happily.

On Good Friday, we went to a nearby village church, where there was a moving performance of The Passion, performed beautifully by a local choir. Then, on Saturday, we spent a busy and enjoyable day cooking, decorating a simnel cake and finishing off the homemade Easter cards and gifts for our children and grandchildren. We packed the car and were all set to travel to our daughter's early on Sunday morning – but this was not to be.

Don woke early on Sunday morning, complaining of pains in his abdomen under his ribs, so severe that he was unable to sit up in bed or even to raise his head without support. He seemed very unwell, with a high temperature, so I contacted the out of hours health service and a GP came out to visit him a couple of hours later. He managed to pull Don up into a sitting position and, after listening to his chest, confirmed another chest infection. The doctor gave us some antibiotics and some codeine tablets to ease the pain and Don spent the rest of the day in bed sleeping while I cancelled our arrangements. The painkillers seemed effective and he was no longer complaining of pain but he was very confused. He didn't seem to be aware of where he was, or what was happening and his response to all questions was , 'I don't know'.

The following day, Easter Monday, Don was still in pain but his temperature had lessened and he was able to get out of bed with a great deal of help and support. It took a lot of time and effort to help him walk a few feet from his bed to the bathroom. Again, like the previous day, he would eat nothing although he managed to drink a little with help, unable to hold a cup himself. He seemed very weak and I had the feeling there was something seriously wrong. On Tuesday, he seemed a little brighter first thing in the morning but deteriorated significantly throughout the day, both physically and mentally, unable to walk or do anything himself. He seemed to have forgotten how to drink and how to swallow tablets and I had to feed him with a little rice pudding to get him to eat something.

Once again, on Wednesday, there was some improvement first thing in the morning and I managed to get him up and washed but he quickly went downhill and it was all I could do to get him back safely to his bed. As he didn't seem to be responding to the antibiotics, which on previous occasions had started to work very quickly on his chest infections, and he was in such a weak, poorly state, I phoned the surgery to request a doctor's visit. His own GP was not there but a duty doctor arrived at lunchtime, by which time Don had a very high temperature, was confused, breathless and in a lot of pain. The doctor prescribed stronger antibiotics and advised me to call the surgery again if there was no improvement.

A similar pattern occurred on Thursday morning; a bright start to the day was soon followed by rapid decline, a high temperature and confusion, as well as pain. Don was refusing all food and drink by this time, so I called for another visit. This time, the doctor on duty happened to be Dr Alice, my GP, whom we knew well. She had seen Don at the surgery on several previous occasions and was the GP who had supported me through my serious depression. I was very glad to see her and to be able to talk to her about what was happening. She recommended sending Don to hospital without further delay, where he could have a chest X-ray, blood tests and be put on a drip to prevent dehydration which was a danger now that he was now refusing to drink. As I was finding it increasingly difficult to manage him at home and as the antibiotics were not working their usual magic, we agreed to this course of action. Dr Alice ordered an ambulance and wrote a full letter to the hospital explaining the circumstances. She also spent time talking to me and warned me to be prepared for anything.

After a lengthy wait, the ambulance finally arrived at about half past seven and Don was admitted to the hospital at about half past nine. Fortunately for us, the A&E department wasn't terribly busy at this time and Don was seen by a doctor fairly quickly. He was sent for an x-ray and, while he was gone, the doctor had a long talk with me about his symptoms, his dementia and about the MDS. He also talked me through a DNR (Do Not Resuscitate) agreement, explaining how unlikely it was that resuscitation would be successful in someone as old and frail as Don, and the damage it could cause. He was a sympathetic, caring doctor and I was very appreciative of the time and effort he spent talking to me. I felt that Don was in a good place, where the hospital staff not only had many resources for the best treatment but actually cared about their patients. When Don was admitted to a ward at about 11.00 pm I went with him and was able to explain to the night duty staff there about his needs. Feeling very relieved that he was now in the best place, I left him there to sleep in a quiet and peaceful bed and made my hour's journey home. It was wonderful to have Llewi there waiting patiently for me, rather than to come home to a completely empty house.

When I telephoned the hospital the following morning, there was no real news, as Don hadn't yet seen the doctor, but I went to visit him in the afternoon, as did my son and daughter who met me there. Don had been moved from where I left him the previous night to a private room where he was sitting up in bed, wearing hospital issue orange pyjamas but looking a little brighter. The staff nurse on duty explained that he was in isolation for his own protection from infection as, due to the MDS and the low level of white blood cells, he had very little immunity. She told me that, when she had told Don I had phoned in the morning, he seemed not to know me or to recognise my name. She thought he was suffering from delirium and also told me, rather apprehensively it seemed, that she had undertaken a mental capacity test, which showed that he had no capacity, so he would be subject to the decisions of the hospital staff. I agreed with this and said that I had Power of Attorney and would bring a copy for the hospital the following day. However, when we arrived at his bedside, Don seemed more alert than we had expected. He recognised all of us and called me by my name. He seemed quite a lot better than the previous day, said he was no longer in pain and he did not seem to be in any distress, though I don't think he had any real idea of where he was. He was just pleased to see us all.

After my children left, I stayed on for a while, until Don became drowsy and fell asleep. When back at home, my children phoned me, saying they were very shocked at how old and frail Don seemed. I suppose I had become used to seeing him looking like this but the change in him was a shock to my son and daughter who had not seen him for several months, since Christmas. I was concerned that Don was in isolation, alone in a room with no company or mental stimulation, but I had to recognise the importance of restricting the likelihood of infection and was impressed with the care he was receiving in the hospital. The nurse had given strict instructions that no-one with a cold, cough or other ailment should visit. He was being well cared for, on a drip to rehydrate him and IV antibiotics, all of which would have been impossible at home. I'd been told to expect a call from the Occupational Therapist to discuss a care package for when Don was discharged, so everything seemed positive at this stage.

The following day, I bought a small battery operated radio to take to Don and I also took in his memory box, in the hope that this might stimulate his mind and comfort him in his strange setting. When I arrived, I found that Don had been moved from the assessment ward to another ward, still in isolation in a private room. He was much less 'vacant' but seemed not to want to talk very much, his attention being taken with an animated film on TV. He sat up and ate a pot of fresh fruit that I'd brought, feeding himself with a spoon, so it was evident that he was feeling much better and the antibiotics seemed to be working.

This pattern of afternoon visits continued over the next week or so. He enjoyed looking at the objects in his memory box and showing them to anyone who visited. I also found some lovely picture books in our local library; these were specifically designed for people with dementia and they proved to be valuable in stimulating conversation and awakening old memories. Two of our friends from the Singing for Fun Group came with me to visit on more than one occasion and we all spent some happy times singing our favourite songs together. As Don was in a room on his own, the hospital staff were very relaxed over visiting times and the number of visitors, for we weren't disturbing the other patients. Sometimes, when they heard us singing, they would sing along outside the door! This made it easy for Don to have at least one visitor every day and sometimes several. I went almost every day, establishing a new routine of doing a few essential things at home in the morning and arranging for various people to feed and take Llewi out in the afternoon, so that

I could visit Don in the hospital. My friends and neighbours were all very kind and helpful.

The occupational therapist contacted me to advise me that, when discharged, Don could have daily visits from the reablement team for up to six weeks; this team would advise on his care needs and organise any aids, equipment and adaptations necessary to care for him at home. She told me that he would be discharged once his blood levels were satisfactory and these were being monitored daily. Once again, it all seemed very positive and I was expecting him to come back home quite soon with suitable support.

The next day though, when I visited, I found Don in bed, as his blood pressure was very low and he was extremely confused, thinking once more that I was his mother. Whilst I was there, his temperature shot up and the consultant was called. She ordered another X-ray for his chest and also for his hand that had become extremely swollen and she prescribed morphine to ease the pain. She said that she would also contact the micro-biology department, as his fever indicated a new infection, in spite of the fact that he was still on IV antibiotics. By the evening, his temperature had come down and Don was cooler and calmer, so I left him to sleep.

Over the next two weeks, this pattern continued, with the symptoms gradually getting worse and more frequent. Don would appear to be responding to the antibiotics and making a recovery when, suddenly, he would develop a high temperature and fever, going downhill rapidly. He became incontinent and was unable to get out of bed, to walk or even to stand unassisted. The swelling on his hand was diagnosed as cellulitis and the infection spread right up his arm, causing him a great deal of additional pain. On some days he was reasonably lucid but on others extremely confused. His blood tests showed no sustained improvement; several blood transfusions helped to increase the haemoglobin level but nothing could be done about the all-important low white cell count.

The consultant haematologist came to see Don and talked to us, explaining that the cellulitis had probably been caused by the catheter in his hand and, whilst this would not have had a serious effect in most people, it was causing a high level of infection in Don, due to his lack of immunity. The hospital dietician also came to see me, as Don was refusing all meals. She offered a feeding tube but Don did not want this and I felt it would just be cruel to insist on it, so we agreed that she would increase his vitamin/protein dose, which sometimes he would drink. He was still eating the portions of fresh fruit that I brought in daily, though I was having to feed him with these by this time, as he was unable to do anything for himself.

On one day the following week, there were signs of improvement. He was still on a drip to prevent dehydration but Don drank half a cup of squash, with help from me, and ate some fresh mango that I'd brought. He'd been able to look at pictures and photos with a friend who had visited, the swelling on his arm and hand had gone down, his temperature, blood pressure and potassium levels had returned to normal. He was able to enjoy listening to a CD of a male voice choir, *Voices in the Valley,* whilst I was there and seemed pain free, in much better spirits. My hopes began to rise again that he was on the mend. Two days later, though, he had deteriorated once more, was back on a drip for fluids and potassium, very confused, sleepy and in considerable pain.

The twelfth of May was Don's eightieth birthday and my son, daughter and I all visited, taking in cards, presents and a birthday cake but it was not really a good day for Don, who was in pain and refusing anything at all to eat. He seemed pleased to see us but really he just wanted to sleep.

This up and down pattern continued relentlessly and it became increasingly difficult to interest him in any food or drink. I had taken to arriving at the hospital in the late morning, before lunch was served, so that I could encourage Don to eat a little ice cream and fruit and to drink some squash or a cup of coffee. It would take about half an hour to manage a drink, just one mouthful at a time. Sometimes he would still respond to look at pictures in a book or magazine but what he liked most of all was to listen to music. I would always leave him in the evening with something suitable to listen to either on the radio or on a personal CD player I had bought for him.

During this time, I kept surprisingly well and adjusted to my new way of life, doing very little, other than visiting Don in hospital and a few essential things at home. The garden became a jungle, with everything growing vigorously during May but I was too busy and preoccupied even to notice. On two occasions, when I did stop rushing around, I became very emotional and tearful but, after a brief cry, managed to pull myself together and get on with all I had to do.

Time marched on relentlessly. Days turned into weeks and spring gradually turned into summer. On my forty mile journey to the hospital each day, I noticed the trees and hedges, bare when I started these trips in April, come into leaf, bluebells and other wild flowers appear in the hedgerows, the blossom appear in the apple orchards and then disappear, the fields turn bright yellow with rapeseed, scenting the air. These were the signs that made me aware that time was passing. In some ways, I think the journey in the car helped me; it was the only time of day that I sat down and relaxed a little and was so thankful for the wonderful music on Radio 3 and Classic FM that I listened to whilst driving. As I approached the hospital each day, I could feel myself tense up with apprehension. How would I find Don today? Even if I'd phoned in the morning for a progress report, he might well have deteriorated by the time I arrived. There seemed no end to the possible complications that he endured and I was worried whether, if he came home, I would be able to cope now that he was so weak, unable to walk and doubly incontinent.

The doctors and the micro-biology department at the hospital continued to try to find effective ways of beating the various infections that arose. I had no idea that there were so many different antibiotics, which all had specific uses and were used to target different types of infection. I could not have asked for better care and commitment from the medical team. He was also well-cared for in other ways, kept clean and comfortable and turned regularly to prevent bed sores, now that he was totally bed-ridden. The nurses and care assistants had all got to know him and chatted away to him cheerfully whenever they went in to see him to carry out their various monitoring and caring tasks.

As time went on, in spite of all the efforts of the hospital staff and the array of antibiotics used to treat Don's infections, it became apparent that his immune system was so weak that he was not going to recover. As soon as any course of antibiotic finished, he would immediately contract another infection, all the time becoming weaker and weaker, unable to eat or drink or to get out of bed. He had lost so much weight that his bones protruded and his arms and legs had little flesh to cover them. He was usually in so much pain that he did not like anyone to touch him. On 'good' days, Don still enjoyed having visits from friends and our children who came several times a week. Sometimes we would sing along to one of Don's CDs or to Golden Oldies on the radio! This was the thing he liked most of all. Musical memory is one of the last parts of memory to deteriorate and he could still remember the words of many of the old songs, even though he had no memory of what he'd done or who he'd seen earlier the same day. Don's elder son, from a previous marriage, made the long journey from Kent and came to visit, bringing with him some old photos and a CD of opera, which made an enjoyable afternoon for both of them. I was pleased that they had this time together before Don became too ill to appreciate anything.

Although I was very happy with the care he was receiving in Hereford, I was spending more and more time there each day, becoming more and more exhausted, and I asked whether it would be possible for Don to be transferred to our local hospital. The staff were shocked at this idea; they felt he was part of their 'family'; he knew them all and they knew and understood him. The level of care available at our local hospital could not fully support Don's needs and I realised that, even if he could make it from the ward to the ambulance, it would be cruel to put him through the trauma of such a journey, so I abandoned the idea.

During the last week of May, I had several conversations with the Consultant and other members of her team, as it became clear that the future was no longer looking positive. I had to accept that the MDS had taken its toll on Don's immune system and, without continual treatment of antibiotics, he would succumb to infection after infection. The grim reality was that he was not going to come home and would spend the rest of his life in hospital. I was faced with making the decision of whether to continue treatment or to stop and let nature take its course.

I knew now, beyond all doubt, that Don's condition was so dire that he was not going to recover, even temporarily, and had to consider whether it was right to continue to put him through continual treatment and blood tests that were increasingly difficult and painful for him. He had said himself on several occasions that he could not face any more and just wanted it all to stop. While we still had hope, it had seemed worthwhile to keep trying to beat the infections but now perhaps the time had come to cease our well-meaning attempts and leave him in peace. I discussed the situation with my children and, although it was very hard to admit, once we had accepted the prognosis, we all agreed that the most important thing was to make Don's final days as comfortable and pain free as possible. Even though I knew what we all thought was right for Don, I still agonised over making the final decision. It is such a serious choice to make on behalf of someone else, whether to let a person die. The consultant was supportive and sympathetic but left the decision up to me and this was the hardest decision I have ever made.

Once treatment was withdrawn, we all continued to visit every day, though often Don would sleep through most of our time with him. He drifted in and out of consciousness but was relaxed and peaceful and, after all he'd been through during the previous six weeks, we were glad to see him in no pain or distress. The consultant and the whole medical team were very supportive and caring to us as a family, as well as to Don, throughout this time.

During the final few days, the hospital staff offered me a bed, so that I could stay overnight and be with Don all the time during the day and only a few yards away if I should be needed in the night. This became a very special time. Now, the priority was pain relief and, because he was on morphine, I was able to touch and hold him without it hurting, to wash his face, comb his hair, cut and manicure his nails, all things I hadn't been able to do for weeks because it had been too painful for him. These simple caring acts and the physical contact brought us very close in those final days. Gradually, his body just closed down. I observed it happening and, although I was sad to be losing him, it seemed to me to be a very natural process and I was convinced it was the right thing to do, to let him go. The end finally came one warm summer evening, when we were listening quietly to a concert on Radio 3. Our children were on their way to visit and Don was quiet, free from pain and relaxed. He died peacefully in his bed, there one minute and drifted away the next, giving up the ghost quietly and naturally with me at his side, only minutes before our son and daughter arrived.

Chapter Nineteen
GRIEF OR DEPRESSION?

After Don died, I was on an emotional roller coaster for many months. The peacefulness and the feeling that his death was a natural end to his long life stayed with me but other feelings sometimes hit and overwhelmed me, often when I was least expecting them.

The first few weeks were very full. Cards, letters, flowers and messages of sympathy arrived each day and it helped to know that so many people were thinking and caring about me. Every time I came home there would be something through the letterbox or on the doorstep. I felt enveloped in love and friendship and this was such a great help. There was also a lot to attend to – registering Don's death, making arrangements for his funeral and notifying all the various organisations that needed to know, so I was kept very busy.

Most of the time, in these early days, I managed quite well and everyone was very supportive and sympathetic. I talked to my son and daughter about all the arrangements and, between us, we put together a lovely funeral, at which we knew Don would have liked to be present. The vicar was kind and helpful, agreeing to all our requests. We wanted to include music that had given Don such pleasure, particularly in those last days of his life, in the service. It was easy to choose hymns that Don loved and which had a special meaning for him; a friend agreed to speak about Don in celebration of his life; another friend offered to play a favourite piece, Gershwin's 'Summertime' on his clarinet; my daughter would play Andrew

Lloyd-Webber's 'Memory' on the church grand piano and the organist would play Bach's 'Prelude Number 1', a piece which Don had always said that he would like played at his funeral. Making these arrangements for his last farewell helped me to keep going; I needed to do this last thing for him, to make it a special, celebratory time, and I found the energy from somewhere.

The only time that grief overcame me was on a visit to the funeral director, when I was asked to choose the clothes in which I would like Don to be buried. My mind caved in, as I was overcome by emotion at this thought. *How can I choose clothes for him to be buried in?* It somehow made his death real and final. I couldn't answer the question and I left the office in tears, distraught at the need to make this decision which I found completely impossible. The memory café was just across the road and, as it was open that afternoon, I stumbled in to seek solace and comfort there with our friends, remaining there until I could gain control of my feelings and face the world again.

The following week, the funeral went smoothly, according to our plans, and many of those who attended told me how lovely they thought the service was. I was touched that my grandson, now fifteen, had agreed to be a bearer. He put aside his usual rebellious, teenage behaviour and carried out his role with dignity and maturity. Another very touching gesture was a picture of grief, drawn by my thirteen-year-old granddaughter, which I put by the coffin. It was so expressive of how we were all feeling. I was moved that she could capture this emotion so sensitively.

It was only after the funeral, when everyone had gone home and back to their normal lives, that I had the time and space to start to take in properly what had happened, what Don's death meant. Well-meaning friends, several of them widows themselves, were advising and encouraging me not to sit at home or become maudlin but to go out, to mix with people and to keep busy, but I felt that I needed time and space to reflect, to grieve, to absorb and process everything. It was not a case of brooding or wallowing in morbidity. My home was my refuge, where I felt secure and safe, and where I still felt Don's presence, even though he was no longer there. His personal belongings were all around me and I made no effort to move them, to tidy up or put them away, as I found it comforting to have them around. I wasn't ready to let go completely yet.

At one point during the next week, I was tempted to drive off, somewhere far away, perhaps to Northumberland, where I could lose myself in some remote place for a time, but the exhaustion of the past two months caught up with me and I simply didn't have the energy or the confidence to do anything so extreme. I didn't cut myself off from everyone but spent as much time as I could walking with the dog and starting to tackle the jungle which my garden had become. These solitary outdoor activities, in the fresh air, helped me to think and just to 'be'. I was experiencing many mixed feelings and needed time to sort these out.

Much of the time, I felt very appreciative and grateful that I had a nice home, a garden, no financial worries and such loving and supportive family and friends. Sometimes these feelings were tinged with guilt, perhaps a sort of mild survivor guilt. Don had died but I was still there, living in our home; now everything we had built together belonged to me; he was gone but I still had a life. There were also some feelings of guilt that I should be so secure and fortunate, when many people in the world had so little. However much I tried to justify this to myself, by reason that I had worked hard all my life and had been careful with money, saving as well as spending, the feelings of guilt persisted and I knew that I would need to do something in the next stage of my life to 'atone' for this, or at least to help those less fortunate in some way.

The worst feeling of all was emptiness. I felt that part of me had died along with Don; there was a large gap inside me. I felt this physically in my body, as well as in my mind and I knew that I would not only have to heal but somehow grow a new part of me to fill this void. I wasn't at all sure how I would go about this, or what I wanted or needed to do, but decided that, instead of rushing out and about, keeping busy or joining groups or activities, I would just take life slowly and quietly for a time to see what transpired. I had the feeling that, if I could be patient, it would become clear to me in time.

I also knew that I was both physically and emotionally exhausted, after the events of the past couple of months, travelling ninety miles a day to visit Don in hospital, with the tension of never knowing what to expect when I arrived and coping with his deterioration during this time. Knowing that I was so tired was more than a bit scary, as I was aware that exhaustion – both physical and mental – were important factors that led to my previous depression, so it was especially important that I allowed myself time to recover. I was suffering from terrible tiredness every day, in spite of sleeping for nine or ten hours a night. By half past eight or nine o'clock every night, I would fall into bed, not able to last out any longer, but at least I was sleeping well and there was no early morning waking to plague me.

When my grandchildren broke up from school in July, my daughter suggested that we all go away for a holiday in her caravan. We didn't want to travel very far and decided upon the Gower Peninsular in South Wales, just a two hour journey for both of us, coming from different directions. The Gower is a wonderful place, mostly unspoilt by development, and it was designated in 1956 as the first Area of Outstanding Natural Beauty in the UK, with its mild climate, rich history and diverse plant habitat. We were fortunate to find a lovely site on a farm, a quiet and peaceful place, near the coast, with good facilities for showers and washing-up but nothing else, just a large field in the countryside with an extra field set aside for dog walking, ideal for us. We booked the caravan in for three weeks, knowing that we need not stay there all the time but could come and go as we wished. For part of the time we were all there together and enjoyed busy family activities together on the beach and in the local area. My youngest grandchild was just four and it was a joy to see him building castles and boats in the sand, exploring the world of rockpools and playing in the sea, all the things my children and I had enjoyed during our childhoods. Eating and living outdoors, close to nature, just playing, walking, sleeping, helped to heal and restore us all. The long, light evenings were accompanied by magnificent sunsets and a huge silver moon appeared each night as it grew dark. It seemed a magical time and place and we all had a wonderful time together. Now and again, my family went home for a few days, when they had appointments or things they needed to do, and then I stayed there on my own, using the opportunity to take long walks with my dog on the Gower Coast Path, enjoying the exercise and the amazing scenery. From Three Cliffs Bay, we walked on vast sandy beaches, with interesting rock formations and caves, to Oxwich and from there through woodlands and cliff tops to Horton; by boardwalk across the dunes to Port Eynon, and over the wild majestic cliffs to Worms Head and Rhossili. I never felt lonely or frightened, just very aware of the beauty all around me and the incredible diversity and power of nature.

This break away from home and the pressures of life provided me with the much needed opportunity to relax and recuperate. By the end of the three weeks, I felt much stronger and went home with renewed energy, ready to face a new life. Of course, I was still sad and often emotional, with the smallest thing likely to trigger tearfulness of one sort or another. Sometimes this would result in sobbing or more gentle weeping; at other times, just a choked up feeling, with tears rolling unstoppably down my face. Whilst this was not a problem in itself, and even though I had not suffered from depression for over a year, I found that I could still be terrified that this was more than grief, that I was in danger of sinking into depression once again.

Like many people, I had read about the five stages of grief – denial, anger, bargaining, depression and acceptance – but, apart from depression (potentially), these didn't seem very relevant to me. (I later found that these five stages, identified by Elisabeth Kubler Ross, were originally identified in patients who were terminally ill and had only later been applied more generally to people grieving a loved one.)

Thinking myself through each of these stages, I knew for certain that I did not experience denial of Don's death. Having lived with him through those last six weeks of illness in hospital and witnessed how his body gradually shut down, eventually ceasing to function completely, it seemed a very natural end to his life. I was simply glad to know that he reached the end of suffering and was in no pain when he died peacefully. Yet, at the moment of death, I did experience some shock, even though I had been expecting him to die. I don't think that you can really be prepared for when death actually occurs; it is such a final end, so hard to believe that the person will never breathe, speak or look at you again.

Nor did I experience any anger about his dying. Don had lived for eighty-seven years, a good age, and he had, for the most part, enjoyed life even over the past few years when his health began to fail. I was relieved and grateful that the treatment and care Don had received both from our local GPs and from the hospital had been excellent. In his case, the NHS had much to be proud of.

Everyone had done all they could to enable him to live his life well until the end and then to have a 'good death', which I had come to realise is so important. I did not resent him dying and I did not feel abandoned by him or deserted, left to face life on my own, partly because, due to his dementia, I had gradually lost the person he had been over a long period of time. During the past two or three years I had, piece by piece, taken over organising our lives, managing our home and garden and caring for our family. Unlike some women of my age, I wasn't faced with not knowing how to drive or how to cope with our financial affairs. In contrast, I felt incredibly grateful that I was left in a comfortable home, with everything I needed, no financial worries, a loving family and many good friends. Don's life had not been cut short like my friend Catherine's, so anger was certainly not part of my experience of grief this time.

Bargaining was never part of my experience. In the week before Don died, I had very much wanted to ensure that he would be kept free from pain and both my children and I did all we could to make his last days pleasant and comfortable but we didn't try to bargain with God or to expect miracles. Being given the time to say our goodbyes and to make his last days happy ones were both important and I think this helped our grieving process immensely. We felt no guilt at never having said the things we wanted to say, or do things we wanted to do for him, and our last memories of Don are happy ones.

Acceptance was more difficult and took much longer for, although I wasn't in denial as I'd been present when Don died and his death was very real, it wasn't until many months later that it fully dawned on me that Don was never coming home again. Although I never denied this rationally, I found that I was keeping things in our home as he would have liked them and I kept thinking of how pleased he would be when the flowers bloomed in the garden, or how he would have laughed at some antic of the dog. In many ways I still felt close to him, as if he was there with me, even though I knew he wasn't. On some emotional level, I think I didn't really accept for some time that he was never coming back to see these things, or to know that I was managing and looking after everything as he would have liked.

Full acceptance of the finality of death took me rather by surprise several months later and caused some belated distress. The feeling that some part of me had died alongside Don was difficult, too; for months I felt incomplete, with this gaping hole inside me, not knowing how to fill it. My friends continued to urge me to keep busy, to go out and mix with others and join in activities. But I still resisted this, as I felt I needed more time to grieve, to reflect and to think about how I wanted to fill this void. It felt as if I were on the brink of a new phase of my life, possibly the last phase in which I would be active, and I wanted to be certain that it would have depth and meaning, not just a mad whirl and rush of social activities.

During this time I continued to attend Evensong regularly, finding peace there; it was a source of continuity and support in my world where everything had changed. Even in my non-religious days, I had never completely abandoned my belief in the existence of 'God', though my belief was in a more spiritual being, rather than a human-like 'father figure' sitting in a heaven above the clouds, surrounded by angels. When I was in my early twenties, on holiday with a friend whose family lived in Kenya, there was one occasion that I still remember vividly when I felt very close to God. One day, as I sat quietly amongst the hills on their farm in the highlands there, admiring the view, I could feel God there, close beside me. I do not now claim to have *seen* God but I was aware of a spiritual presence there, close beside me. It is hard to describe something invisible but which you know is there, rather like the wind. The experience of this perception had never left me in all the intervening years. At that point in my life I had been troubled, at a crossroads, not knowing which direction to take. After this experience of being with God on that day, I came away feeling that

God would somehow show me what I must do and indeed, it seemed as if that was what happened when I returned to the UK. Everything fell into place.

Now, all these years later, I was at another crossroads and, over the next few months, it seemed that the words of the sermons I heard in church had direct relevance to me: it was as if God was speaking to me personally through those taking the services. Use your talents for the good of others; be patient; show humility and listen to what God tells or shows you, rather than thinking you know best. These were the messages that I heard and which resonated with me.

I tried to identify what my talents were and how they might be used, and waited patiently for God to show me the way forward. I really prayed for the first time for many years, not just saying the words of prayers but truly asking for help and guidance about how I could best help other people during the next phase of my life. This time there was no flash of inspiration, no pieces miraculously falling into place and I was left trying to be patient, to hear or to be shown an answer to my prayer but, in the meantime, floundering.

Still confused and being apprehensive about the possibility of going under with depression, at the beginning of September I saw a course advertised at our local 'Mind' and decided to go along. The course was entitled 'Thrive', which seemed to me to hold out some hope of finding a positive way to live. It was a challenging and powerful course, during which I had several painful and emotional experiences but, with the professional support of the trainers and the sharing which took place between the participants, I found it very rewarding. It helped me to sort out in my own confused mind the difference between grief and depression and to accept – even to value – the emotions I was going through. We did several creative activities there which I found useful, one of which was to write a poem. We had no warning that we were to be asked to undertake this task. The course leader read a poem to us and then suggested that we all try to write one of our own, there and then. It came as a shock to be put on the spot like that – writing poetry is not something I do every day – but, attempting to show willing, I picked up my pen and held it poised over a sheet of paper. To my great surprise, I just started to write fluently, without stopping to think. It was as if my hand took control and wrote the words that came spilling out of my brain, with no conscious effort, no thinking, no searching for words or phrases, no pauses for thought or reflection. It was hard to believe what was happening. Once we had finished, we were invited to share our efforts with each other. Some people had written a lot, others just a few lines, one person nothing at all and, although we had all been inspired by the same poem read to us at the start of the exercise, everyone's work was completely different. Here is what I wrote that afternoon:

Poem 18, September 2017

I am sinking, slithering in dark slimy mud,
Down into a deep dark pit.
Heavy, black clouds overhead push me down, down.
How far will I sink?
I think I have been here before.
It all seems horribly familiar but this time
I will not let the clouds, mud and slime engulf me.
I call for help, softly at first, but then
Louder and more determined.
Someone answers.
They cannot pull me out, I'm too far down.
But just knowing they are there
Makes all the difference.

They believe in me and encourage me
To start to climb,
Grabbing hold of anything that can help pull me up,
Just a little at a time.
Small steps and then a rest.
Each step brings a sense of achievement.
The clouds at the top have moved on, blown away.
I can see a shaft of light and then
Faint glimmers of sunshine.
I breathe fresh air, a warm breeze gently caressing my face
Instead of cold dankness, mud and slime.
Don't rush, don't panic, I tell myself
Even when I slip back a bit.
I can hear church bells ringing in the distance.
Is it Sunday, are they calling me to church?
Or is it the mournful tolling for my funeral
Dong, dong, dong, dong.
Close to the top now,
My head emerges into the world again.
My fingers grip the surface, I'm nearly out.
One final effort is needed to heave myself up
And rejoin the world.
But is this what I want?
Or should I let go
And slide down, back into the familiar dark pit?
A helping hand appears and words of welcome
Ring in my ears.
There are people glad to see me, smiling, clapping, cheering.
I make the choice.
I make the effort
Knowing that
I will survive and live my life again.

When I read my poem afterwards, I could see that I was no longer in any real danger of succumbing to depression or suicidal thoughts. By writing this poem I learnt more about myself and I called it 'Resilience'. Although I was still sad and grieving, I knew that I had found the strength to overcome the pit of despair and hopelessness. It was this exercise that helped me particularly to separate out grief from depression and to know that, in spite of the difficulties of the past six months, I had recovered.

Chapter Twenty
RECOVERY

Do you ever recover fully from depression? I think people can and do recover fully. Just because you may become ill with depression again doesn't necessarily mean that you didn't recover the previous time, any more than catching a cold or flu many times over your lifetime. You recover fully from these illnesses but, having done so, doesn't always make you immune to further bouts. Once recovered, it is so important to look after your mental health, as research shows that it is more difficult and takes longer to recover from each successive depressive illness and you are more likely to succumb to depression if you have experienced an earlier episode. If you do all you can to look after your mental health, as with your physical health, you are less likely to succumb again but you can't prevent a recurrence completely, any more than with a physical illness.

How do you know when you have recovered? This is a difficult question to answer. You may feel well one day or one week but then, a few days later, you feel low and are not so sure that you are better. It seems that one of the difficulties with depression is that the signs and symptoms are not always clear and that people who have experienced the horrors and terrors of a bad depression remain apprehensive and perhaps over-vigilant because they dread the return of those dark days. So it is sometimes difficult to end the counselling, the therapy, the anti-depressants, even though you may feel perfectly well and in good mental health. These treatments may not be physically addictive but you can become psychologically dependent on them or unwilling to take the risk when you are so apprehensive and afraid.

For many months, I felt well and strong but still hesitated to say I was 'better', meaning 'completely recovered', but I learnt to cope. On good days, when I felt fit, well and strong, I was confident and could not imagine that I would ever again experience the depths of depression. Yet, on not so good days, mainly when I was physically unwell or very tired, I worried that I might be stepping onto that slippery slope once again.

In my case, I have identified two things – being tired and being unwell – as my 'triggers' or danger points. Although I do everything I can to avoid or minimise them, I cannot control them completely but being aware of what they are helps me prevent them becoming too serious. It also helps me to know that these physical states of tiredness or illness will pass and, when they have passed, I will feel much better again. Of course, it is often hard to convince yourself of this at the time and hard to be patient, to give yourself time to get better. It is very important not to end treatment – whether this be anti-depressants or some sort of therapy – too early, but there inevitably comes a point where you may feel you need to stop and rejoice in being well again.

How do you recover from depression? I don't think anyone really knows the answer to this, not least because it seems to vary so much from person to person. Just as what causes depression in an individual is complicated and depends on many factors, so is recovery.

On one occasion, I was taken aback when my GP said to me, 'You have worked so hard to get better'. It had never occurred to me that I was working hard to recover but, when I thought about it, I had put a tremendous amount of effort into recovery. Even in those dark, early days when I had no strength or motivation to do very much, I listened carefully to everything I was told by my GP, my psychiatrists, my counsellors, and I read avidly about the subject of depression, trying to understand what had happened to me and what I might do to get better. Reading was difficult at first and, even more difficult, was understanding and processing information but I was gradually able to read more and more and progressed from short articles on the internet to more in-depth studies and books. I think this is why I found Dr Cantopher's book so helpful because, even though he is dealing with a complicated subject, he manages to write simply and clearly and he even suggests that you skip certain chapters if you are at an early stage in a serious depression. It was soon after reading this book that I first came across books written by others who had experienced this illness; these were personal accounts and it was those memoirs that touched me deeply and helped me to find hope in recovery. Some of them also contain much general information about depressive illness, which is of great interest once you are fit enough to cope with this, and they contain many useful references to other works if you wish to read more widely. Andrew Solomon's *The Noonday Demon – An Anatomy of Depression* is a huge mine of information. As well as telling of his own agonising experiences of breakdowns and depression, he looks at the subject much more widely, at the history, the politics, the implications of poverty and addiction, how the illness manifests itself in other countries and cultures as well as at treatments and alternatives. It is a weighty tome and one which I could not cope with until I was well on the road to recovery.

As I read, I found many recommendations and suggestions of things that have been shown to aid recovery and, as I grew a little stronger, I was desperate to try everything that was recommended as a potential way of helping. Some of them, for example walking and gardening, I had already discovered for myself, before finding out how beneficial they were considered to be by health professionals.

Others, such as socialising, volunteering to help others and learning a new skill, I had to think about and decide when and how to put these into practice and fit them into my life without overcrowding it, whilst Mindfulness was something completely new to me and gave me a great deal to think about.

For me, walking has been one of the most important and powerful remedies, particularly since I learnt about mindfulness and have learnt to take more care in observing what I see, hear, smell and feel, whilst on a walk. Even the same walk is different on different days, times of day, in different seasons of the year, in different weathers and there is so much to observe if you concentrate and set your mind to the experience, instead of thinking about some problem or what you are going to do once you get home. Keeping yourself grounded in the present is the key, not ruminating about things you should have done differently in the past, or worrying about the future, but just 'being' where you are, noticing everything around you and how it affects you, observing yourself and your senses' reactions to your surroundings.

Other people have found important solace, support and healing from many different activities. Rachel Kelly describes in *Black Rainbow* how she found hers in poetry and later in religion. Alongside medication and various types of psychotherapy, many different people have found gardening, yoga, reading, writing, painting or music to be helpful. Everyone needs to find their individual source, an activity which must not just entertain but completely absorb them for a time.

In recent years, we have all often been exhorted to take more exercise to improve our physical and mental health. I've tried to adopt a good balance, going swimming and doing pilates every week but it is my daily walking that keeps me in good mental as well as physical health. As I have already described in earlier chapters, I started walking, just short distances at first, getting longer, more demanding and interesting as time went on, walking with friends, with different groups and eventually with my dog.

Some people find walking boring and prefer to go to the gym, take a dance or aerobics class or perhaps play football or badminton or learn judo. I don't think it matters what the exercise is and there is so much choice today. The important thing is for everyone to find what works for them, to do it regularly and to enjoy the experience for the pleasure it brings in itself, not just because you think it is 'doing you good.'

Psychiatrists and neuroscientists now recognise the beneficial effects of exercise on mental as well as physical health. They have found that exercise not only helps to protect against heart disease, diabetes and high blood pressure but different types of exercise also have other important influences on our bodies and minds. High intensity exercise is known to release endorphins which make people feel good, whilst low intensity exercise sustained over time spurs the release of proteins which cause nerve cells to grow and make new connections. Such improvements in brain function make you feel better and can help to relieve depression.

Of particular interest to me is the fact that low-intensity exercise, like walking, is particularly good for depression. This is a great relief for someone of my age, who would find more vigorous high impact exercise difficult. Another advantage of walking is that is costs very little, although it is important to invest in some good quality walking shoes or boots and some effective weatherproof clothing to keep warm and dry if, to get the most benefit from it, you walk in all weathers.

Soon after I was introduced to Mindfulness, I started to record what I had noticed on my walks. It wasn't a special walk, just one I did most days but now I did it with enhanced awareness and, instead of trudging along, eyes not really seeing, allowing my mind to dwell on something that had happened or planning what I would do when I got home, I now focused all my senses on what was happening around me in the present:

Early February

> A mild day, full of sunshine and showers but very windy. Sudden gusts would rake through our hair, making the dog run wildly with excitement. We walked across fields, the wet grass glinting in the sunshine, and watched clouds scudding rapidly across the sky and rainbows arching their pale colours across the land, bending down to the ground in the misty distance. Tiny catkins have appeared on alder trees; some are grey, others a rosy pink and those most advanced, a crimson red. The hazel catkins are longer and larger, hanging fluffy and yellow, deserving of their name as 'lambs tails'. As we returned, I was conscious of the wind soughing through a copse of tall Scots Pine trees, reminding me of one of my favourite childhood stories of *Heidi*, who used to run out of Nunky's cabin in the Swiss mountains to hear the wind in the pines, a sound she pined for during her homesickness in Germany.

Taking exercise outside, in the fresh air and amidst nature, brings additional benefits. Numerous recent studies have highlighted the healing power of nature and the benefits are beginning to be more widely recognised. One study by researchers at the University of Essex found that of a group of people suffering from depression, ninety percent felt a higher level of self-esteem after taking a walk through a country park, and almost three quarters felt less dispirited after the walk.

In 2018, GPs on the Shetland Islands began issuing nature prescriptions which instruct patients with chronic conditions to take strolls on beaches and moors, with a list of bird and plant species to look out for as they wander.

There have also been experiments in counselling whilst walking and it has been found that people often find it easier to open up when talking outside; they feel less self-conscious talking about feelings or personal issues and it is also easier to cope with silence, which can be part of the healing process. It is believed that walking side by side, which means only fleeting eye contact, makes them feel less exposed. Being outside, the views can be uplifting and the sights and sounds of nature, especially water, can be calming, helping people to access inner space and peace.

Similarly, the therapeutic value of getting close to nature through gardening is also gaining acceptance. Although gardening and agriculture were sometimes used as occupational therapy long ago in some asylums and mental hospitals, the therapeutic value of working with nature fell out of use as new drugs and therapies were discovered from the 1950s and 60s onwards, and many of the old hospitals were closed down. Gardening was certainly something that I found to be beneficial, almost by accident, and in recent months I have found that there is an increasing body of research that is making it popular again in the treatment of those with mental health issues. In the early stages of my illness, I attended to the garden more as a chore than a pleasure or a therapy. It was something that had to be done, like housework indoors, but it was not long before I discovered that I felt so much better after a spell working in the garden. Cutting and slashing brambles or nettles or vigorously pruning bushes and hedges is a good way of releasing anger or frustration, whilst more gentle nurturing tasks like planting and watering are soothing and satisfying. I became more aware of myself and my place in the natural world through gardening, the relentless round of life beginning as a small seed or bulb, growing, developing, fruiting and dying down as winter approaches. Everything has a season; nothing lasts for ever but life will start afresh the following year.

In her book *Shoot the Damn Dog*, Sally Brampton, who endured several years of major depression, describes how, when living in a flat, she bought a piece of land, wild and overgrown, and transformed it into a garden. Many other writers, too, have discovered, to a greater or lesser extent, the therapeutic value of gardening.

Whilst writing this chapter, in September 2019, I happened to watch a particular programme of *Gardeners' World* which focused on the close relationship between gardening and wellbeing and which found that the idea of 'Green Medicine' and social prescribing of gardening is not only on the increase but is working well, with a prediction that over the next five years it will increase to 900,000 appointments per year. On a visit to the Blackthorn Trust in Kent, participants at this therapeutic environment stated that, by working in the large garden there, they felt more grounded and connected, that it had reduced their social isolation and anxiety and given them a sense of hope for the future. There, the activity of gardening is based on Dr Rudolf Steiner's principles that plants and people benefit each other in a symbiotic way and that people benefit from the beauty of the flowers, the peace to be found in the garden and the ability to become absorbed, to get lost in what they are doing.

The programme reported on the research of an American journalist, Florence Williams, who has travelled worldwide to gather scientific evidence, which is changing the way we think about the impact of nature, green spaces and gardening on human beings. She found that in Japan, the idea of 'Forest Bathing' is being promoted by the government to alleviate stress. Participants follow therapy trails in the forests, where they concentrate on engaging all of their senses. In other words, they practise mindfulness outside in a natural environment. After as short a period of fifteen minutes, opening up their senses in the healing forests, physiological changes can be observed – the lowering of blood pressure, the calming of respiratory levels and lowering of the stress hormone, cortisol.

She also reported that recent research in England has shown that a total of two hours a week of time spent outside communing with nature is beneficial to health and wellbeing.

What other things are helpful in recovery and staying well? Loving relationships are known to be key factors in maintaining good mental health. There are many kinds of love, that between parents and children, brothers and sisters, friends and sometimes colleagues, as well as love that has a sensual element between husbands, wives and partners. My first psychiatrist told me that most mental illness has a root cause in some relationship breakdown or difficulty, past or present. In the main, I have been lucky with relationships, both within my family and outside. I had loving, caring parents, grandparents, aunts and uncles. Growing up in the 1940s and 50s, when families were not as demonstrative as today and we rarely, if ever, talked about feelings, I nevertheless always felt loved and valued as a person. I never suffered from neglect, cruelty or abuse and was never bullied at school or at work. My schools were caring places where we were taught, mainly by the example of teachers and older pupils, to respect others and to be thoughtful, kind and compassionate. From a young age, I always had good friends and sometimes I befriended children who seemed to be finding life difficult.

In spite of this secure, stable background I have, from a young age, gone to great lengths to keep my most private feelings hidden from other people, particularly if I felt in any way hurt, jealous, rejected, humiliated, unwanted. I never confided in anyone, nor wore my heart on my sleeve; it was as if I was ashamed or felt that to have such feelings somehow made me less worthy, less likeable or weak. I would listen to other people's problems, anxieties and fears and encourage them to talk to me but rarely shared my own. During my depression I had to spend much time and effort trying to be more open, less private; talking about difficulties, instead of trying to hide them or deal with them secretly; recognising how important people are to each other, being kind even with just a smile; listening to and supporting those who are close to me but also letting them support and help me when necessary. This was the hardest and most difficult work I've ever done.

If I'm not careful, I still tend to revert to my old ways but have learnt the dangers of doing this.

My counselling sessions helped me to understand and to accept myself, to realise that I do not have to manage and control everything, that other people also have responsibilities and can share the bad and the difficult as well as the good. This doesn't mean going around telling my woes and worries to everyone I meet. That is not me and never will be but I can talk about and share my feelings better now with a few people that I trust, and I recognise the value in doing this. I've come to realise that, actually, people seem to like you better if you show you're fallible sometimes and are not 'perfect'.

Socialising is another important factor in helping recovery from depression and, indeed, lack of social contact can be a cause or contributing factor in developing depression in the first place. In the early days of my illness, socialising was one of the most difficult things for me. Like many others who have suffered depression, I just wanted to withdraw into myself, to avoid people and, if faced with people, to avoid communicating with them. It really was hard work to learn to engage again and something I had to build up very gradually, starting with just one or two individuals whom I trusted, before re-joining groups.

Even though I now thoroughly enjoy engaging in group activities, there are still days, perhaps when I'm tired or slightly unwell, when I feel like opting out and not going to a group. I have to make a concerted effort but usually enjoy it when I get there and end up being pleased that I went.

At the other extreme, I have to be careful to balance my social life and not to rush into too many activities, which would result in me becoming too busy and overcharged, likely to end in burnout or breakdown. I have had to recognise my limitations; I think I've achieved a good balance now and have to be content with that. There are so many more things I would like to do but not enough time or energy. Now, well into my seventies, I cannot do as much as I could ten or twenty years ago and must recognise that and live my life within sensible limits.

Helping other people is also something that has been found good for people suffering from depression. I loved the voluntary work I did, listening to children reading in a local primary school and I was sorry to have to give it up when my husband needed more of my time. After Don died, I thought long and hard about doing some sort of voluntary work again but was conscious that it had to be the right kind of work for me. It would have to be sustainable, something that interested me, where I could use my skills or even learn new ones to help people but something that would not put too much pressure on me. In the end I decided that writing this book should be my priority for now and I hope that it will one day help someone else.

Accepting life for what it is has been very important to me in recovery and staying well. I know I'm lucky to have the time, now that I've retired, to slow down, to choose how I spend most of my time, to stand and stare, to think, relax, reflect and meditate, to notice and appreciate small things around me. Recently, it struck me, when out walking in the rain, that life is very like the weather; it changes frequently, nothing lasts for ever and we have no control over it. It can be bright, warm and cheerful or dull, cold and gloomy but, sooner or later, the sun will pass behind clouds or the blackest clouds will blow away to show blue sky and the sun will come out again. Everything passes. Sometimes, we even appreciate the light and sunshine more after a few days of dreary dampness; or, after a long spell of dry hot weather, it is a pleasure to see, feel and smell the rain.

Mindfulness has taught me that, if we can use our senses to the full, it is possible for much of the time to enjoy the weather, to feel raindrops on our faces, the wind in our hair, to marvel at clouds scudding across the sky on a windy day, to relax in the warmth of a sunny day. After the rain it can be wonderful to find the drops sparkling on twigs in the hedge, to see colourful reflections in puddles, to hear a rushing stream or watch a fast running river or tumbling waterfall, to squelch along a boggy path or crunch your way along a path of diamonds on a crisp, icy morning after snowfall. I also try to appreciate the ups and downs in life in the same way and to view my dark thoughts as clouds which come, sometimes do their worst, but always blow away.

Faith is something that seems somehow to have crept back into my life through the back door. I feel a stronger person for it and not completely alone, floundering about in this world. Through suffering depression, I have developed a new sense of belonging – to my family, to my friends, to my community, and have accepted my place in the world.

Faith is about having trust, about believing in something or someone very strongly. The word has its origin in the Old French word feid, meaning 'belief, trust, confidence'. It is often, though not always, applied to religion where belief is based on spiritual conviction rather than hard evidence. In the Bible, faith is defined as 'the substance of things hoped for, the evidence of things not seen' (Hebrews 11:1). In this sense, faith becomes your spiritual link with God – whoever or whatever you believe that 'God' to be.

In recent years, I have regained a belief and a relationship with God, though not the same 'God' that I believed in during my younger days, and I consider myself to be a Christian, even though I do not accept or believe in all the rules and rituals laid out in the Bible or by the Anglican Church. I still have many questions and continue on a journey, searching for answers, but have been helped greatly by a retired Anglican priest with surprisingly liberal views. He was extremely kind to me during Don's final illness and in the time following his death. We meet now and then for a coffee and theological discussion, based on the books he lends me, and I am finding a new way forward, though I recognise it is likely to be a long and often difficult journey.

Although I had started to attend church only to accompany my husband, since he died I have continued to attend regularly. Initially, I found comfort and security in the structure of the church service, something that was unchanging, secure and stable in the upheaval of my world. Church is a place where I can easily feel God's presence and I like to set aside a time every week when I think about and pray to God. One of the most special parts of Evensong for me is just before the service starts, when people sit quietly and reflectively, the organ playing wonderful music, while the candles burn and shed their light in this lovely building, with its beautiful architecture and stained glass windows. All of this appeals to my senses and puts me into a receptive mood to be aware of God, to listen, to pray, to seek forgiveness and guidance. In great contrast, once a month, I also enjoy the contemporary worship service. This is not a peaceful service but one where we sing modern songs, to the accompaniment of a small band, but where the sincerity of those involved shines through and inspires me. In church, sometimes it seems that God speaks to me through the sermon, or perhaps through a hymn, a psalm, a passage read from the Bible, or even something that a member of the congregation might do or say, which makes me aware of the goodness and compassion in human beings. I have come to love the Church in

Wales, although I find the preoccupation with 'sin' unhelpful and would like to see parts of the Creed and the set prayers updated with a more positive message. Even Jesus didn't dwell so heavily on asking forgiveness for our sins. In the Lord's Prayer, Jesus simply asks of God, 'Forgive us our trespasses' and then goes on to add, 'as we forgive those who trespass against us', an important part of forgiveness. I think it is right that we take time to reflect on what we have said and done over the past week or weeks and to ask for help to do better in the future, but to describe the people who make up the congregation as 'sinners in thought, word and deed' not just once but at several points during the service seems unnecessarily guilt-inducing and potentially damaging. None of us is perfect and to strive always for perfection, or to set ourselves unrealistically high standards, can lead to disaster. We know, too, that we do not have control over our thoughts; anyone who has tried mindfulness or meditation will know that thoughts come and go as they will, often unbidden and sometimes shocking. In meditation, we have to learn to bring our minds back from our thoughts. The important thing is not the thoughts themselves but how we react to them; what we *can* control is our actions.

It is not only in church that I'm aware of God's presence and I find my relationship is strongest when I am outside in the natural world. For me, a walk in the hills or woods, by streams or rivers, on cliffs or beaches, is often a spiritual experience, one that 'restores my soul'. I'm also aware of the presence of 'holiness' in the kindness, compassion or care of people for one another. I was very taken by what I heard in one sermon, where the vicar was talking about the Trinity – the Father, Son and Holy Spirit. Most people can understand and picture God the Father and God the Son but it is the Holy Spirit that is most difficult to grasp. This vicar promoted the idea that the Holy Spirit resides in all of us. It is that part of us that is 'goodness' or 'grace'. In some people it might become well-hidden, shut away or damaged by events and their life circumstances, whilst in others it is very evident. I have come to believe that all human beings have the capacity for spirituality and we neglect this part of us at our peril.

My recovery from depression has taken much time and effort. I cannot pinpoint a moment in time when I 'recovered'. It was much more of a gradual process. Help from medical professionals played a hugely important part in this, as did anti-depressant medication. I know that I have been extremely fortunate in the quality of help that I've received from individuals through the NHS, for which I shall be eternally grateful. Alongside the medical help during my crisis points, the support from friends and family has been so valuable in sustaining me on an ongoing basis, making me feel that life is worth living and I would not have recovered so well without their patience and kindness.

The activities described in this chapter have helped me to find a new joy in life, to make me stronger, so far warding off any further depression. They are my personal way of coping; they will not be the way for everyone but they are my means of salvation.

I know that, in the future, life will bring times of sadness, illness, grief, worry, anxiety, even misery and I hope that I shall not be overwhelmed by such times. Yet, strangely, I do not now regret my experience of depression. It has given me a richer awareness of life; a better knowledge of myself; an understanding of suffering and of the joy of recovery; a deeper appreciation of the importance of people to each other, of love and kindness, of the many wonderful things around us in nature, in the creativity of human beings, and, above all, of the need for all people to cling to that sometimes elusive but essential emotion of hope.

AFTERWORD

This book is about *me* and *my experiences*; it is not about my family, friends or the medical professionals who have helped me, though clearly they all have played important roles during my illness and in helping me recover. In most cases I have used fictitious names to preserve their identity and I have also used a pen-name for the same reason; the names have been allocated alphabetically, in the order in which they appear and bear no resemblance to actual names.

I have kept details of events where they have played a part to a minimum, only including details where they are relevant to how they affected me.

Several friends have given me permission to use their real names but I have been unable to contact everyone as some have retired or moved away or I am no longer in contact with them. Whoever they are I shall be eternally grateful to them all for their care and support and for literally helping to save my life.

USEFUL BOOKS, ARTICLES AND WEBSITES

Some books, articles and websites that I have found particularly useful are listed below. I have referred to some of these in my writing, while others have been helpful in informing my knowledge, thinking and understanding in general:

Books

Shoot the Damn Dog by Sally Brampton.

Depressive Illness The Curse of the Strong by Dr Tim Cantopher.

The Other Side of Silence by Linda Gask.

Plot 29 by Allan Jenkins.

Sunbathing in the Rain by Gwyneth Lewis.

The Devil Within by Stephanie Merritt.

Underneath the Lemon Tree by Mark Rice-Oxley.

The Noonday Demon by Andrew Solomon.

Malignant Sadness by Lewis Wolpert.

Mindfulness a Practical Guide to Finding Peace in a Frantic World by Mark Williams and Danny Penman with Foreword by Jon Kabat-Zinn.

Mindfulness 25 Ways to Live in the Moment Through Art by Christophe André.

Understanding the Process of Suicide Through Accounts of Experience – A new focus for suicide prevention – Article from SANE website.

Websites

www.bcap.co.uk – information on counselling and therapy, different types, how they can help and how to access them.

www.cruse.org.uk – information, support and advice on coping with grief, helpline, chat.

www.mind.org.uk – helpline, local drop-in centres, counselling.

www.samaritans.org – information, helpline, phone/email/text support, research.

www.sane.org.uk – emotional support, helpline, resources, research.

www.nhs.uk – articles on sleep, benefits of exercise and mindfulness, help for suicidal thoughts.

www.getselfhelp.co.uk/stopp.htm – 'cbt in a nutshell', online course, worksheets .

ACKNOWLEDGEMENTS

When I look back over this period of my life I can still feel the pain and anguish of the darkest moments but my overwhelming emotion is one of gratitude and appreciation. Experiencing depression and recovery has brought so much good to my life and I am immensely grateful to the many people who played a part in this, some of whom I would never have met or got to know so well had this not happened. I have already paid tribute to some of them within the book itself but there are even more who deserve acknowledgement.

First of all I am grateful to my family, to my son and daughter for being the kind, caring and generous people they are and to my grandchildren who have brought me so much pleasure and fun in my later years, making life worth living. I could not have done it without you.

I owe a huge debt of gratitude to all the medical staff who helped me come through depression through their care and professionalism. I'm sure that I was not the easiest patient to deal with at times and I thank them for their patience and for never giving up on me. I have not used their real names in this book but they will know who they are.

Thank you to my closest, very dear friends, Margaret Mason and Ann Wheatley, who have both been there for me through many trials and tribulations and whose friendship and support made such a difference. I remember and thank Catherine Clarke too, who is sadly no longer with us.

Then there are the many friends who, probably unknown to

most of them, have have also played a critical part in my recovery through their friendship; thanks especially to: Ewart and Joy Hilsden, Berwyn Woolnough, Patsy Godfrey, Ann Morgan, Jill Mouncer, Karyn Evans, Joan Annetts, Martha Wooldridge, all at U3A; to Hazel Bird, Anne Read, Shirley Evans, Jane Jarvis at the Memory Café; to Lucy Wills, Mercia and Margaret at Pilates; to Roy Palmer at Holy Trinity Church.

Thank you to the staff at Mid Powys Mind for the courses and activities there and to Malissa Craig-Smedley and Nic Williams for their help in looking after Don and for giving me time to find myself again.

Last but by no means least, I must thank those who made this book possible. A big thank you to Nic Williams who walked my dog every Tuesday and Thursday afternoon for many months, giving me dedicated time to write; to Margaret Mason for inspiring me with her enthusiasm and for giving me advice and encouragement to pursue publication; to Revd Bob Shorter, not only for the loan of books from his theological library and for many hours of discussion over cups of coffee, but also for his encouragement and initial proof reading of the drafts of my work.

Thank you to Mary Sim for support, encouragement and recommendation to my publisher, Aspect Design; to Valerie Ball, my editor and professional proof reader for her painstaking work and her words of wisdom; to my granddaughter for her ideas and initial illustration for the book cover; and finally, to Dan at Aspect Design for his expertise in bringing it all to fruition.